Peer Review of the Automatic Exchange of Financial Account Information 2024 Update

OECD
BETTER POLICIES FOR BETTER LIVES

This report was approved by the AEOI Peer Review Group on 31 October 2024 and adopted by the AEOI Peers on 25 November 2024. It was prepared for publication by the Secretariat of the Global Forum on Transparency and Exchange of Information for Tax Purposes.

Please cite this publication as:
OECD (2024), *Peer Review of the Automatic Exchange of Financial Account Information 2024 Update*, OECD Publishing, Paris, https://doi.org/10.1787/1aa02413-en.

ISBN 978-92-64-55510-5 (print)
ISBN 978-92-64-62529-7 (PDF)
ISBN 978-92-64-77271-7 (HTML)
ISBN 978-92-64-42551-4 (epub)

Revised version, December 2024
Details of revisions available at: https://www.oecd.org/en/publications/support/corrigenda.html

Photo credits: Cover © OECD with cover illustration by Renaud Madignier.

Corrigenda to OECD publications may be found at: https://www.oecd.org/en/publications/support/corrigenda.html.

Foreword

The Global Forum on Transparency and Exchange of Information for Tax Purposes (the Global Forum) provides a multilateral response to tackle offshore tax evasion by promoting and assessing the implementation of international standards for exchange of information for tax purposes. It brings together 171 jurisdictions dedicated to improving transparency and cooperation for tax purposes. The Global Forum promotes and ensures the effective implementation of two complementary international standards: the exchange of information on request (EOIR) and the automatic exchange of financial account information (AEOI). In addition, the Global Forum has been tasked with ensuring the widespread implementation of the new Crypto-Asset Reporting Framework (CARF). These Standards provide for closer co-operation between tax authorities worldwide so that they can obtain information necessary to ensure tax compliance.

The OECD, working with G20 countries, developed the Standard for Automatic Exchange of Financial Account Information in Tax Matters (AEOI Standard) in 2014. It provides for the annual exchange between tax authorities of a predefined set of information on financial accounts held by individuals and entities that are tax resident of one jurisdiction and that hold financial accounts in another jurisdiction. The Global Forum has been supporting, monitoring and reviewing the implementation of the AEOI Standard since its inception, including the necessary legal, technical and administrative frameworks to ensure the effective implementation of the Standard. The Global Forum has published detailed yearly reports on the implementation of the AEOI Standard by all participating jurisdictions since exchanges commenced in 2017 and, since 2020, has published the results of its peer reviews.

The peer review report published in 2022 contained the results of the reviews of the domestic and international legal frameworks put in place by the first 106 jurisdictions that implemented the AEOI Standard. It also included, for the first time, the results of the initial reviews in relation to the effectiveness of the implementation of the AEOI Standard in practice for the first 99 jurisdictions to implement it. Subsequent reports have included the peer review reports for the later jurisdictions to commit to implement the AEOI Standard. In this regard an update was produced in 2023 to supplement the 2022 report. This included new assessments for later jurisdictions to commit and reassessments where jurisdictions had made changes to their legal frameworks implementing the AEOI Standard. This report is the 2024 update. It includes similar updates to those contained in the 2023 update, as well as the results of the additional checks on the legal frameworks jurisdictions have in place to ensure that Reporting Financial Institutions implement the requirements effectively in practice.

This report demonstrates a high level of completeness in the legal frameworks in place, with 95% (108 out of 114) of jurisdictions assessed as having legal frameworks that are "In Place" or "In Place But Needs Improvement." Furthermore, a majority of jurisdictions have received a rating of "On Track" in terms of their implementation in practice (67 out of 104). However, the Global Forum has noted that further efforts are required to ensure the effectiveness of the AEOI Standard, particularly ensuring its effective implementation by Reporting Financial Institutions. It is therefore conducting a second round of AEOI effectiveness reviews.

Table of contents

Abbreviations and acronyms

AEOI	Automatic Exchange of Information
AEOI Standard	Standard for Automatic Exchange of Financial Account Information in Tax Matters
AML	Anti-Money Laundering
APRG	AEOI Peer Review Group
CARF	Crypto-Asset Reporting Framework
CFT	Combating the Financing of Terrorism
CR	Core Requirement
CRS	Common Reporting Standard
CRS MCAA	CRS Multilateral Competent Authority Agreement
CTS	Common Transmission System
EOIR	Exchange of Information on Request
FATCA	Foreign Account Tax Compliance Act
FATF	Financial Action Task Force
G20	The Group of Twenty
Global Forum	Global Forum on Transparency and Exchange of Information for Tax Purposes
KYC	Know Your Customer
Model CAA	Model Competent Authority Agreement
OECD	Organisation for Economic Co-operation and Development
RFI	Reporting Financial Institution
SR	Sub-requirement

Executive summary

As the financial system has become increasingly globalised and it has become easier for taxpayers to move their financial affairs across borders, it has become an increasing priority for jurisdictions to ensure that the evolution of the financial system does not undermine the correct payment of tax. This is to ensure that the public finances are not eroded and that the public's trust in the tax system is preserved. International cooperation to provide tax authorities with transparency across borders has therefore become increasingly the norm, providing jurisdictions with the necessary tools to ensure that taxpayers with offshore financial activities meet their domestic tax obligations.

One key tool is the automatic exchange of information amongst tax authorities on financial assets held offshore, under the Standard for Automatic Exchange of Financial Account Information in Tax Matters (AEOI Standard), which was developed by the OECD, working with G20 countries, and adopted by the Global Forum on Transparency and Exchange of Information for Tax Purposes (Global Forum). The AEOI Standard provides for the annual automatic exchange of information on Financial Accounts held by taxpayers outside their jurisdiction of tax residence, with the tax authority in the jurisdiction in which they are tax resident. In certain cases, this includes where Financial Accounts are held through Entities that the taxpayers control. This helps ensure that tax evaders are at greater risk than ever of being caught and deters potential tax evaders from failing to properly declare their financial activities.

Information exchange commenced under the AEOI Standard in 2017. By 2024, tax authorities from 111 jurisdictions have automatically exchanged information on financial accounts. Information on over 134 million financial accounts was exchanged automatically in 2023, covering total assets of almost EUR 12 trillion. More jurisdictions are also expected to implement the AEOI Standard in the coming years. This move to AEOI has had a dramatic impact on taxpayer behaviour and the ability of tax authorities to ensure tax compliance. So far, over EUR 130 billion in tax, interest and penalties have been raised by jurisdictions through voluntary disclosure programmes and other offshore tax compliance initiatives with the vast majority linked to the commitments made to implement the AEOI Standard. Furthermore, research has shown that financial investments held in international financial centres have decreased by 20% over the same time, which is linked to the implementation of the AEOI Standard.[1]

This change is the result of significant investments by governments across the world, all of which introduced legislation to require Reporting Financial Institutions to conduct the detailed due diligence and reporting rules to ensure the Financial Account information is reported, put in place international exchange agreements to exchange the information and implemented technical and operational solutions to deliver the exchanges in practice. In addition, legal, operational and technical frameworks have been needed to keep the information confidential and secure. Investments have also been needed by the financial sector to ensure compliance.

1 O'Reilly P., Parra Ramirez K. and Stemmer M.A. (2019), "Exchange of Information and Bank Deposits in International Financial Centres", OECD Taxation Working Papers No. 46

To realise the full benefits of the AEOI Standard, including maximising the deterrent effect and the usability of the information exchanged, it must be ensured that the AEOI Standard is implemented effectively and on a widespread basis. This is why the G20 called on the Global Forum to monitor and review its global implementation. This started by seeking to ensure all relevant jurisdictions commit to implement the AEOI Standard (i.e. all Global Forum members, except developing countries that do not host a financial centre) and moved to peer reviews of the legal frameworks in place and the effectiveness of implementation in practice, including the frameworks in place to ensure compliance by Reporting Financial Institutions.

Having commenced the publication of annual monitoring reports in 2017, in 2020 the Global Forum began publishing the results of its peer reviews of the legal frameworks implementing the AEOI Standard starting with the first 99 jurisdictions to commit to commence exchanging under the AEOI Standard and to commence exchanges in 2017 or 2018. The results have been updated each year thereafter, to include later jurisdictions to commit to implement the AEOI Standard and the results of reassessments, where changes have been made to the legal frameworks implementing the AEOI Standard, including to address recommendations made. In 2022, the Global Forum published the results of its initial peer reviews of the effectiveness in practice of the implementation of the AEOI Standard, including ratings, for the first 99 jurisdictions.[2] An update was subsequently published in 2023, again to reflect the results for jurisdictions that subsequently committed to implement the AEOI Standard and the results of reassessments of the AEOI legal frameworks. This 2024 report provides a further such update.

This update contains the latest situation on the assessments of the legal frameworks implementing the AEOI Standard, reflecting the results for a total of 114 jurisdictions, including an additional five jurisdictions since 2023 and reassessments in relation to 46 jurisdictions. These include reassessments carried out as the result of specific targeted checks made in the context of the ongoing second round of AEOI effectiveness reviews that the Global Forum is conducting, which are focused on the completeness of the compliance and enforcement frameworks jurisdictions have in place in their domestic legal frameworks. This update shows that, amongst the 114 jurisdictions assessed, 108 or 95% have in place domestic and international legal frameworks that are fully or substantially complete and that have been determined to be “In Place” or “In Place But Needs Improvement.” Notwithstanding that, three jurisdictions still have fundamental deficiencies in their legal frameworks, and three jurisdictions have no legal frameworks in place at all, leading to six jurisdictions being issued an overall determination of “Not In Place.” These jurisdictions should therefore urgently address the issues identified to deliver an effective AEOI Standard based on a level playing field for governments and business.

This update also sets out the latest results of the initial peer reviews of the effectiveness of the implementation of the AEOI Standard in practice, for a total of 104 jurisdictions, which includes an additional three jurisdictions since 2023. The update shows that, amongst the 104 jurisdictions assessed, 67 of jurisdictions are rated as “On Track” with their implementation. This includes implementing administrative compliance frameworks that appear to be on track to effectively ensure compliance by Reporting Financial Institutions and ensuring the smooth operation of the exchanges in practice. Notwithstanding that, there is also clearly more to do to ensure the effectiveness of the AEOI Standard in practice, including to ensure the completeness and effectiveness of the administrative compliance frameworks in place to ensure compliance with the AEOI Standard.

To retain this focus, the Global Forum put in place a framework for a second round of peer reviews in relation to the effective implementation of the AEOI Standard. These commenced in 2023 and are designed to obtain a deeper level of comfort that jurisdictions are implementing the AEOI Standard effectively,

---

[2] OECD (2022), *Peer Review of the Automatic Exchange of Financial Account Information 2022*, OECD Publishing, Paris, https://doi.org/10.1787/36e7cded-en.

including onsite visits by Assessment Teams where key stakeholders from the public and private sectors are met.

In this regard the Global Forum has extended the period within which it will conduct the second round of AEOI effectiveness reviews. While it was intended that the review of the effectiveness of the implementation of the AEOI Standard would be fully completed in relation to the first 99 jurisdictions to implement the AEOI Standard within three years of the conclusion of the initial effectiveness reviews, the Global Forum has allowed for an additional year for the relevant processes. This is to support the effective and sustainable implementation of the AEOI Standard, including by continuing to disseminate the best practices observed and to ensure that the peer review process can best assess the implementation of the AEOI Standard.

This report is structured as follows:

- Chapter 1 provides the latest results of the Global Forum's monitoring and peer review processes in relation to the AEOI Standard.
- Chapter 2 sets out the methodologies for the Global Forum's peer reviews, including of the AEOI legal frameworks and the initial reviews of the effectiveness of the implementation of the AEOI Standard in practice. It also provides details of the in-depth effectiveness reviews being conducted under the second round of AEOI effectiveness reviews.
- Chapter 3 contains the jurisdiction-specific peer review reports completed and updated since the publication of the 2023 AEOI Review Report, including the analysis, findings and recommendations.
- Annex A provides information on the exchange agreements the jurisdictions that have been newly assessed on their legal frameworks implementing the AEOI Standard have in place to exchange information under the AEOI Standard.
- Annex B contains the AEOI Terms of Reference, which provides the basis for the AEOI reviews.

The information in this report is up to date as of 25 November 2024. Updates are available on the Global Forum website (https://www.oecd.org/tax/transparency) and the relevant communication channels that each jurisdiction has in place domestically.

1. Ensuring the effective implementation of the AEOI Standard: the monitoring and peer review results

126 jurisdictions, including developed and developing countries, have either commenced exchanges under the AEOI Standard or have committed to do so soon. Maximising the benefits of the AEOI Standard requires its widespread and effective implementation based on a level playing field. The Global Forum seeks to deliver this through its monitoring and peer review processes, as well as through capacity building.

The OECD, working with G20 countries, developed the AEOI Standard in 2014. The G20 then asked the Global Forum to monitor the implementation of the AEOI Standard worldwide. As a first step, the Global Forum initiated a commitment process to ensure the widespread implementation of the AEOI Standard.

The Global Forum's AEOI commitment process

The Global Forum's first step to deliver the widespread and effective implementation of the AEOI Standard based on a level playing field was to put in place a commitment process. As a consequence, all Global Forum members, except for developing countries that did not host a financial centre, were invited to commit to implement the AEOI Standard to specific timelines. This led to around 100 jurisdictions committing to:

- implement the AEOI Standard;
- exchange information with all Interested Appropriate Partners (which are all jurisdictions interested in receiving information from a jurisdiction and that meet the expected standards in relation to confidentiality and data safeguards); and
- commence exchanges in 2017 or 2018.

Since then, a further 26 jurisdictions have committed to implement the AEOI Standard, with commencement dates between 2019 and 2027. This mainly consists of developing countries that do not host a financial centre but that want to benefit from AEOI in relation to Financial Accounts, although does also include jurisdictions subsequently identified through the Global Forum's "jurisdiction of relevance" process, designed to maintain a level playing field. The continually increasing number of jurisdictions committing to, and commencing, exchanges under the AEOI Standard, demonstrates the growing significance of AEOI to enhance tax transparency and ensure the correct payment of tax.

Monitoring the timeliness of delivery

Once commitments are made, the Global Forum monitors the timeliness of the delivery of each aspect of the implementation process. These include:

- putting in place a domestic legislative framework requiring Reporting Financial Institutions to collect and report the information for exchange, in accordance with the detailed due diligence and reporting rules contained in the AEOI Standard;
- putting in place an international legal framework that allows the automatic exchange of information with a jurisdiction's exchange partners, which includes an underlying legal basis for exchange and an administrative agreement containing the detailed specificities. The overwhelming majority of exchanges are conducted under the multilateral frameworks of the multilateral Convention on Mutual Administrative Assistance in Tax Matters (the Convention) and the associated Multilateral Competent Authority Agreement (MCAA); and
- establishing a technical infrastructure to receive the information from Reporting Financial Institutions and to process and transmit it to exchange partners. All jurisdictions use the Common Transmission System (CTS), procured by the OECD and managed by the Global Forum, to transmit the information.

In addition, both before and after jurisdictions receive information from their partners, their confidentiality and data safeguards frameworks are assessed to provide assurance that the information exchanged will be kept safe and only be used for the purposes set out in the international exchange agreement. Where substantive issues are identified in the confidentiality and data safeguards assessments, they must be addressed for the jurisdiction to receive, or continue to receive, information. Assistance is provided where necessary.

Delivery of the commitments

Table 1.1 presents details of the numbers of partners to which information was successfully sent by each implementing jurisdiction from 2018 to 2024. The data presented includes jurisdictions that received information as well as all instances where the necessary (domestic and international) legal frameworks were in place containing an obligation on Reporting Financial Institutions to report information with respect to tax residents of an exchange partner, but where no relevant Reportable Accounts were identified in practice (i.e. essentially a nil return).

97% of jurisdictions have delivered their commitment to exchange information under the AEOI Standard.

Table 1.1. Jurisdictions that exchanged information from 2018 to 2024

Jurisdiction	Year of commitment to first AEOI exchanges	Number of partners to which data was sent (Year Data Exchanged (EY) / Underlying Reportable Year (RY))						
		EY: 2018 RY: 2017	EY: 2019 RY: 2018	EY: 2020 RY: 2019	EY: 2021 RY: 2020	EY: 2022 RY: 2021	EY: 2023 RY: 2022	EY: 2024 RY: 2023
1. Albania[a,e]	2021	N/A	N/A	59	69	75	74	79
2. Andorra	2018	39	59	69	62	67	79	79
3. Anguilla	2017	4	52	52	55	57	67	67
4. Antigua and Barbuda	2018	36	35	30	33	23	40	40
5. Argentina	2017	56	67	71	76	78	82	82
6. Aruba	2018	50	58	66	64	65	62	73
7. Australia	2018	57	64	70	72	76	76	81
8. Austria	2018	46	61	68	71	77	79	84
9. Azerbaijan[a]	2018	33	53	52	70	74	79	83
10. Bahamas	2018	36	48	56	60	66	66	67
11. Bahrain	2018	38	50	59	63	65	70	72
12. Barbados	2018	57	53	61	64	62	68	71
13. Belgium	2017	66	69	72	77	80	83	87
14. Belize	2018	47	59	64	63	67	69	70
15. Bermuda	2017	52	61	60	64	70	73	75
16. Brazil	2018	56	67	69	76	76	77	77
17. British Virgin Islands	2017	50	64	67	65	61	73	76
18. Brunei Darussalam	2018	27	27	33	41	61	62	67
19. Bulgaria	2017	60	65	71	73	77	80	86
20. Canada	2018	56	59	57	66	65	68	73
21. Cayman Islands	2017	57	64	70	73	73	79	83
22. Chile	2018	48	63	69	72	71	78	86
23. China (People's Republic of)	2018	52	64	69	75	76	77	80
24. Colombia	2017	60	65	70	77	77	83	85
25. Cook Islands	2018	45	62	68	68	72	79	80
26. Costa Rica	2018	49	67	69	71	44	61	79
27. Croatia	2017	60	65	70	76	77	79	83
28. Curaçao	2018	57	57	66	51	71	71	78

29.	Cyprus[h]	2017	59	67	72	74	77	80	84
30.	Czechia	2017	60	60	66	74	80	83	81
31.	Denmark	2017	66	69	73	76	78	83	86
32.	Dominica	2018	0	0	0	56	65	62	57
33.	Ecuador[a]	2021	N/A	N/A	N/A	46	65	72	79
34.	Estonia	2017	62	66	69	73	74	78	85
35.	Faroe Islands	2017	57	67	67	73	72	77	80
36.	Finland	2017	66	69	70	77	81	82	83
37.	France	2017	62	66	68	71	75	80	83
38.	*Including New Caledonia*	2020	N/A	N/A	29	33	36	59	67
39.	Georgia[a]	2024	N/A	N/A	N/A	N/A	N/A	N/A	34
40.	Germany	2017	63	68	68	74	77	80	83
41.	Ghana[a]	2019	N/A	56	64	62	68	72	73
42.	Gibraltar	2017	51	59	69	72	75	77	77
43.	Greece	2017	67	68	69	74	76	82	85
44.	Greenland	2018	57	67	69	77	76	82	79
45.	Grenada	2018	55	54	65	61	59	57	17[g]
46.	Guernsey	2017	61	64	70	73	78	82	85
47.	Hong Kong, China	2018	40	45	50	67	71	75	80
48.	Hungary	2017	57	66	72	72	73	82	81
49.	Iceland	2017	59	64	67	70	73	76	83
50.	India	2017	60	67	68	74	77	81	82
51.	Indonesia	2018	59	66	69	72	77	76	83
52.	Ireland	2017	66	69	73	78	80	81	84
53.	Isle of Man	2017	57	64	68	75	78	82	84
54.	Israel	2018	41	55	61	67	71	65	70
55.	Italy	2017	64	67	71	76	75	79	83
56.	Jamaica[a]	2022	N/A	N/A	N/A	N/A	13	44	51
57.	Japan	2018	55	67	70	75	77	82	83
58.	Jersey	2017	58	65	69	73	76	79	80
59.	Jordan[c]	2023	N/A	N/A	N/A	N/A	N/A	-	-
60.	Kazakhstan[c]	2021	N/A	N/A	N/A	44	58	53	56
61.	Kenya[a]	2024	N/A	N/A	N/A	N/A	N/A	N/A	-[f]
62.	Korea	2017	59	67	70	74	76	81	86
63.	Kuwait[b]	2019	34	52	67	62	72	0[g]	81
64.	Latvia	2017	56	66	69	75	78	81	80
65.	Lebanon	2018	27	59	50	60	-[f]	-[f]	-[f]
66.	Liechtenstein	2017	50	60	68	75	74	79	82
67.	Lithuania	2017	63	66	70	70	75	79	80
68.	Luxembourg	2017	66	69	72	77	79	83	86
69.	Macau (China)	2018	36	48	60	67	70	73	78
70.	Malaysia	2018	42	64	65	69	73	76	82
71.	Maldives[a]	2022	N/A	N/A	N/A	N/A	35	56	73
72.	Malta	2017	61	67	73	73	73	83	80
73.	Marshall Islands	2018	1	57	59	60	58	62	66
74.	Mauritius	2018	58	65	69	74	75	77	80
75.	Mexico	2017	60	67	67	73	75	79	79
76.	Moldova[a]	2024	N/A	N/A	N/A	N/A	N/A	N/A	8[g]
77.	Monaco	2018	34	58	63	65	66	70	80
78.	Montenegro[c]	2023	N/A	N/A	N/A	N/A	N/A	-	-
79.	Montserrat	2017	12	16	60	0	57	60	65
80.	Nauru[d]	2018	No RFIs	No RFIs	No RFIs	No RFIs	No RFIs	No RFIs	No RFIs
81.	Netherlands	2017	61	65	68	70	77	82	82

82. New Zealand	2018	55	65	66	73	77	82	83
83. Nigeria[a]	2020	N/A	N/A	25	63	73	74	76
84. Niue[d]	2018	No RFIs	No RFIs	No RFIs	No RFIs	No RFIs	No RFIs	No RFIs
85. Norway	2017	64	68	71	75	77	82	86
86. Oman[b]	2020	N/A	N/A	28	28	39	58	61
87. Pakistan[a]	2018	40	55	57	61	55	69	73
88. Panama	2018	32	62	63	67	69	68	74
89. Peru[a]	2020	N/A	N/A	15	45	61	73	81
90. Poland	2017	66	69	71	74	76	78	86
91. Portugal	2017	66	69	71	76	75	80	84
92. Qatar	2018	9	49	49	58	59	65	61
93. Romania	2017	59	65	67	71	77	74	82
94. Russia	2018	50	58	63	69	No data	No data	No data
95. Saint Kitts and Nevis	2018	25	62	57	59	61	80	84
96. Saint Lucia	2018	40	61	65	68	69	75	75
97. Saint Vincent and the Grenadines	2018	65	56	0	0	21	76	75
98. Samoa	2018	45	59	64	66	63	69	71
99. San Marino	2017	57	63	68	71	74	82	85
100. Saudi Arabia	2018	56	65	68	74	72	78	84
101. Seychelles	2017	55	66	63	25	69	72	72
102. Singapore	2018	50	63	66	70	75	77	82
103. Sint Maarten	2018	0	0	0	0	49	69	70
104. Slovak Republic	2017	62	67	68	77	77	81	85
105. Slovenia	2017	64	69	72	78	80	83	87
106. South Africa	2017	57	63	68	76	77	82	85
107. Spain	2017	66	71	72	78	80	83	86
108. Sweden	2017	61	66	70	73	78	81	82
109. Switzerland	2018	36	62	66	72	73	81	81
110. Thailand[c]	2023	N/A	N/A	N/A	N/A	N/A	33	56
111. Trinidad and Tobago[c]	2018	-	-	-	-	-	-	-
112. Türkiye	2018	1	1	52	68	73	78	81
113. Turks and Caicos Islands	2017	44	0	63	67	68	75	74
114. Ukraine[a]	2024	N/A	N/A	N/A	N/A	N/A	N/A	53
115. United Arab Emirates	2018	43	53	68	70	75	79	79
116. United Kingdom	2017	62	68	70	72	76	81	85
117. Uruguay	2018	59	67	70	74	77	83	81
118. Vanuatu	2018	20	42	53	53	61	67	70

Note:

The United States has undertaken automatic information exchanges pursuant to FATCA from 2015 and entered into intergovernmental agreements (IGAs) with other jurisdictions to do so. The Model 1A IGAs entered into by the United States acknowledge the need for the United States to achieve equivalent levels of reciprocal automatic information exchange with partner jurisdictions. They also include a political commitment to pursue the adoption of regulations and to advocate and support relevant legislation to achieve such equivalent levels of reciprocal automatic exchange.

[a] Jurisdictions that are developing countries that were not asked to commit to implementing the AEOI Standard to a particular timeline but did so voluntarily.

[b] Developed jurisdictions that joined the Global Forum after the commitment process was conducted in 2014 and were therefore asked to commit to a particular timeline upon joining.

[c] Jurisdiction that were identified through the Global Forum process aimed at identifying jurisdictions of relevance for the implementation of the AEOI Standard and subsequently voluntarily committed to implement the AEOI Standard.

[d] As established through the peer review process, there are no Reporting Financial Institutions (RFIs) located in this jurisdiction.

[e] Albania voluntarily committed to commence exchanges in 2021 but did so in 2020.

[f] This jurisdiction is delayed in undertaking exchanges. It is expected to carry out the exchanges in the near future.

[g] This jurisdiction has conducted exchanges, but the figure provided is provisional and subject to changes as the exchanges are not yet fully verified.

[h] Note by the Republic of Türkiye: The information in this document with reference to "Cyprus" relates to the southern part of the Island. There is no single authority representing both Turkish and Greek Cypriot people on the Island. Türkiye recognises the Turkish Republic of Northern Cyprus (TRNC). Until a lasting and equitable solution is found within the context of the United Nations, Türkiye shall preserve its position concerning the "Cyprus issue".

Note by all the European Union Member States of the OECD and the European Union: The Republic of Cyprus is recognised by all members of the United Nations with the exception of Türkiye. The information in this document relates to the area under the effective control of the Government of the Republic of Cyprus.

N/A: Not applicable since the year is prior to the commitment date.

Jurisdictions yet to commence exchanges as committed to

As set out above, the vast majority (97%) of jurisdictions that committed to commence exchanges under the AEOI Standard have fulfilled their commitment.

There are nevertheless some jurisdictions that were invited to commence exchanges from a certain date, either under the original commitment process (**Trinidad and Tobago** that committed to commence exchanges from 2018) or that were identified later through the Global Forum's jurisdictions of relevance process (**Jordan and Montenegro** that committed to commence exchanges from 2023) that have not yet delivered on the commitments made.

A fully effective AEOI Standard requires a level playing field and the Global Forum therefore continues to work closely with these jurisdictions to facilitate the delivery of their commitments.

Commitments to commence exchanges in the future

Nine jurisdictions have committed to commencing the exchanges under the AEOI Standard in 2025 or in subsequent years. These are set out in Table 1.2 below.

Table 1.2. Jurisdictions committed to commencing exchanges in the near future

Year of commitment to first exchanges	Jurisdiction
2025	Armenia, Morocco, Rwanda, Senegal, Tunisia, Uganda
2026	Cameroon
2027	Mongolia, Papua New Guinea

Note: All jurisdictions committed to commencing AEOI exchanges from 2025 onwards are developing countries that do not host a financial centre and that were not asked to commit to a specific date to exchange information, but that have done so voluntarily.

Peer reviews of the effectiveness of implementation

While the timeliness of implementation is critical, all of the requirements must be implemented in a complete and effective manner for the potential benefits of the AEOI Standard be fully delivered. To ensure this, the Global Forum conducts peer reviews with respect to the quality of the implementation of all aspects of the AEOI Standard. Conclusions are drawn on the completeness of the domestic and international legal frameworks and on the effectiveness in practice of the domestic collection of the information and its international exchange.

Below is an analysis of the peer review results to date, after which the results are set out in full.

An analysis of the peer review results to date

The results of the reviews of the AEOI legal frameworks

Chapter 3 of this Report contains the new and amended jurisdiction reports. It includes five new reports on the AEOI legal frameworks in the jurisdictions that committed to commence exchanges from 2022 (Jamaica and the Maldives) and 2023 (Jordan, Montenegro and Thailand). It also contains revised reports for 46 jurisdictions that underwent a reassessment, either due to the additional checks carried out in 2023, mainly in relation to the compliance and enforcement frameworks, or at the request of the jurisdiction following amendments to their legal frameworks, including to address recommendations previously made.

In total, across all 114 jurisdictions whose legal frameworks have been assessed to date, 936 recommendations have been made, including 107 recommendations following the additional checks made in 2023. A total of 82 jurisdictions have brought into force amendments to their legal frameworks to address recommendations made through the Global Forum peer reviews, with 706 recommendations having been successfully addressed.

The peer review results show that there is a very high level of compliance in relation to the legal frameworks put in place to implement the AEOI Standard. Of the 114 jurisdictions committed to commencing exchanges by 2023, virtually all of them (111, or 97%) have an international legal framework that is fully in accordance with the AEOI Terms of Reference. The Global Forum has therefore issued 111 jurisdictions with a determination of “In Place” for Core Requirement 2. Furthermore, the majority of jurisdictions (60, or 53%) have domestic legislative frameworks that are also fully in accordance with the AEOI Terms of Reference. The Global Forum has therefore issued these jurisdictions with a determination of “In Place” for Core Requirement 1. 60 (or 53%) of jurisdictions have therefore received an overall determination of “In Place” for their legal frameworks implementing the AEOI Standard.

By far the next largest group of jurisdictions (48, or 42%) are those for which the Global Forum issued a determination of “In Place” for Core Requirement 2 and “In Place But Needs Improvement” for Core Requirement 1. Their peer review reports include one or more recommendations to amend their domestic legislative framework in order for it to be fully consistent with the AEOI Terms of Reference. Consequently, 48 jurisdictions received an overall determination of “In Place But Needs Improvement”. In total, 108 out of 114 (or 95%) of the jurisdictions assessed therefore have domestic and international legal frameworks that are fully or substantially in place. This demonstrates a high level of compliance with the AEOI Terms of Reference.

> Following the actions taken, 95% of jurisdictions have been determined to have domestic and international legal frameworks that are **fully** or **substantially** in accordance with the AEOI Terms of Reference

Of the remaining jurisdictions, three have implemented a domestic legislative framework which contains many of the requirements, but that include significant deficiencies. Three jurisdictions (Jordan, Montenegro and Trinidad and Tobago) have not yet implemented a domestic legal framework. Six jurisdictions have therefore received an overall determination of “Not In Place”.

Figure 1.1 summarises the distribution of the peer review results.

Figure 1.1. Overall legal determinations at a glance

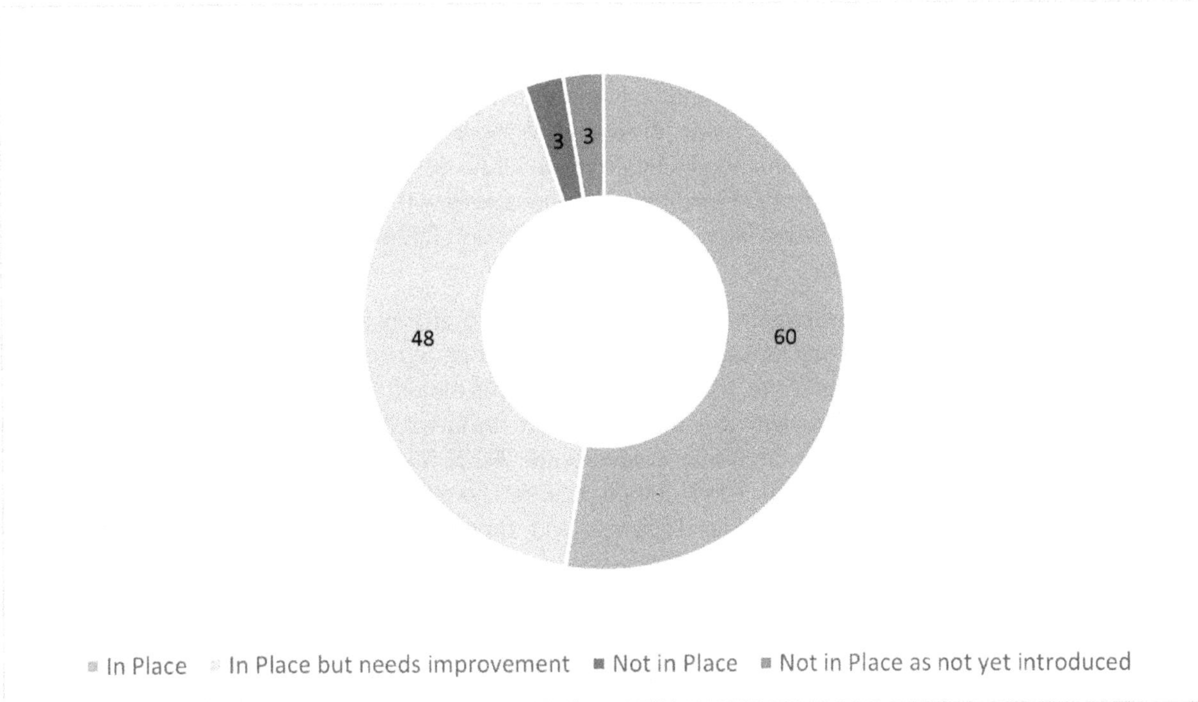

Common issues identified

While compliance with the requirements is generally high, there are some common issues where recommendations remain. They most commonly relate to the following:

- The largest category of remaining recommendations relates to jurisdiction-specific Non-Reporting Financial Institutions and Excluded Accounts that are not in accordance with the requirements of the AEOI Standard.
- The legal frameworks for compliance and enforcement have also been found to have issues in several cases, including issues identified through the additional targeted checks in relation to the compliance and enforcement frameworks conducted in the context of the second round of AEOI reviews in relation to effectiveness in practice. These include gaps in:
    - the powers to address avoidance of the due diligence and reporting requirements;
    - the ability to impose sanctions on Reporting Financial Institutions across the full expected range of instances of failures to comply with the due diligence and reporting obligations;
    - the ability to sanction Account Holders and Controlling Persons for submitting false self-certifications; and
    - the applicable record-keeping obligations.

It is noted that all the jurisdictions with legal frameworks that have been determined to be "Not In Place" have multiple recommendations with respect to their legal frameworks for compliance and enforcement.

Several more specific recommendations have also been made in cases where jurisdictions have summarised the detailed definitions in the AEOI Standard with the omission of relevant details that are needed to ensure their full and proper operation.

The Global Forum continues to work with the jurisdictions concerned to assist them in addressing the issues where recommendations have been made.

The results of the reviews of the effectiveness in practice

Chapter 3 of this report contains the jurisdiction-specific reports. It contains three additional initial effectiveness review reports on the implementation in practice of the AEOI Standard by jurisdictions that committed to commence exchanges from 2020: Nigeria, Oman and Peru. Note that, under the usual process, the initial effectiveness review report in relation to New Caledonia would have been published this year as New Caledonia also commenced exchanges in 2020, as it committed to. However, the Global Forum has deferred the finalisation of the initial effectiveness review for New Caledonia by one year due to the severe political and social issues faced by New Caledonia in 2024, including the civil unrest and the imposition of a state of emergency.

Overall, the results of the initial effectiveness reviews show that most jurisdictions are delivering as expected. Moreover, it is understood that significant progress continues to be made since the assessments have been carried out. The results of the initial reviews show that almost two thirds (67, or 64%) of the 104 jurisdictions that have been reviewed so far, have been rated as "On Track" with respect to their frameworks and activities to ensure the effectiveness of the AEOI Standard in practice. This means that they have developed complete administrative compliance frameworks to ensure that Reporting Financial Institutions effectively implement the due diligence and reporting obligations, which they are also implementing. Furthermore, these jurisdictions are also successfully conducting the exchanges in practice, addressing any issues as they emerged.

A further 17 (or 16%) jurisdictions have been found to have credible frameworks and plans in place and were generally successfully exchanging the information in accordance with the technical requirements, but need to further implement their plans. These jurisdictions have therefore been rated as "Partially Compliant". The implementation in many of these jurisdictions is expected to mature significantly in the near future, provided that the plans they have in place are followed through.

Finally, 20 (or around 19%) jurisdictions have been found to have fundamental deficiencies in their frameworks (i.e. they are not yet fully developed) and have therefore been found to be "Non-Compliant". Of the "Non-Compliant" jurisdictions, four have since addressed the significant gaps in their legal compliance and enforcement frameworks that drove the result of the initial effectiveness reviews. For these jurisdictions, while the exchanges are taking place each year, they have not yet completed operational frameworks to verify and enforce the compliance by Reporting Financial Institutions with all of the due diligence and reporting requirements.

Figure 1.2 summarises the distribution of the peer review results.

Figure 1.2. Overall initial effectiveness ratings at a glance

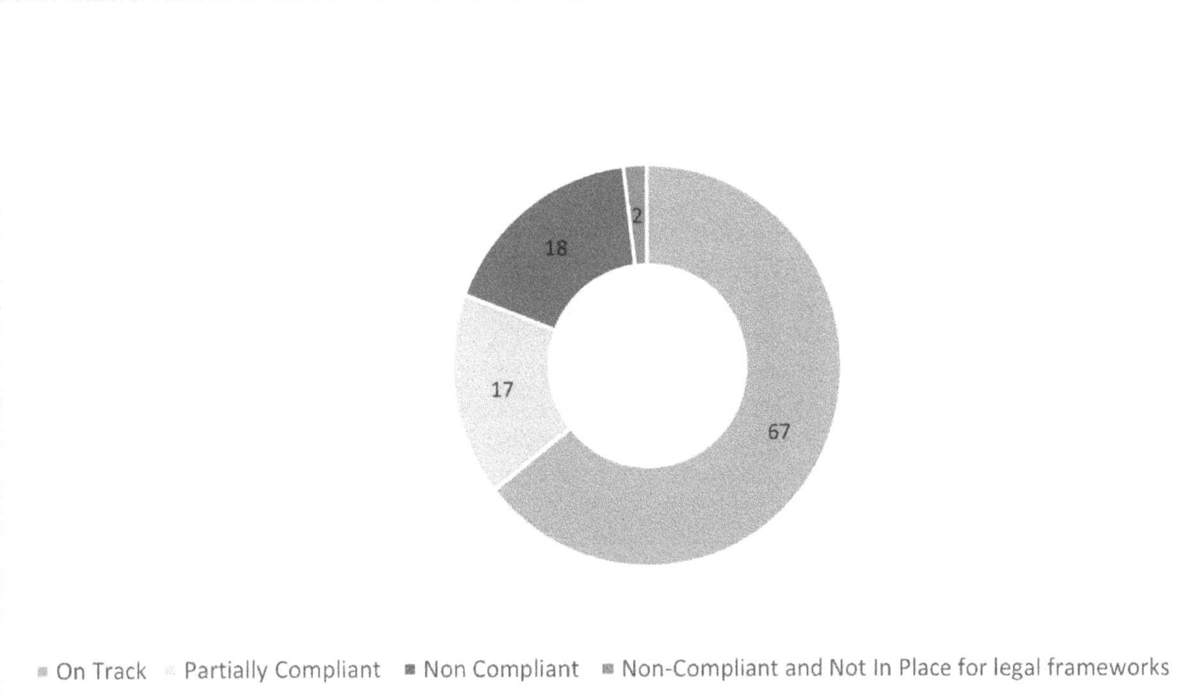

In general, the rate of advancement and the increasing maturity in implementation continues at pace. In this regard, a significant majority of jurisdictions had seen improvements in their ability to match the information received, indicating an increase in the quality of the information being sent. Furthermore, in recent years, three-quarters of jurisdictions have seen improvements in the collection of Tax Identification Numbers, as well as reductions in the numbers of undocumented accounts reported. Furthermore, the rate of the collection and exchange of dates of birth is close to 100%. These are all critical aspects to the matching of the information exchanged with domestic taxpayer records. As regards the exchanges themselves, while there are sometimes delays and issues with the preparation of the files, these tend to be quickly and effectively addressed.

Common issues identified

While around two thirds of jurisdictions assessed have been found to be “On Track” with their implementation, amongst the remaining jurisdictions, several common issues were identified.

The most significant issues identified relate to the lack of a complete framework to enforce the requirements. In many cases some activities had been conducted to ensure Reporting Financial Institutions are reporting information as required (e.g. by cross checking relevant lists of regulated entities), but there has been limited activities to ensure that the information being reported is complete and accurate. These jurisdictions generally committed to quickly work to address the deficiencies identified. Furthermore, support is being given by the Global Forum Secretariat, which has developed a Model Administrative Compliance Strategy, organised knowledge sharing events and recently released additional tools to support its bilateral technical assistance programme. It is therefore expected that these issues be successfully addressed in the near term. It will generally take longer for jurisdictions that need to address constraints in their legal frameworks to enforce the requirements, in order to complete the necessary legislative processes.

There is another group of jurisdictions that have credible plans in place but that have only very recently started implementing them. For example, the checks to ensure that the information being reported is complete and accurate is not yet very mature, such as being limited to analysing the information reported but not yet including reviewing the policies, procedures and account documentation of individual Reporting Financial Institutions.

As mentioned earlier, with respect to the exchanges in practice, the level of implementation has been very high and, where issues emerge, they are generally promptly addressed.

A summary of the peer reviews to date

Table 1.3 contains an overall summary of: (i) the determinations made with respect to legal frameworks introduced by each jurisdiction to implement the AEOI Standard, and (ii) the ratings made following the initial review of the effectiveness of their implementation in practice. Further details on the analysis and reasons for the determinations for each jurisdiction can be found in Peer Review of the Automatic Exchange of Financial Account Information 2022 (https://www.oecd-ilibrary.org/taxation/peer-review-of-the-automatic-exchange-of-financial-account-information-2022_36e7cded-en) which has been supplemented by the reports in Chapter 3 of the 2023 report for the assessments and reassessments completed in 2023 and in Chapter 3 of this report for the assessments and reassessments conducted in 2024.

Table 1.3. Overview of the determinations on the legal frameworks and the ratings on effectiveness in practice for the assessed jurisdictions

Jurisdiction	Review of the AEOI legal frameworks			Initial review of effectiveness in practice of AEOI		
	Core Requirement 1 (domestic legal framework)	Core Requirement 2 (international legal framework)	Overall determination	Core Requirement 1 (domestic information collection and reporting)	Core Requirement 2 (international information exchange)	Overall rating
1. Albania	In Place But Needs Improvement	In Place	In Place But Needs Improvement	Not yet reviewed		
2. Andorra	In Place But Needs Improvement	In Place	In Place But Needs Improvement	On Track	On Track	On Track
3. Anguilla	In Place But Needs Improvement	In Place	In Place But Needs Improvement	Partially Compliant	On Track	Partially Compliant
4. Antigua and Barbuda	In Place But Needs Improvement	In Place	In Place But Needs Improvement	Non-Compliant	Partially Compliant	Non-Compliant
5. Argentina	In Place But Needs Improvement	In Place	In Place But Needs Improvement	Partially Compliant	On Track	Partially Compliant
6. Aruba	In Place But Needs Improvement	In Place	In Place But Needs Improvement	Non-Compliant	On Track	Non-Compliant
7. Australia	In Place But Needs Improvement	In Place	In Place But Needs Improvement	On Track	On Track	On Track
8. Austria	In Place	In Place	In Place	On Track	On Track	On Track

Jurisdiction	Review of the AEOI legal frameworks			Initial review of effectiveness in practice of AEOI		
	Core Requirement 1 (domestic legal framework)	Core Requirement 2 (international legal framework)	Overall determination	Core Requirement 1 (domestic information collection and reporting)	Core Requirement 2 (international information exchange)	Overall rating
9. Azerbaijan	In Place But Needs Improvement	In Place	In Place But Needs Improvement	On Track	On Track	On Track
10. Bahamas	In Place But Needs Improvement	In Place	In Place But Needs Improvement	Non-Compliant	On Track	Non-Compliant
11. Bahrain	In Place	In Place	In Place	On Track	On Track	On Track
12. Barbados	In Place	In Place	In Place	On Track	Partially Compliant	On Track
13. Belgium	In Place	In Place	In Place	On Track	On Track	On Track
14. Belize	In Place	In Place	In Place	Non-Compliant	On Track	Non-Compliant
15. Bermuda	In Place	In Place	In Place	On Track	On Track	On Track
16. Brazil	In Place	In Place	In Place	On Track	On Track	On Track
17. British Virgin Islands	In Place But Needs Improvement	In Place	In Place But Needs Improvement	Partially Compliant	On Track	Partially Compliant
18. Brunei Darussalam	In Place But Needs Improvement	In Place	In Place But Needs Improvement	Partially Compliant	On Track	Partially Compliant
19. Bulgaria	In Place But Needs Improvement	In Place	In Place But Needs Improvement	On Track	On Track	On Track
20. Canada	In Place But Needs Improvement	In Place	In Place But Needs Improvement	On Track	On Track	On Track
21. Cayman Islands	In Place	In Place	In Place	On Track	On Track	On Track
22. Chile	In Place But Needs Improvement	In Place	In Place But Needs Improvement	Non-Compliant	Partially Compliant	Non-Compliant
23. China (People's Republic of)	In Place	In Place	In Place	On Track	On Track	On Track
24. Colombia	In Place	In Place	In Place	On Track	On Track	On Track
25. Cook Islands	In Place But Needs Improvement	In Place	In Place But Needs Improvement	Non-Compliant	On Track	Non-Compliant
26. Costa Rica	In Place	In Place	In Place	Non-Compliant	Partially Compliant	Non-Compliant
27. Croatia	In Place But Needs Improvement	In Place	In Place But Needs Improvement	Non-Compliant	On Track	Non-Compliant

Jurisdiction	Review of the AEOI legal frameworks			Initial review of effectiveness in practice of AEOI		
	Core Requirement 1 (domestic legal framework)	Core Requirement 2 (international legal framework)	Overall determination	Core Requirement 1 (domestic information collection and reporting)	Core Requirement 2 (international information exchange)	Overall rating
28. Curaçao	In Place	In Place	In Place	Non-Compliant	Partially Compliant	Non-Compliant
29. Cyprus	In Place	In Place	In Place	On Track	On Track	On Track
30. Czechia	In Place	In Place	In Place	On Track	On Track	On Track
31. Denmark	In Place	In Place	In Place	On Track	On Track	On Track
32. Dominica	In Place	In Place	In Place	Non-Compliant	Partially Compliant	Non-Compliant
33. Ecuador	In Place	In Place	In Place	Not yet reviewed		
34. Estonia	In Place But Needs Improvement	In Place	In Place But Needs Improvement	Partially Compliant	On Track	Partially Compliant
35. Faroe Islands	In Place	In Place	In Place	Partially Compliant	On Track	Partially Compliant
36. Finland	In Place	In Place	In Place	On Track	On Track	On Track
37. France	In Place But Needs Improvement	In Place	In Place But Needs Improvement	On Track	Partially Compliant	On Track
38. Germany	In Place But Needs Improvement	In Place	In Place But Needs Improvement	On Track	On Track	On Track
39. Ghana	In Place But Needs Improvement	In Place	In Place But Needs Improvement	Partially Compliant	On Track	Partially Compliant
40. Gibraltar	In Place	In Place	In Place	Partially Compliant	On Track	Partially Compliant
41. Greece	In Place	In Place	In Place	On Track	On Track	On Track
42. Greenland	In Place	In Place	In Place	On Track	On Track	On Track
43. Grenada	In Place	In Place	In Place	Non-Compliant	Partially Compliant	Non-Compliant
44. Guernsey	In Place	In Place	In Place	On Track	On Track	On Track
45. Hong Kong (China)	In Place	In Place	In Place	On Track	On Track	On Track
46. Hungary	In Place But Needs Improvement	In Place	In Place But Needs Improvement	On Track	On Track	On Track
47. Iceland	In Place	In Place	In Place	On Track	On Track	On Track

Jurisdiction	Review of the AEOI legal frameworks			Initial review of effectiveness in practice of AEOI		
	Core Requirement 1 (domestic legal framework)	Core Requirement 2 (international legal framework)	Overall determination	Core Requirement 1 (domestic information collection and reporting)	Core Requirement 2 (international information exchange)	Overall rating
48. India	In Place	In Place	In Place	On Track	On Track	On Track
49. Indonesia	In Place	In Place	In Place	On Track	On Track	On Track
50. Ireland	In Place	In Place	In Place	On Track	On Track	On Track
51. Isle of Man	In Place	In Place	In Place	On Track	On Track	On Track
52. Israel	In Place But Needs Improvement	In Place	In Place But Needs Improvement	Partially Compliant	On Track	Partially Compliant
53. Italy	In Place	In Place	In Place	On Track	On Track	On Track
54. Jamaica	In Place But Needs Improvement	In Place	In Place But Needs Improvement	Not yet reviewed		
55. Japan	In Place But Needs Improvement	In Place	In Place But Needs Improvement	On Track	On Track	On Track
56. Jersey	In Place	In Place	In Place	On Track	On Track	On Track
57. Jordan	Not In Place	Not In Place	Not In Place	Not yet reviewed		
58. Kazakhstan	Not In Place	In Place	Not In Place	Not yet reviewed		
59. Korea	In Place	In Place	In Place	On Track	On Track	On Track
60. Kuwait	Not In Place	In Place	Not In Place	Non-Compliant	On Track	Non-Compliant
61. Latvia	In Place But Needs Improvement	In Place	In Place But Needs Improvement	On Track	On Track	On Track
62. Lebanon	In Place	In Place	In Place	On Track	On Track	On Track
63. Liechtenstein	In Place	In Place	In Place	On Track	On Track	On Track
64. Lithuania	In Place But Needs Improvement	In Place	In Place But Needs Improvement	On Track	On Track	On Track
65. Luxembourg	In Place	In Place	In Place	On Track	On Track	On Track
66. Macau (China)	In Place	In Place	In Place	On Track	On Track	On Track
67. Malaysia	In Place	In Place	In Place	On Track	On Track	On Track

Jurisdiction		Review of the AEOI legal frameworks			Initial review of effectiveness in practice of AEOI		
		Core Requirement 1 (domestic legal framework)	Core Requirement 2 (international legal framework)	Overall determination	Core Requirement 1 (domestic information collection and reporting)	Core Requirement 2 (international information exchange)	Overall rating
68.	Maldives	Not In Place	In Place	Not In Place	Not yet reviewed		
69.	Malta	In Place	In Place	In Place	Partially Compliant	On Track	Partially Compliant
70.	Marshall Islands	In Place	In Place	In Place	Partially Compliant	On Track	Partially Compliant
71.	Mauritius	In Place	In Place	In Place	On Track	On Track	On Track
72.	Mexico	In Place	In Place	In Place	Partially Compliant	Partially Compliant	Partially Compliant
73.	Monaco	In Place	In Place	In Place	On Track	On Track	On Track
74.	Montenegro	Not In Place	Not In Place	Not In Place	Not yet reviewed		
75.	Montserrat	In Place But Needs Improvement	In Place	In Place But Needs Improvement	Non-Compliant	Non-Compliant	Non-Compliant
76.	Nauru	In Place But Needs Improvement	In Place	In Place But Needs Improvement	On Track	On Track	On Track
77.	Netherlands	In Place	In Place	In Place	On Track	On Track	On Track
78.	New Caledonia	In Place But Needs Improvement	In Place	In Place But Needs Improvement	Not yet reviewed		
79.	New Zealand	In Place	In Place	In Place	On Track	On Track	On Track
80.	Nigeria	In Place But Needs Improvement	In Place	In Place But Needs Improvement	On Track	On Track	On Track
81.	Niue	In Place	In Place	In Place	On Track	On Track	On Track
82.	Norway	In Place	In Place	In Place	On Track	On Track	On Track
83.	Oman	In Place	In Place	In Place	Partially Compliant	Partially Compliant	Partially Compliant
84.	Pakistan	In Place	In Place	In Place	Partially Compliant	Partially Compliant	Partially Compliant
85.	Panama	In Place But Needs Improvement	In Place	In Place But Needs Improvement	Non-Compliant	Partially Compliant	Non-Compliant
86.	Peru	In Place But Needs Improvement	In Place	In Place But Needs Improvement	On Track	On Track	On Track
87.	Poland	In Place But Needs Improvement	In Place	In Place But Needs Improvement	On Track	On Track	On Track

Jurisdiction	Review of the AEOI legal frameworks			Initial review of effectiveness in practice of AEOI		
	Core Requirement 1 (domestic legal framework)	Core Requirement 2 (international legal framework)	Overall determination	Core Requirement 1 (domestic information collection and reporting)	Core Requirement 2 (international information exchange)	Overall rating
88. Portugal	In Place But Needs Improvement	In Place	In Place But Needs Improvement	On Track	On Track	On Track
89. Qatar	In Place	In Place	In Place	On Track	On Track	On Track
90. Romania	In Place	In Place	In Place	Partially Compliant	On Track	Partially Compliant
91. Russia	In Place But Needs Improvement	In Place	In Place But Needs Improvement	No data available		
92. Saint Kitts and Nevis	In Place But Needs Improvement	In Place	In Place But Needs Improvement	On Track	On Track	On Track
93. Saint Lucia	In Place But Needs Improvement	In Place	In Place But Needs Improvement	On Track	On Track	On Track
94. Saint Vincent and the Grenadines	In Place But Needs Improvement	In Place	In Place But Needs Improvement	Non-Compliant	Non-Compliant	Non-Compliant
95. Samoa	In Place But Needs Improvement	In Place	In Place But Needs Improvement	On Track	On Track	On Track
96. San Marino	In Place	In Place	In Place	On Track	On Track	On Track
97. Saudi Arabia	In Place	In Place	In Place	On Track	On Track	On Track
98. Seychelles	In Place But Needs Improvement	In Place	In Place But Needs Improvement	Non-Compliant	Non-Compliant	Non-Compliant
99. Singapore	In Place	In Place	In Place	On Track	On Track	On Track
100. Sint Maarten	In Place But Needs Improvement	In Place	In Place But Needs Improvement	Non-Compliant	Non-Compliant	Non-Compliant
101. Slovak Republic	In Place	In Place	In Place	On Track	On Track	On Track
102. Slovenia	In Place But Needs Improvement	In Place	In Place But Needs Improvement	On Track	On Track	On Track
103. South Africa	In Place	In Place	In Place	Partially Compliant	On Track	Partially Compliant
104. Spain	In Place	In Place	In Place	On Track	On Track	On Track
105. Sweden	In Place But Needs Improvement	In Place	In Place But Needs Improvement	On Track	On Track	On Track
106. Switzerland	In Place But Needs Improvement	In Place	In Place But Needs Improvement	On Track	On Track	On Track

Jurisdiction	Review of the AEOI legal frameworks			Initial review of effectiveness in practice of AEOI		
	Core Requirement 1 (domestic legal framework)	Core Requirement 2 (international legal framework)	Overall determination	Core Requirement 1 (domestic information collection and reporting)	Core Requirement 2 (international information exchange)	Overall rating
107. Trinidad and Tobago	Not In Place	Not In Place	Not In Place	Non-Compliant	Non-Compliant	Non-Compliant
108. Thailand	In Place But Needs Improvement	In Place	In Place But Needs Improvement	Not yet reviewed		
109. Türkiye	In Place	In Place	In Place	Partially Compliant	Partially Compliant	Partially Compliant
110. Turks and Caicos Islands	In Place But Needs Improvement	In Place	In Place But Needs Improvement	Non-Compliant	On Track	Non-Compliant
111. United Arab Emirates	In Place	In Place	In Place	On Track	On Track	On Track
112. United Kingdom	In Place But Needs Improvement	In Place	In Place But Needs Improvement	On Track	On Track	On Track
113. Uruguay	In Place	In Place	In Place	On Track	On Track	On Track
114. Vanuatu	In Place But Needs Improvement	In Place	In Place But Needs Improvement	Non-Compliant	On Track	Non-Compliant

The second round of AEOI effectiveness reviews

With the completion of the initial peer reviews of the effectiveness of the implementation of the AEOI Standard for the first 99 jurisdictions in 2022, the Global Forum put in place a framework to carry out a second round of AEOI effectiveness reviews. These are designed to obtain a more in-depth assurance in relation to the effectiveness of the implementation of the AEOI Standard in practice and include onsite visits by Assessment Teams to meet with all relevant public and private sector stakeholders.

The second round of AEOI effectiveness reviews commenced in 2023 and involve a detailed and deeper assessment of the administrative strategies and frameworks jurisdictions have in place to ensure compliance by Reporting Financial Institutions, as well as the actions taken and the results of those actions. Onsite visits are being conducted during which assessment teams meet with the officials involved in ensuring compliance by Reporting Financial Institutions as well as with the regulatory authorities and representatives of the financial sector. There is also an annual peer input process to obtain the feedback from each jurisdiction's exchange partners to inform the peer review process. All 99 jurisdictions that committed to commence exchanges in 2017 or 2018 are being assessed simultaneously, according to a schedule for the onsite visits, with all reports being updated at the end of the process to reflect the most up to date situation in the jurisdictions.

The second round of AEOI effectiveness reviews has been a hugely beneficial learning process, both for implementing jurisdictions and the Global Forum more generally. The collective knowledge of the practices of governmental and private sector stakeholders has expanded considerably, and the expectations of AEOI Peers as to what constitutes an effective implementation of the AEOI Standard have been developed and refined. Ultimately, the objective of the Global Forum is to have a global implementation of the AEOI Standard that is as effective as possible to provide the greatest expected benefit to the international community. This is supported by continuing to disseminate the best practices observed to all jurisdictions and allowing time for their sustainable implementation and review. With this in mind, the Global Forum has extended the period within which it will conduct the second round of AEOI effectiveness reviews of the first 99 jurisdictions to implement the AEOI Standard by one year. An update on the processes being conducted will be published in the 2025 AEOI Peer Review Report and the final results of the second round AEOI effectiveness reviews for all 99 jurisdictions will be published in the 2026 AEOI Peer Review Report.

Further details of the frameworks used for the AEOI peer reviews can be found in Chapter 2.

2. Methodologies for the Global Forum's AEOI peer review processes

This chapter provides an overview of the methodologies used by the Global Forum for its peer review processes, including explanations of how to interpret the determinations in relation to the legal frameworks for AEOI and the ratings of the effectiveness in practice.

To ensure that the implementation of the AEOI Standard is both complete and effective, the Global Forum conducts peer reviews in relation to all of the key areas of the AEOI Standard. These are conducted in accordance with the agreed Terms of Reference for the AEOI reviews, which are contained in Annex B of this report. As set out therein, the Terms of Reference comprise of Core Requirement 1 in relation to the domestic collection and reporting of the information by Reporting Financial Institutions, Core Requirement 2 in relation to the international exchange of the information between tax authorities and Core Requirement 3 in relation to confidentiality and data safeguards.

Global Forum AEOI peer reviews: covering all relevant areas

Properly implementing the AEOI Standard requires various legal, technical and operational requirements to be put in place and for them to operate effectively in practice. The Global Forum has therefore designed and conducted a range of peer review processes specifically suited to assess each area. The processes are as follows:

- **Reviews of the domestic and international legal frameworks in place**: The AEOI Standard requires complete domestic and international legal frameworks to be in place. Domestically, Reporting Financial Institutions must be required to conduct the prescribed due diligence procedures in the AEOI Standard and to report the specified information to their tax authority. Internationally, jurisdictions must also have a legal basis in place to exchange the information, in the required manner, with all their Interested Appropriate Partners (which are jurisdictions interested in receiving information from another jurisdiction and that meet the expected standards in relation to confidentiality and data safeguards). The Global Forum conducts peer reviews of the domestic and international legal frameworks in place to ensure that they are complete and provide a sound basis for the effective operation of the AEOI Standard.
- **Reviews of the effectiveness of the implementation of the AEOI Standard in practice**: In addition to having complete legal frameworks, jurisdictions must ensure that the legal frameworks operate effectively in practice, including that they are properly complied with by Reporting Financial Institutions. The Global Forum therefore reviews each jurisdiction's implementation of the AEOI Standard in practice, including the administrative frameworks in place, and the associated activities undertaken, to ensure compliance by Reporting Financial Institutions and the functioning of the exchanges in practice. These reviews are done in two stages: (i) initial desk-based reviews of effectiveness in practice to assess whether jurisdictions are "On Track", and (ii) deeper reviews of effectiveness that include an on-site visit to obtain a deeper level of assurance.
- **Assessments of confidentiality and data safeguards frameworks**: The information exchanged, which includes sensitive information identifying taxpayers and their international financial activities, must be properly safeguarded and used only for the purpose set out in the international exchange agreements. The Global Forum therefore conducts reviews of the legal and operational arrangements jurisdictions have in place to safeguard data before they can receive information through AEOI. Assistance is given where needed. The Global Forum again reviews the arrangements in place once exchanges are underway, to ensure the requirements are met on an ongoing basis and has recently adopted a framework for a new third round of reviews to ensure ongoing compliance with the requirements. This Global Forum process includes a mechanism to react to breaches of confidentiality or the safeguarding of data. Due to their confidential nature, the results of these assessments are not published.

Further details in relation to the assessments and work of the Global Forum with respect to confidentiality and data safeguards can be found in the *Terms of Reference for the Confidentiality and Data Safeguards Assessments*[1] and the *Confidentiality and Information Security Management Toolkit*.[2] With respect to the other reviews, further details on their scope and the process can be found below.

Peer reviews of the AEOI legal frameworks

A key early step in the implementation process is putting in place complete domestic and international legal frameworks, in accordance with the AEOI Standard and the commitments made. The Global Forum reviews the frameworks once they are put in place to allow any issues to be identified early so they can be promptly addressed.

The requirements

The AEOI Terms of Reference group the requirements with respect to the legal frameworks into two Core Requirements. These are set out below:

- **Core Requirement 1**: Jurisdictions should have a domestic legislative framework in place that requires all Reporting Financial Institutions to conduct the due diligence and reporting procedures in the CRS, and that provides for the effective implementation of the CRS as set out therein.
- **Core Requirement 2**: Jurisdictions should have exchange relationships in effect with all Interested Appropriate Partners as committed to and that provide for the exchange of information in accordance with the Model CAA.

Each Core Requirement is split into detailed Sub-Requirements, which are contained in Annex B.

How the requirements are reviewed

For each of the review processes in relation to the AEOI legal frameworks, the following steps are conducted:

- The Global Forum Secretariat conducts an initial in-depth analysis of the legal texts and drafts proposed recommendations where issues are identified.
- The analysis and draft recommendations are sent to all AEOI Peers[3] for input, which is incorporated as appropriate.
- The analysis and proposed recommendations are sent to the AEOI Peer Review Group (APRG)[4] for approval.
- The approved analysis and recommendations are submitted to all AEOI Peers for adoption.

What is reviewed in relation to Core Requirement 1

Core Requirement 1 in the AEOI Terms of Reference refer to the detailed due diligence and reporting procedures that Reporting Financial Institutions must follow. These are standardised procedures to ensure that Reporting Financial Institutions report the correct information on Financial Accounts and their Account Holders to the tax authority in a uniform manner. It is therefore crucial that each jurisdiction properly reflects these requirements in its domestic legislative framework. The specific elements reviewed are as follows:

- **The due diligence and reporting rules**: This involves a review of how each jurisdiction has: (i) defined the scope of Reporting Financial Institutions, (ii) defined the scope of the Financial Accounts that must be reviewed, (iii) implemented the detailed due diligence procedures that must be applied to identify Reportable Accounts, and (iv) defined the information that must be reported. If a jurisdiction relies on non-AEOI legislation that defines "beneficial owners" to identify Controlling Persons with respect to the AEOI Standard, this legislation is also reviewed.
- **Jurisdiction-specific Non-Reporting Financial Institutions and Excluded Accounts**: This consists of a specific review of each entry to ensure that the Non-Reporting Financial Institutions and Excluded Accounts provided for by each jurisdiction meet the requirements of the AEOI Standard and pose a low-risk of use for tax evasion purposes.

- **The framework to enforce the requirements**: This includes, amongst other aspects, a review of the provisions that jurisdictions have in place to: (i) prevent the circumvention of the AEOI Standard, (ii) require Reporting Financial Institutions to maintain appropriate records; and (iii) enforce the requirements and address non-compliance. Where the provisions relied upon are included in non-AEOI legal frameworks, these provisions are also reviewed, to the extent they are relevant for the implementation of the requirements of the AEOI Standard.

Where gaps are identified, recommendations are made.

What is reviewed in relation to Core Requirement 2

Core Requirement 2 in the AEOI Terms of Reference contains requirements with respect to both the contents of the international agreements used to exchange the information and the scope of the networks of exchange relationships. These requirements are therefore also essential to ensure the effective operation of the AEOI Standard, based on a level playing field. The processes conducted are as follows:

- **The contents of the exchange agreements**: The contents of the exchange agreements put in place are reviewed to ensure their provisions are in accordance with the requirements. This includes the international agreement that provides the legal basis for the exchange and the administrative agreement containing the detailed specificities.
- **Ensuring exchange networks are complete**: It is ensured that each jurisdiction's exchange network includes all its Interested Appropriate Partners (i.e. the jurisdictions interested in receiving information from a jurisdiction and that meet the expected standards in relation to confidentiality and data safeguards). The process includes facilitating jurisdictions in putting agreements in place, which can be escalated into a peer review mechanism that jurisdictions can trigger if they become concerned about delays with respect to the putting in place of an agreement with a particular partner.

Again, where gaps are identified, recommendations are made.

Drawing conclusions and issuing determinations on the completeness of the AEOI legal frameworks

The determinations on the AEOI legal frameworks are made with respect to each Core Requirement and overall. They are either: "**In Place**", "In Place But **Needs Improvement**" or "**Not In Place**", with the determination for each Core Requirement and the overall determination reflecting all relevant factors (i.e. it is not a mechanical exercise). Further details on how to interpret each of these determinations, along with an indication of the relevant considerations, are set out in Table 2.1 below.

Table 2.1. The determinations made in relation to the AEOI legal frameworks

Determination	Description
In Place	A jurisdiction's legal framework is determined as being "**In Place**" where the review of its legal framework does not identify any gaps that need to be addressed in order for the legal framework to be in accordance with the AEOI Terms of Reference. This is the case where the peer review processes have not resulted in any recommendations. It is possible, although unusual, for a legal framework to be determined to be In Place even where there is a recommendation. This is only the case where the gap is viewed as so minor that it would have a highly limited impact on the operation of the AEOI Standard.
In Place But **Needs Improvement**	A jurisdiction's legal framework is determined as being "In Place But **Needs Improvement**" where the review of its legal framework concludes that the legal framework is in place but certain aspects need improvement in order for it to be fully in accordance with the AEOI Terms of Reference.

Determination	Description
	This is the case where the peer review processes have identified one or more deficiencies material to the proper functioning of elements of the AEOI Standard. The determination of In Place But Needs Improvement is therefore a broad category. It includes jurisdictions with one recommendation, as well as jurisdictions with multiple recommendations. In all cases, the deficiencies are viewed collectively as material to the proper functioning of certain elements of the AEOI Standard, but not to its overall operation.
Not In Place	A jurisdiction's legal framework is determined as being "**Not In Place**" where the review of its legal framework shows that the legal framework needs to be significantly improved in order to be in accordance with the AEOI Terms of Reference. At the extreme, this is the case where a jurisdiction has not implemented the relevant legal framework. More commonly, this is where the peer review processes have resulted in recommendations viewed collectively as having a material impact on the overall operation of the AEOI Standard. It is important to note, aside from the jurisdictions that have not implemented a legal framework, a determination of Not In Place does not mean that a jurisdiction's legal framework is not in effect. In fact, several aspects of that legal framework are likely to be in place as required. The determination instead means that the impact of the deficiencies found are viewed as creating a material risk to the overall proper functioning of the AEOI Standard (e.g. a jurisdiction's legal framework to enforce the due diligence requirements is substantively incomplete).

Peer reviews of the effectiveness in practice of AEOI implementation

Having complete legal frameworks is not sufficient to ensure that the AEOI Standard is effective and delivers the potential benefits it has to offer. It must also be ensured that the requirements are being implemented effectively in practice. The Global Forum therefore carries out peer reviews to assess the effectiveness in practice of each jurisdiction's implementation of the AEOI Standard.

The peer reviews in relation to the effectiveness in practice of the implementation of the AEOI Standard are carried out in two stages. Firstly, there in an initial assessment to verify whether the jurisdiction is "On Track" and, secondly, there is a deeper review to obtain a deeper level of assurance.

The requirements

Similarly to the legal frameworks, the AEOI Terms of Reference group the requirements with respect to effectiveness in practice into the same two Core Requirements. The requirements are the same for the initial and in-depth reviews. These are set out below:

- **Core Requirement 1**: Jurisdictions should have an administrative framework to ensure the effective implementation of the CRS and ensure that in practice Reporting Financial Institutions correctly implement the due diligence and reporting procedures in the CRS.
- **Core Requirement 2**: Jurisdictions should exchange the information effectively in practice, in a timely manner, including by sorting, preparing, validating and transmitting the information in accordance with the AEOI Standard.

Each Core Requirement is again split into detailed Sub-Requirements, as set out in Annex B.

How the requirements are reviewed during the initial reviews

For the initial reviews of effectiveness in practice (the first round of AEOI effectiveness reviews), the following procedures are carried out:

- Each jurisdiction provides a detailed description of the operational compliance frameworks they have implemented to ensure the effective implementation of the AEOI Standard by Financial

Institutions, including information on the strategy adopted and details of the compliance activities carried out, the outcomes achieved as well as any follow-up actions undertaken.

- All AEOI Peers are invited to provide input in relation to their experiences of the exchanges in practice with each of their exchange partners, including the timeliness and technical aspects, as well as any issues experienced when trying to utilise the information received. Input is also provided on the level of co-operation experienced with each exchange partner when looking to address any such issues that arise.
- Expert assessors from AEOI Peers, supported by the Global Forum Secretariat, conduct a desk-based review to analyse the information provided and other relevant information and follow up with each jurisdiction and its exchange partners with respect to any omissions or uncertainties. Once a clear view of the situation is established, the analysis is finalised and a short report is prepared on the jurisdiction being reviewed.
- The reports are provided to each jurisdiction for comment before they are submitted to the APRG for discussion and approval. They are then sent to all AEOI Peers for adoption, prior to their publication.

Statistics in relation to the operational activities to ensure compliance domestically and in relation to the various aspects of the exchanges in practice play an important role in the assessment, including through benchmarking certain key areas across all jurisdictions. In this regard, it should be noted that the statistics used are based on the disclosure and interpretation of each jurisdiction. Therefore, especially with respect to certain aspects of the domestic compliance frameworks, the statistics are shaped by the framework implemented by individual jurisdictions and may therefore not always be directly comparable. They are nevertheless useful indicators when considered alongside the other information available and have been collected annually from 2021.

How the requirements are reviewed during the deeper reviews

For the deeper reviews of effectiveness in practice under the second round of AEOI effectiveness reviews, the procedures are as above, aside from with the following additions:

- With respect to Core Requirement 1, Assessment Teams consisting of two expert assessors from AEOI Peers, supported by the Global Forum Secretariat, review and analyse the information provided and other relevant information and conduct onsite visits where all key governmental and private sector stakeholders, such as representatives of the financial sector, are met and interviewed. Once a clear view of the situation is established, the analysis is finalised and a report is prepared on the jurisdiction being reviewed, which is provided to the jurisdiction for comment.
- With respect to Core Requirement 2, all AEOI Peers are invited to provide input on an annual basis, over a multi-year period, in relation to their experiences of the exchanges in practice and covering the same areas as during the initial reviews. The Assessment Teams analyse the information received and decide which issues to follow-up on. There is engagement with the jurisdictions and their exchange partners to understand the situation and a horizontal report is prepared each year.
- All the reports are submitted to the APRG for discussion and approval. At the end of the multi-year schedule, the analysis is updated and the reports with respect to Core Requirements 1 and 2 are brought together. Consolidated reports are then prepared and submitted to the APRG for approval. The reports are then sent to all AEOI Peers for adoption, prior to publication.

What is reviewed in relation to Core Requirement 1

The AEOI Terms of Reference refer to jurisdictions ensuring that, in practice, Reporting Financial Institutions are effectively implementing the detailed due diligence and reporting procedures specified in the AEOI Standard. Various specific elements in relation to the required framework are set out, such as various components of the administrative compliance framework that must be put in place, some of which are referred to below.

- **Having an effective administrative framework to ensure compliance**: Various components of each jurisdiction's compliance framework are assessed in detail, including their implementation in practice. Each jurisdiction is therefore asked for details of, amongst other things: (i) the compliance strategy it has in place, including whether it is based on a risk assessment specific to their jurisdiction that takes into account a range of relevant information sources, (ii) the procedures the jurisdiction has implemented and the actions taken to ensure that Reporting Financial Institutions are reporting information as required, including to identify incorrect non-reporting and to follow-up to ensure compliance, (iii) the verification procedures implemented in practice and the actions taken to ensure that the information being reported is complete and accurate, including analysis of the information reported and details of the desk-based and onsite reviews conducted, and (iv) the enforcement activities carried out, including the application of penalties as appropriate and their impact. Each jurisdiction's exchange partners are also asked for any issues with respect to compliance by Reporting Financial Institutions that they might have identified when using the data received.
- **International collaboration to ensure effectiveness**: There are provisions in the AEOI Standard for collaboration between exchange partners to address errors or non-compliance by Reporting Financial Institutions identified by exchange partners. Feedback is therefore also obtained from each jurisdiction's exchange partners on how effective the cooperation has been in practice.

Where deficiencies or areas for improvement are identified, then recommendations are made.

What is reviewed in relation to Core Requirement 2

The AEOI Terms of Reference also contain requirements in relation to the processing of the information reported by Reporting Financial Institutions and its subsequent transmission to exchange partners. Some of the key elements are below.

- **Preparing and validating the information**: Once reported by Reporting Financial Institutions, the information must be sorted, prepared and validated in accordance with the technical requirements set out in the AEOI Standard (e.g. the Common Reporting Standard User Guide and XML Schema). Each jurisdiction's exchange partners are therefore asked about any errors they might have been when trying to utilise the information received. The cause of the issue(s) is identified, including to establish whether there are deficiencies in the jurisdiction's systems to process and send the information reported.
- **Using secure channels to exchange the information**: It is of vital importance that the information is kept safe while it is being transmitted. This is ensured using the CTS, which utilises industry leading security standards and which is used by all jurisdictions. This requirement has therefore always been found to be met in practice.
- **Timeliness in the exchanges and follow-up**: The timeliness of the exchanges is also reviewed, including the timeliness of any response to follow-up from a jurisdiction's partners and the provision of additional or amended information as necessary. Again, feedback on these issues is obtained from each jurisdiction's exchange partners.

Where deficiencies or areas for improvement are identified, then recommendations are made.

Drawing conclusions and issuing ratings on the effectiveness of the implementation of AEOI in practice

Ratings issued during the initial reviews

The ratings issued following the initial reviews of the effectiveness in practice of AEOI implementation (the first round of AEOI effectiveness reviews) are also made with respect to each Core Requirement and overall. They are either: "**On Track**", "**Partially Compliant**" or "**Non-Compliant**", with the rating for each Core Requirement and the overall rating considering all relevant factors (i.e. it is not a mechanical exercise). The terminology for the ratings reflects the fact that these are initial reviews and that the frameworks to ensure effectiveness in practice are not yet fully mature. For these reasons the effectiveness ratings are issued separately to the determinations with respect to the AEOI legal frameworks (which are relatively mature), although legal gaps with a direct influence on the framework to ensure the effective implementation of the requirements by Financial Institutions are considered in the initial reviews of effectiveness. Further details on how to interpret each of these ratings, along with an indication of the relevant considerations, are set out in Table 2.2 below.

Table 2.2. The ratings issued during the initial reviews of the effectiveness in practice of AEOI

Rating	Description
On Track	The effectiveness in practice of jurisdiction's implementation of the AEOI Standard is rated as "**On Track**" where the initial review of its implementation in practice establishes that: (i) the jurisdiction has developed and commenced implementing a complete administrative compliance framework to ensure that Financial Institutions effectively implement their due diligence and reporting obligations and there is an absence of evidence to suggest that it will not be effective in practice, and (ii) the exchanges successfully take place in accordance with the technical requirements and on time, or where issues arise then they are addressed in a timely manner. Given that this rating framework is used for the initial reviews in relation to the effectiveness of operational frameworks that are not yet fully mature, the On Track category is broad. In general, it is given where the review has not identified issues significant to the proper functioning of a Core Requirement or the AEOI Standard, taking into account the general maturity of implementation. The review might nevertheless have identified areas for improvement, beyond simply continuing to implement the framework as envisaged, in which case recommendations for improvement are made.
Partially Compliant	The effectiveness in practice of jurisdiction's implementation of the AEOI Standard in practice is rated as "**Partially Compliant**" where the initial review of its implementation in practice establishes that: (i) the jurisdiction has developed a complete administrative compliance framework to ensure that Financial Institutions effectively implement their due diligence and reporting obligations, although it has not yet begun to fully implement it, and/or (ii) the exchanges are generally taking place successfully, but significant issues have arisen that are often not been addressed in a timely manner. In such cases the assessment has found deficiencies that are significant to the proper functioning of a Core Requirement of the AEOI Standard as a whole.
Non-Compliant	The effectiveness in practice of jurisdiction's implementation of the AEOI Standard in practice is rated as "**Non-Compliant**" where the initial review of its implementation in practice establishes that: (i) the jurisdiction has not yet developed a complete administrative compliance framework to ensure that Financial Institutions effectively implement their due diligence and reporting obligations, and/or (ii) the exchanges are generally not taking place successfully and fundamental issues have arisen that are often not been addressed in a timely manner. In such cases the assessment has found deficiencies that are fundamental to the proper functioning of a Core Requirement of the AEOI Standard as a whole. In this regard, the effectiveness rating takes into account fundamental deficiencies in a jurisdiction's legal framework for AEOI (e.g. jurisdictions with a legal determination of Not In Place), that will likely result in there being fundamental deficiencies in practice. This could be the case where a jurisdiction has not implemented a legal framework or where it has gaps in key areas relating to the enforcement of the requirements.

Ratings issued during the deeper reviews

Under the deeper reviews, effectiveness ratings are given that take into account and incorporate the determinations on the AEOI legal frameworks. Furthermore, a four-tier rating system will be used, mirroring the approach used for the Exchange of Information on Request (EOIR). The ratings used will therefore be: "**Compliant**", "**Largely Compliant**", "**Partially Compliant**" or "**Non-Compliant**". These reflects the greater maturity in the implementation of the AEOI Standard.

Note

[1] *Terms of Reference for the Confidentiality and Data Safeguards Assessments,* https://www.oecd.org/tax/transparency/documents/confidentiality-data-safeguards-assessments-tor.pdf.

[2] OECD (2020), *Confidentiality and Information Security Management Toolkit*, Global Forum on Transparency and Exchange of Information for Tax Purposes, Global Forum on Transparency and Exchange of Information for Tax Purposes, Paris, https://www.oecd.org/tax/transparency/documents/confidentiality-ism-toolkit_en.pdf.

[3] All jurisdictions committed to implementing the AEOI Standard and that have passed domestic legislation to that effect.

[4] A peer review group of the Global Forum consisting of 33 members which replaced the former AEOI Group (https://web-archive.oecd.org/tax/transparency/who-we-are/structure/).

3. Jurisdiction specific reports

Albania

Overall findings

Albania's legal framework implementing the AEOI Standard is in place but needs improvement in order to be fully consistent with the requirements of the AEOI Terms of Reference. While Albania's international legal framework to exchange the information with all of Albania's Interested Appropriate Partners (CR2) is consistent with the requirements, its domestic legislative framework requiring Reporting Financial Institutions to conduct the due diligence and reporting procedures (CR1) has deficiencies significant to the proper functioning of elements of the AEOI Standard. More specifically, the deficiencies relate to the approach to non-Participating Jurisdictions and to the enforcement framework.

The methodology used for the peer reviews and that therefore underpins this report is outlined in Chapter 2.

Overall determination on the legal framework: In Place **But Needs Improvement**

Conclusions on the legal framework

General context

Albania commenced exchanges under the AEOI Standard in 2020.

In order to provide for Reporting Financial Institutions to collect and report the information to be exchanged, Albania:

- enacted Law No. 4/2020 "For Automatic Exchange of Financial Accounts Information" as approved on 30.01.2020 and amended as approved on 29.07.2020; and
- introduced Decision No. 613, Dated 29.7.2020 on the implementing provisions of Law No. 4/2020, "On Automatic Exchange of Financial Account Information".

Under this framework Reporting Financial Institutions were required to commence the due diligence procedures in relation to New Accounts from 1 January 2019. With respect to Preexisting Accounts, Reporting Financial Institutions were required to complete due diligence procedures on High Value Individual Accounts by 31 December 2019 and on Lower Value Individual Accounts and Entity Accounts by 31 December 2020.

Following the initial Global Forum peer review, Albania amended its legislative framework to address issues identified, effective from 28 December 2023.

With respect to the exchange of information under the AEOI Standard, Albania is a Party to the Convention on Mutual Administrative Assistance in Tax Matters and activated the associated CRS Multilateral Competent Authority Agreement in time for exchanges in 2020.

Detailed findings

The detailed findings for Albania are below, organised per Core Requirement (CR) and sub-requirement (SR), as extracted from the AEOI Terms of Reference (see Annex B).

CR1 Domestic legal framework: Jurisdictions should have a domestic legislative framework in place that requires all Reporting Financial Institutions to conduct the due diligence and reporting procedures in the CRS, and that provides for the effective implementation of the CRS as set out therein.

Overall determination on the legal framework: In Place **But Needs Improvement**

Albania's domestic legislative framework is in place and contains most of the key aspects of CRS and its Commentary requiring Reporting Financial Institutions to conduct the due diligence and reporting procedures, but it needs improvement in relation to the due diligence procedures to be applied (SR 1.2) and the framework to enforce the requirements (SR 1.4). More specifically, Albania's domestic legislative framework does not define the term Participating Jurisdiction in accordance with the requirements and does not include rules to prevent circumvention of due diligence and reporting obligations.

SR 1.1 Jurisdictions should define the scope of Reporting Financial Institutions consistently with the CRS.

Albania has defined the scope of Reporting Financial Institutions in its domestic legislative framework in accordance with the CRS and its Commentary.

Recommendations:

No recommendations made.

SR 1.2 Jurisdictions should define the scope of Financial Accounts and Reportable Accounts consistently with the CRS and incorporate the due diligence procedures to identify them.

Albania has defined the scope of the Financial Accounts that are required to be reported in its domestic legislative framework and incorporated the due diligence procedures that must be applied to identify them in a manner that is largely consistent with the CRS and its Commentary. However, a deficiency has been identified. More specifically, Albania's legislative framework does not incorporate the requirements in relation to certain Entities not located in Participating Jurisdictions in line with the AEOI Standard. This deficiency is material to the proper functioning of the AEOI Standard as it does not ensure that all Investment Entities that are not in Participating Jurisdictions are subject to the "look-through" approach to identify their Controlling Persons.

Recommendations:

Albania should amend its domestic legislative framework to ensure that the approach taken with respect to the 19 jurisdictions defined as Participating Jurisdictions and with which Albania does not have an agreement to exchange CRS information with, is in accordance with the AEOI Standard.

SR 1.3 Jurisdictions should incorporate the reporting requirements contained in Section I of the CRS into their domestic legislative framework.

Albania has incorporated the reporting requirements in its domestic legislative framework in accordance with the CRS and its Commentary.

Recommendations:

No recommendations made.

SR 1.4 Jurisdictions should have a legislative framework in place that allows for the enforcement of the requirements of the CRS in practice.

Albania has a legislative framework in place to enforce the requirements in a manner that is largely consistent with the CRS and its Commentary. However, a deficiency has been identified. More specifically, Albania's legislative framework does not include rules to prevent all Financial Institutions, persons or intermediaries from adopting practices intended to circumvent the due diligence and reporting procedures as required.

This is a key element of the required enforcement framework and is therefore material to the proper functioning of the AEOI Standard

Recommendations:

Albania should amend its domestic legislative framework to include rules to prevent all Financial Institutions, persons and intermediaries from adopting practices intended to circumvent the due diligence and reporting procedures, rather than just those on whom the AEOI Standard imposes an obligation.

CR2 International legal framework: Jurisdictions should have exchange relationships in effect with all Interested Appropriate Partners as committed to and that provide for the exchange of information in accordance with the Model CAA.

Determination: In Place

Albania's international legal framework to exchange the information is in place, is consistent with the Model CAA and its Commentary and provides for exchange with all of Albania's Interested Appropriate Partners (i.e. all jurisdictions that are interested in receiving information from Albania and that meet the required standard in relation to confidentiality and data safeguards) (SRs 2.1 – 2.3).

SR 2.1 Jurisdictions should have exchange agreements in effect with all Interested Appropriate Partners that permit the automatic exchange of CRS information.

Albania has exchange agreements that permit the automatic exchange of CRS information in effect with all its Interested Appropriate Partners.

Recommendations:

No recommendations made.

SR 2.2 Such an exchange agreement should be put in place without undue delay, following the receipt of an expression of interest from an Interested Appropriate Partner.

Albania put in place its exchange agreements without undue delay.

Recommendations:

No recommendations made.

SR 2.3 Jurisdictions should ensure that the exchange agreements in effect provide for the exchange of information in accordance with the requirements of the Model CAA.

Albania's exchange agreements provide for the exchange of information in accordance with the requirements of the Model CAA.

Recommendations:

No recommendations made.

Comments by the assessed jurisdiction

No comments made.

Anguilla

Overall findings

Anguilla's legal framework implementing the AEOI Standard is in place but needs improvement in order to be fully consistent with the requirements of the AEOI Terms of Reference. While Anguilla's international legal framework to exchange the information with all of Anguilla's Interested Appropriate Partners (CR2) is consistent with the requirements, its domestic legislative framework requiring Reporting Financial Institutions to conduct the due diligence and reporting procedures (CR1) has a deficiency significant to the proper functioning of elements of the AEOI Standard. More specifically, a deficiency has been identified in relation to Anguilla's enforcement framework.

The methodology used for the peer reviews and that therefore underpins this report is outlined in Chapter 2.

Overall determination on the legal framework: In Place But **Needs Improvement**

Conclusions on the legal framework

General context

Anguilla initially intended to commence exchanges under the AEOI Standard in 2017 but due to the impact of the hurricanes in the region instead commenced exchanging in 2018.

In order to provide for Reporting Financial Institutions to collect and report the information to be exchanged, Anguilla:

- enacted the Tax Information Exchange (International Cooperation) Act;
- introduced the International Tax Compliance (CRS) Regulations; and
- issued further guidance (referred to as Guidance Notes), which is not legally binding.

Under this framework Reporting Financial Institutions were required to commence the due diligence procedures in relation to New Accounts from 1 July 2016. With respect to Preexisting Accounts, Reporting Financial Institutions were required to complete the due diligence procedures on High Value Individual Accounts by 31 December 2016 and on Lower Value Individual Accounts and Entity Accounts by 31 December 2017.

With respect to the exchange of information under the AEOI Standard, Anguilla:

- has the Convention on Mutual Administrative Assistance in Tax Matters in place[1] and activated the associated CRS Multilateral Competent Authority Agreement in time for exchanges in 2018; and
- put in place three bilateral agreements.[2]

Detailed findings

The detailed findings for Anguilla are below, organised per Core Requirement (CR) and sub-requirement (SR), as extracted from the AEOI Terms of Reference (see Annex B).

CR1 Domestic legal framework: Jurisdictions should have a domestic legislative framework in place that requires all Reporting Financial Institutions to conduct the due diligence and reporting procedures in the CRS, and that provides for the effective implementation of the CRS as set out therein.

Determination: In Place But **Needs Improvement**

Anguilla's domestic legislative framework is in place and contains all of the key aspects of the CRS and its Commentary requiring Reporting Financial Institutions to conduct the due diligence and reporting procedures, but it needs improvement in relation to the framework to enforce the requirements (SR 1.4). More specifically, Anguilla does not have an explicit legal basis to impose or enforce a sanction for non-compliance if the Reporting Financial Institution is a legal arrangement.

SR 1.1 Jurisdictions should define the scope of Reporting Financial Institutions consistently with the CRS.

Anguilla has defined the scope of Reporting Financial Institutions in its domestic legislative framework in accordance with the CRS and its Commentary.

Recommendations:

No recommendations made.

SR 1.2 Jurisdictions should define the scope of Financial Accounts and Reportable Accounts consistently with the CRS and incorporate the due diligence procedures to identify them.

Anguilla has defined the scope of the Financial Accounts that are required to be reported in its domestic legislative framework and incorporated the due diligence procedures that must be applied to identify them in accordance with the CRS and its Commentary.

Recommendations:

No recommendations made.

SR 1.3 Jurisdictions should incorporate the reporting requirements contained in Section I of the CRS into their domestic legislative framework.

Anguilla has incorporated the reporting requirements in its domestic legislative framework in accordance with the CRS and its Commentary.

Recommendations:

No recommendations made.

SR 1.4 Jurisdictions should have a legislative framework in place that allows for the enforcement of the requirements of the CRS in practice.

Anguilla has a legislative framework in place to enforce the requirements in a manner that is largely consistent with the CRS and its Commentary. However, a deficiency has been identified. More specifically, Anguilla's legislative framework does not include an explicit legal basis to enforce a sanction where a Reporting Financial Institution is a legal arrangement. This deficiency relates to a key element of the AEOI Standard and is therefore material to its proper functioning.

Recommendations:

Anguilla should amend its legislative framework to ensure that there is an explicit legal basis to enforce a sanction when there is non-compliance by a Reporting Financial Institution that is a legal arrangement.

CR2 International legal framework: Jurisdictions should have exchange relationships in effect with all Interested Appropriate Partners as committed to and that provide for the exchange of information in accordance with the Model CAA.

Determination: In Place

Anguilla's international legal framework to exchange the information is in place, is consistent with the Model CAA and its Commentary and provides for exchange with all of Anguilla's Interested Appropriate Partners (i.e. all jurisdictions that are interested in receiving information from Anguilla and that meet the required standard in relation to confidentiality and data safeguards) (SRs 2.1 – 2.3).

SR 2.1 Jurisdictions should have exchange agreements in effect with all Interested Appropriate Partners that permit the automatic exchange of CRS information.

Anguilla has exchange agreements that permit the automatic exchange of CRS information in effect with all its Interested Appropriate Partners.

Recommendations:

No recommendations made.

SR 2.2 Such an exchange agreement should be put in place without undue delay, following the receipt of an expression of interest from an Interested Appropriate Partner.

Anguilla put in place its exchange agreements without undue delay.

Recommendations:

No recommendations made.

SR 2.3 Jurisdictions should ensure that the exchange agreements in effect provide for the exchange of information in accordance with the requirements of the Model CAA.

Anguilla's exchange agreements provide for the exchange of information in accordance with the requirements of the Model CAA.

Recommendations:

No recommendations made.

Comments by the assessed jurisdiction

No comments made.

Notes

[1] Through a territorial extension by the United Kingdom.

[2] With Guernsey, the Isle of Man and the United Kingdom.

Antigua and Barbuda

Overall findings

Antigua and Barbuda's legal framework implementing the AEOI Standard is in place but needs improvement in order to be fully consistent with the requirements of the AEOI Terms of Reference. While Antigua and Barbuda's international legal framework to exchange the information with all of Antigua and Barbuda's Interested Appropriate Partners (CR2) is consistent with the requirements, its domestic legislative framework requiring Reporting Financial Institutions to conduct the due diligence and reporting procedures (CR1) has deficiencies significant to the proper functioning of elements of the AEOI Standard. Most significantly, Financial Account is not defined in accordance with the AEOI Standard and deficiencies have been identified in relation to Antigua and Barbuda's enforcement framework.

The methodology used for the peer reviews and that therefore underpins this report is outlined in Chapter 2.

Overall determination on the legal framework: In Place But **Needs Improvement**

Conclusions on the legal framework

General context

Antigua and Barbuda commenced exchanges under the AEOI Standard in 2018.

In order to provide for Reporting Financial Institutions to collect and report the information to be exchanged, Antigua and Barbuda:

- enacted the Automatic Exchange of Financial Account Information Act 2016 (No. 11 of 2016);
- enacted the Automatic Exchange of Financial Account Information (Amendment) Act 2017 (No. 39 of 2017); and
- introduced the Automatic Exchange of Financial Account Information Regulations 2017, (Statutory Instrument No. 18 of 2017).

Under this framework Reporting Financial Institutions were required to commence the due diligence procedures in relation to New Accounts from 1 January 2017. With respect to Preexisting Accounts, Reporting Financial Institutions were required to complete the due diligence procedures on High Value Individual Accounts by 31 December 2017 and on Lower Value Individual Accounts and Entity Accounts by 31 December 2018.

With respect to the exchange of information under the AEOI Standard, Antigua and Barbuda is a Party to the Convention on Mutual Administrative Assistance in Tax Matters and activated the associated CRS Multilateral Competent Authority Agreement in time for exchanges in 2018.

Detailed findings

The detailed findings for Antigua and Barbuda are below, organised per Core Requirement (CR) and sub-requirement (SR), as extracted from the AEOI Terms of Reference (see Annex B).

CR1 Domestic legal framework: Jurisdictions should have a domestic legislative framework in place that requires all Reporting Financial Institutions to conduct the due diligence and reporting procedures in the CRS, and that provides for the effective implementation of the CRS as set out therein.

Determination: In Place But **Needs Improvement**

Antigua and Barbuda's domestic legislative framework is in place and contains most of the key aspects of the CRS and its Commentary requiring Reporting Financial Institutions to conduct the due diligence and reporting procedures, but it needs improvement in relation to the scope of Financial Accounts required to be reported and the due diligence procedures to identify them (SR 1.2), the reporting requirements (SR 1.3) and the framework to enforce the requirements (SR 1.4). Most significantly, Financial Account is not defined in accordance with the requirements, there are no sanctions on Account Holders and Controlling Persons for the provision of false self-certifications and Antigua and Barbuda does not have an explicit legal basis to enforce a sanction for non-compliance if the Reporting Financial Institution is a legal arrangement.

SR 1.1 Jurisdictions should define the scope of Reporting Financial Institutions consistently with the CRS.

Antigua and Barbuda has defined the scope of Reporting Financial Institutions in its domestic legislative framework in accordance with the CRS and its Commentary.

Recommendations:

No recommendations made.

SR 1.2 Jurisdictions should define the scope of Financial Accounts and Reportable Accounts consistently with the CRS and incorporate the due diligence procedures to identify them.

Antigua and Barbuda has defined the scope of the Financial Accounts that are required to be reported in its domestic legislative framework and incorporated the due diligence procedures that must be applied to identify them in a manner that is largely consistent with the CRS and its Commentary. However, a deficiency has been identified. Most significantly, Antigua and Barbuda's domestic legislative framework omits several key details of the definition of Financial Account, which is material to the proper functioning of the AEOI Standard.

Recommendations:

Antigua and Barbuda should amend its domestic legislative framework to define Financial Account in accordance with the AEOI Standard, rather than defining it by exclusion as is currently the case (i.e. an account that is not (a) a retirement or pension account; (b) a non-retirement tax favoured account; (c) a term life insurance contract; (d) a estate account; (e) a depository account due to not-returned over payments and (g) a low risk excluded account).

Antigua and Barbuda should amend its domestic legislative framework to ensure that the approach taken with respect to the two jurisdictions defined as Participating Jurisdictions and with which Antigua and Barbuda does not have an agreement to exchange CRS information with (one of which has not implemented the AEOI Standard), is in accordance with the AEOI Standard.

SR 1.3 Jurisdictions should incorporate the reporting requirements contained in Section I of the CRS into their domestic legislative framework.

Antigua and Barbuda has incorporated the reporting requirements in its domestic legislative framework in accordance with the CRS and its Commentary. While a deficiency has been identified with respect to the timing of the measurement of the balance of a Reportable Account, given the account is still required to be reported along with its balance, the deficiency is considered to be relatively minor and its impact not to be material.

Recommendations:

Antigua and Barbuda should amend its domestic legislative framework to specify that Reporting Financial Institutions should always report the balance or value of a Reportable Account as at the end of the calendar year.

SR 1.4 Jurisdictions should have a legislative framework in place that allows for the enforcement of the requirements of the CRS in practice.

Antigua and Barbuda has a legislative framework in place to enforce the requirements in a manner that is largely consistent with the CRS and its Commentary. However, deficiencies have been identified. Most significantly, Antigua and Barbuda's legislative framework does not impose sanctions for the provision of false self-certifications by Account Holders and Controlling Persons and it does not include an explicit legal basis to enforce a sanction where a Reporting Financial Institution is a legal arrangement. These deficiencies relate to key elements of the enforcement framework and are therefore material to the proper functioning of the AEOI Standard.

Recommendations:

Antigua and Barbuda should amend its domestic legislative framework to include sanctions on Account Holders and Controlling Persons for providing false self-certifications.

Antigua and Barbuda should ensure that it has rules in its domestic legislative framework that provide relevant authorities access to records for the purposes of verifying compliance with the AEOI Standard, without first requiring that there be a suspicion of noncompliance. Antigua and Barbuda amend its legislative framework to ensure that there is an explicit legal basis to enforce a sanction when there is non-compliance by a Reporting Financial Institution that is a legal arrangement.

Antigua and Barbuda should amend its domestic legislative framework to require Reporting Financial Institutions to maintain records of self-certifications for at least five years from the deadline to report the information, rather than five years from the date when an account is closed.

CR2 International legal framework: Jurisdictions should have exchange relationships in effect with all Interested Appropriate Partners as committed to and that provide for the exchange of information in accordance with the Model CAA.

Determination: In Place

Antigua and Barbuda's international legal framework to exchange the information is in place, is consistent with the Model CAA and its Commentary and provides for exchange with all of Antigua and Barbuda's Interested Appropriate Partners (i.e. all jurisdictions that are interested in receiving information from Antigua and Barbuda and that meet the required standard in relation to confidentiality and data safeguards) (SRs 2.1 – 2.3).

SR 2.1 Jurisdictions should have exchange agreements in effect with all Interested Appropriate Partners that permit the automatic exchange of CRS information.

Antigua and Barbuda has exchange agreements that permit the automatic exchange of CRS information in effect with all its Interested Appropriate Partners.

Recommendations:

No recommendations made.

SR 2.2 Such an exchange agreement should be put in place without undue delay, following the receipt of an expression of interest from an Interested Appropriate Partner.

Antigua and Barbuda put in place its exchange agreements without undue delay.

Recommendations:

No recommendations made.

SR 2.3 Jurisdictions should ensure that the exchange agreements in effect provide for the exchange of information in accordance with the requirements of the Model CAA.

Antigua and Barbuda's exchange agreements provide for the exchange of information in accordance with the requirements of the Model CAA.

Recommendations:

No recommendations made.

Comments by the assessed jurisdiction

Antigua and Barbuda has conducted remedial action and submitted legislative amendments to the Automatic Exchange of Financial Account Information Act 2016 as amended and the Automatic Exchange of Financial Account Information Regulations 2017, in accordance with the stated recommendations. Accordingly, the said amendments will be subjected to the Parliamentary process of debate and passage in 2020.

Argentina

Overall findings

Argentina's legal framework implementing the AEOI Standard is in place but needs improvement in order to be fully consistent with the requirements of the AEOI Terms of Reference. While Argentina's international legal framework to exchange information with all of Argentina's Interested Appropriate Partners (CR2) is consistent with the requirements, its domestic legislative framework requiring Reporting Financial Institutions to conduct the due diligence and reporting procedures (CR1) has a deficiency significant to the proper functioning of elements of the AEOI Standard. More specifically, a deficiency has been identified with respect to Argentina's enforcement framework.

The methodology used for the peer reviews and that therefore underpins this report is outlined in Chapter 2.

Overall determination on the legal framework: In Place But **Needs Improvement**

Conclusions on the legal framework

General context

Argentina commenced exchanges under the AEOI Standard in 2017.

In order to provide for Reporting Financial Institutions to collect and report the information to be exchanged, Argentina:

- relies on Section 7 of the Decree No. 618/1997;
- enacted the AFIP General Resolution No. 4.056/2017, that replaced the AFIP General Resolution 3.826/2015, and its amendments, including the Resolutions No. 4.422/2019, 4.888/2020, 5065/2021, 5303/2022 and 5.537/2024;
- introduced the FIU Resolutions 112/2021, 14/2023, 78/2023 and 126/2023; and
- issued further guidance, which is not legally binding.

Under this framework Reporting Financial Institutions were required to commence the due diligence procedures in relation to New Accounts from 1 January 2016. With respect to Preexisting Accounts, Reporting Financial Institutions were required to complete the due diligence procedures on High Value Individual Accounts by 31 December 2016 and on Lower Value Individual Accounts and Entity Accounts by 31 December 2017.

Following the initial Global Forum peer review, Argentina made various amendments to its legislative framework to address issues identified, the last of which was effective from 1 August 2024.

With respect to the exchange of information under the AEOI Standard, Argentina is a Party to the Convention on Mutual Administrative Assistance in Tax Matters and activated the associated CRS Multilateral Competent Authority Agreement in time for exchanges in 2017.

Detailed findings

The detailed findings for Argentina are below, organised per Core Requirement (CR) and sub-requirement (SR), as extracted from the AEOI Terms of Reference (see Annex B).

CR1 Domestic legal framework: Jurisdictions should have a domestic legislative framework in place that requires all Reporting Financial Institutions to conduct the due diligence and reporting procedures in the CRS, and that provides for the effective implementation of the CRS as set out therein.

Determination: In Place But **Needs Improvement**

Argentina's domestic legislative framework is in place and contains most of the key aspects of the CRS and its Commentary requiring Reporting Financial Institutions to conduct the due diligence and reporting procedures, but it needs improvement in relation to the framework to enforce the requirements (SR 1.4). More specifically, Argentina's legal framework does not impose sanctions on Account Holders and Controlling Persons for the provision of false self-certifications.

SR 1.1 Jurisdictions should define the scope of Reporting Financial Institutions consistently with the CRS.

Argentina has defined the scope of Reporting Financial Institutions in its domestic legislative framework in accordance with the CRS and its Commentary.

Recommendations:

No recommendations made.

SR 1.2 Jurisdictions should define the scope of Financial Accounts and Reportable Accounts consistently with the CRS and incorporate the due diligence procedures to identify them.

Argentina has defined the scope of the Financial Accounts that are required to be reported in its domestic legislative framework and incorporated the due diligence procedures that must be applied to identify them in accordance with the CRS and its Commentary.

Recommendations:

No recommendations made.

SR 1.3 Jurisdictions should incorporate the reporting requirements contained in Section I of the CRS into their domestic legislative framework.

Argentina has incorporated the reporting requirements in its domestic legislative framework in accordance with the CRS and its Commentary.

Recommendations:

No recommendations made.

SR 1.4 Jurisdictions should have a legislative framework in place that allows for the enforcement of the requirements of the CRS in practice.

Argentina has a legislative framework in place to enforce the requirements in a manner that is largely consistent with the CRS and its Commentary. However, a deficiency has been identified. More specifically, Argentina's legislative framework does not impose sanctions for the provision of false self-certifications by Account Holders and Controlling Persons. This is a key element of the required enforcement framework and is therefore material to the proper functioning of the AEOI Standard.

Recommendations:

Argentina should amend its domestic legislative framework to include sanctions on Account Holders and Controlling Persons for the provision of a false self-certification.

CR2 International legal framework: Jurisdictions should have exchange relationships in effect with all Interested Appropriate Partners as committed to and that provide for the exchange of information in accordance with the Model CAA.

Determination: In Place

Argentina's international legal framework to exchange the information is in place, is consistent with the Model CAA and its Commentary and provides for exchange with all of Argentina's Interested Appropriate Partners (i.e. all jurisdictions that are interested in receiving information from Argentina and that meet the required standard in relation to confidentiality and data safeguards) (SRs 2.1 – 2.3).

SR 2.1 Jurisdictions should have exchange agreements in effect with all Interested Appropriate Partners that permit the automatic exchange of CRS information.

Argentina has exchange agreements that permit the automatic exchange of CRS information in effect with all its Interested Appropriate Partners.

Recommendations:

No recommendations made.

SR 2.2 Such an exchange agreement should be put in place without undue delay, following the receipt of an expression of interest from an Interested Appropriate Partner.

Argentina put in place its exchange agreements without undue delay.

Recommendations:

No recommendations made.

SR 2.3 Jurisdictions should ensure that the exchange agreements in effect provide for the exchange of information in accordance with the requirements of the Model CAA.

Argentina exchange agreements provide for the exchange of information in accordance with the requirements of the Model CAA.

Recommendations:

No recommendations made.

Comments by the assessed jurisdiction

No comments made.

Aruba

Overall findings

Aruba's legal framework implementing the AEOI Standard is in place but needs improvement in order to be fully consistent with the requirements of the AEOI Terms of Reference. While Aruba's international legal framework to exchange the information with all of Aruba's Interested Appropriate Partners (CR2) is consistent with the requirements, its domestic legislative framework requiring Reporting Financial Institutions to conduct the due diligence and reporting procedures (CR1) has deficiencies significant to the proper functioning of elements of the AEOI Standard. Most significantly, Aruba's legislative framework does not set out some of the key due diligence timelines and the procedures and evidence that may be relied upon for the determination of the status of Financial Institutions depart from those set out in the AEOI Standard.

The methodology used for the peer reviews and that therefore underpins this report is outlined in Chapter 2.

Overall determination on the legal framework: In Place **But Needs Improvement**

Conclusions on the legal framework

General context

Aruba commenced exchanges under the AEOI Standard on a non-reciprocal basis in 2018 (i.e. it sends but does not receive information).

In order to provide for Reporting Financial Institutions to collect and report the information to be exchanged, Aruba:

- enacted Ordinance No. 74 of 2017, amended with effect from 1 July 2023;
- introduced State Decree No. 76 of 2017;
- issued further guidance, which is not legally binding; and
- relies on its legal framework implementing the FATF Recommendations for the purposes of the identification of Controlling Persons under the AEOI Standard.

Under this framework Reporting Financial Institutions were required to commence the due diligence procedures in relation to New Accounts from 1 January 2017. With respect to Preexisting Accounts, the non-binding guidance states that the review of High Value Individual Accounts should be completed in time for the 2018 reporting deadline and by 31 December 2018 in the cases of Lower Value Individual Accounts and Entity Accounts.

Following the initial Global Forum peer review, Aruba amended its legislative framework to address issues identified, the last of which was effective from 1 July 2023.

With respect to the exchange of information under the AEOI Standard, Aruba has the Convention on Mutual Administrative Assistance in Tax Matters[1] in place and activated the associated CRS Multilateral Competent Authority Agreement in time for exchanges in 2018.

Detailed findings

The detailed findings for Aruba are below, organised per Core Requirement (CR) and sub-requirement (SR), as extracted from the AEOI Terms of Reference (see Annex B).

CR1 Domestic legal framework: Jurisdictions should have a domestic legislative framework in place that requires all Reporting Financial Institutions to conduct the due diligence and reporting procedures in the CRS, and that provides for the effective implementation of the CRS as set out therein.

Determination: In Place **But Needs Improvement**

Aruba's domestic legislative framework is in place and contains most of the key aspects of the CRS and its Commentary requiring Reporting Financial Institutions to conduct the due diligence and reporting procedures, but it needs improvement in relation to the scope of Reporting Financial Institutions required to report information (SR 1.1) and the scope of Financial Accounts required to be reported and the due diligence procedures to be applied (SR 1.2). Most significantly, the due diligence provisions in Aruba's legislative framework do not include some key dates determining the application of the due diligence obligations and the procedures and evidence that may be relied upon for the determination of the status of Financial Institutions depart from those set out in the AEOI Standard.

SR 1.1 Jurisdictions should define the scope of Reporting Financial Institutions consistently with the CRS.

Aruba has defined the scope of Reporting Financial Institutions in its domestic legislative framework in a manner that is largely consistent with the AEOI Standard and its Commentary. However, a deficiency has been identified. More specifically, Aruba's legislative framework does not specify the date as of when Qualified Credit Card Issuers that are treated as Non-Reporting Financial Institutions are required to implement policies requiring the returning of overpayments made.

The scope of Reporting Financial Institutions, including the specification of Non-Reporting Financial Institutions, is material to the proper functioning of the AEOI Standard.

Recommendations:

Aruba should amend its domestic legislative framework to require Qualified Credit Card Issuers to implement policies with respect to the returning of overpayments from a specified date in order to be treated as Non-Reporting Financial Institutions.

SR 1.2 Jurisdictions should define the scope of Financial Accounts and Reportable Accounts consistently with the CRS and incorporate the due diligence procedures to identify them.

Aruba has not defined the scope of the Financial Accounts that are required to be reported in its domestic legislative framework and has not incorporated the due diligence procedures that must be applied to identify them in a manner that is consistent with the AEOI Standard and its Commentary as significant deficiencies have been identified. More specifically, Aruba's legislative framework:

- does not specify the date as of when the Qualified Credit Card Issuers need to implement policies for the returning of overpayments, which is required for Depository Accounts due to not-returned overpayments to be treated as Excluded Accounts;
- does not follow the conditions set out in the AEOI Standard for when Reporting Financial Institutions can use existing classifications as Documentary Evidence with respect to Preexisting Entity Accounts;
- does not specify the date on which a Preexisting Entity Account is first to be identified; and
- does not specify the dates by when the due diligence procedures on High and Lower Value Preexisting Individual Accounts as well as Preexisting Entity Accounts are to be completed; the non-binding guidance indicates that these procedures should be completed in time for 2018 reporting deadline in the case of High Value Individual Accounts and by 31 December 2018 in the cases of Lower Value Individual Accounts and Entity Accounts.

The scope of Financial Accounts and the due diligence procedures to identify them are material to the proper functioning of the AEOI Standard.

Recommendations:

Aruba should amend its domestic legislative framework to require Qualified Credit Card Issuers to implement policies with respect to the returning of overpayments from a specified date in order for Depository Accounts due to not-returned overpayments to be treated as Excluded Accounts.

Aruba should amend its domestic legislative framework to require Reporting Financial Institutions to only use Documentary Evidence in relation to the due diligence procedures for Preexisting Entity Accounts in accordance with the conditions in the AEOI Standard.

Aruba should amend its domestic legislative framework to specify the date on which a Preexisting Entity Account is first to be identified using the USD 250 000 balance or value threshold.

Aruba should amend its legislative framework to specify the completion dates for the reviews of: (i) Preexisting High Value Individual Accounts; (ii) Preexisting Lower Value Individual Accounts; and (iii) Preexisting Entity Accounts.

SR 1.3 Jurisdictions should incorporate the reporting requirements contained in Section I of the CRS into their domestic legislative framework.

Aruba has incorporated the reporting requirements in its domestic legislative framework in accordance with the CRS and its Commentary. While a deficiency has been identified with respect to the reporting of the currency denomination, it is considered to be relatively minor as the CRS XML Schema will compel the reporting of a currency type.

Recommendations:

Aruba should amend its domestic legislative framework to require Reporting Financial Institutions to identify the currency in which each account is denominated.

SR 1.4 Jurisdictions should have a legislative framework in place that allows for the enforcement of the requirements of the CRS in practice.

Aruba has a legislative framework in place to enforce the requirements in accordance with the CRS and its Commentary. While a deficiency has been identified with respect to a lack of an explicit legal basis to enforce a sanction where a Reporting Financial Institution is a legal arrangement, it is considered relatively minor and does not materially undermine the implementation of SR 1.4. This is because such Reporting Financial Institutions have so far not been known to exist in Aruba and are considered unlikely to exist under Aruba's financial and legal frameworks.

Recommendations:

Aruba should amend its legislative framework to ensure that there is an explicit legal basis to enforce a sanction when there is non-compliance by a Reporting Financial Institution that is a legal arrangement.

CR2 International legal framework: Jurisdictions should have exchange relationships in effect with all Interested Appropriate Partners as committed to and that provide for the exchange of information in accordance with the Model CAA.

Determination: In Place

Aruba's international legal framework to exchange the information is in place, is consistent with the Model CAA and its Commentary and provides for exchange with all of Aruba's Interested Appropriate Partners (i.e. all jurisdictions that are interested in receiving information from Aruba and that meet the required standard in relation to confidentiality and data safeguards) (SRs 2.1 – 2.3).

SR 2.1 Jurisdictions should have exchange agreements in effect with all Interested Appropriate Partners that permit the automatic exchange of CRS information.

Aruba has exchange agreements that permit the automatic exchange of CRS information in effect with all its Interested Appropriate Partners.

Recommendations:

No recommendations made.

SR 2.2 Such an exchange agreement should be put in place without undue delay, following the receipt of an expression of interest from an Interested Appropriate Partner.

Aruba put in place its exchange agreements without undue delay.

Recommendations:

No recommendations made.

SR 2.3 Jurisdictions should ensure that the exchange agreements in effect provide for the exchange of information in accordance with the requirements of the Model CAA.

Aruba's exchange agreements provide for the exchange of information in accordance with the requirements of the Model CAA.

Recommendations:

No recommendations made.

Comments by the assessed jurisdiction

No comments made.

Note

[1] Through a territorial extension by the Netherlands.

Australia

Overall findings

Australia's legal framework implementing the AEOI Standard is in place but needs improvement in order to be fully consistent with the requirements of the AEOI Terms of Reference. While Australia's international legal framework to exchange the information with all of Australia's Interested Appropriate Partners (CR2) is consistent with the requirements, its domestic legislative framework requiring Reporting Financial Institutions to conduct the due diligence and reporting procedures (CR1) has a deficiency significant to the proper functioning of an element of the AEOI Standard. More specifically, Australia's legal framework includes a category of jurisdiction-specific Excluded Account that is not in accordance with the AEOI Standard, and the enforcement framework does not fully provide for sanctions on Reporting Financial Institutions for failing to carry out the due diligence procedures.

The methodology used for the peer reviews and that therefore underpins this report is outlined in Chapter 2.

Overall determination on the legal framework: In Place But **Needs Improvement**

Conclusions on the legal framework

General context

Australia commenced exchanges under the AEOI Standard in 2018.

In order to provide for Reporting Financial Institutions to collect and report the information to be exchanged, Australia:

- enacted the Tax Laws Amendment (Implementation of the Common Reporting Standard) Act 2015 (TLA(ICRS) 2015); and
- issued further guidance, which is not legally binding.

Under this framework Reporting Financial Institutions were required to commence the due diligence procedures in relation to New Accounts from 1 July 2017. With respect to Preexisting Accounts, Reporting Financial Institutions were required to complete the due diligence procedures on High Value Individual Accounts by 31 July 2018 and on Lower Value Individual Accounts and Entity Accounts by 31 July 2019 and 31 July 2018 respectively.

Following the initial Global Forum peer review, Australia made various amendments to its legislative framework to address issues identified, the last of which was effective from 18 December 2020.

With respect to the exchange of information under the AEOI Standard, Australia:

- is a Party to the Convention on Mutual Administrative Assistance in Tax Matters and activated the associated CRS Multilateral Competent Authority Agreement in time for exchanges in 2018; and
- put in place a bilateral agreement.[1]

Detailed findings

The detailed findings for Australia are below, organised per Core Requirement (CR) and sub-requirement (SR), as extracted from the AEOI Terms of Reference (see Annex B).

CR1 Domestic legal framework: Jurisdictions should have a domestic legislative framework in place that requires all Reporting Financial Institutions to conduct the due diligence and reporting procedures in the CRS, and that provides for the effective implementation of the CRS as set out therein.

Determination: In Place But **Needs Improvement**

Australia's domestic legislative framework is in place and contains most of the key aspects of the CRS and its Commentary requiring Reporting Financial Institutions to conduct the due diligence and reporting procedures, but it needs improvement in relation to the scope of Financial Accounts required to be reported (SR 1.2), and the framework to enforce the requirements (SR 1.4). More specifically, Australia's legislative framework provides for a category of jurisdiction-specific Excluded Account that does not meet all the requirements, and the enforcement framework does not fully provide for sanctions on Reporting Financial Institutions for failing to carry out the due diligence procedures.

SR 1.1 Jurisdictions should define the scope of Reporting Financial Institutions consistently with the CRS.

Australia has defined the scope of Reporting Financial Institutions in its domestic legislative framework in accordance with the CRS and its Commentary.

Recommendations:

No recommendations made.

SR 1.2 Jurisdictions should define the scope of Financial Accounts and Reportable Accounts consistently with the CRS and incorporate the due diligence procedures to identify them.

Australia has defined the scope of the Financial Accounts that are required to be reported in its domestic legislative framework and incorporated the due diligence procedures that must be applied to identify them in a manner that is largely consistent with the CRS and its Commentary. However, a deficiency has been identified. More specifically, Australia provides for a jurisdiction-specific Excluded Account that is not in accordance with the requirements, as it does not provide for effective penalties for withdrawals that do not meet the criteria of the account. The definition of Financial Accounts, including the provision of Excluded Accounts, is material to the proper functioning of the AEOI Standard.

Recommendations:

Australia should amend its domestic legislative framework to remove the Scholarship Plans from its jurisdiction-specific list of Excluded Accounts, as they do not meet the requirements in the AEOI Standard, such as by not having penalties for withdrawals from the accounts for non-educational purposes.

SR 1.3 Jurisdictions should incorporate the reporting requirements contained in Section I of the CRS into their domestic legislative framework.

Australia has incorporated the reporting requirements in its domestic legislative framework in accordance with the CRS and its Commentary.

Recommendations:

No recommendations made.

SR 1.4 Jurisdictions should have a legislative framework in place that allows for the enforcement of the requirements of the CRS in practice.

Australia has a legislative framework in place to enforce the requirements in a manner that is largely consistent with the CRS and its Commentary. While a deficiency has been identified in that it does not fully provide for sanctions on Reporting Financial Institutions for failing to carry out the due diligence procedures, it is considered relatively minor and does not materially undermine the implementation of SR

1.4. This is because the gap is largely mitigated by having in place penalty provisions for failing to report, failing to obtain a valid self-certification and failing to keep records.

Recommendations:

While Australia is able to impose penalties for failing to report, for reporting incorrect information, failing to obtain a self-certification and failing to keep the required records, it is recommended to amend its legislative framework to ensure it is able to also impose penalties for all failures to carry out due diligence.

CR2 International legal framework: Jurisdictions should have exchange relationships in effect with all Interested Appropriate Partners as committed to and that provide for the exchange of information in accordance with the Model CAA.

Determination: In Place

Australia's international legal framework to exchange the information is in place, is consistent with the Model CAA and its Commentary and provides for exchange with all of Australia's Interested Appropriate Partners (i.e. all jurisdictions that are interested in receiving information from Australia and that meet the required standard in relation to confidentiality and data safeguards) (SRs 2.1 – 2.3).

SR 2.1 Jurisdictions should have exchange agreements in effect with all Interested Appropriate Partners that permit the automatic exchange of CRS information.

Australia has exchange agreements that permit the automatic exchange of CRS information in effect with all its Interested Appropriate Partners.

Recommendations:

No recommendations made.

SR 2.2 Such an exchange agreement should be put in place without undue delay, following the receipt of an expression of interest from an Interested Appropriate Partner.

Australia put in place its exchange agreements without undue delay.

Recommendations:

No recommendations made.

SR 2.3 Jurisdictions should ensure that the exchange agreements in effect provide for the exchange of information in accordance with the requirements of the Model CAA.

Australia's exchange agreements provide for the exchange of information in accordance with the requirements of the Model CAA.

Recommendations:

No recommendations made.

Comments by the assessed jurisdiction

No comments made.

Note

[1] With Singapore. Australia has also activated a relationship under the CRS MCAA with Singapore.

Azerbaijan

Overall findings

Azerbaijan's legal framework implementing the AEOI Standard is in place but needs improvement in order to be consistent with the requirements of the AEOI Terms of Reference. While Azerbaijan's international legal framework to exchange the information with all of Azerbaijan's Interested Appropriate Partners (CR2) is consistent with the requirements, its domestic legislative framework requiring Reporting Financial Institutions to conduct the due diligence and reporting procedures (CR1) has deficiencies significant to the proper functioning of the AEOI Standard. More specifically, deficiencies have been identified with respect to Azerbaijan's enforcement framework.

The methodology used for the peer reviews and that therefore underpins this report is outlined in Chapter 2.

Overall determination on the legal framework: In Place **But Needs Improvement**

Conclusions on the legal framework

General context

Azerbaijan commenced exchanges under the AEOI Standard in 2018.

In order to provide for Reporting Financial Institutions to collect and report the information to be exchanged, Azerbaijan:

- enacted Limits and Regulations for provision of information on financial transactions carried out by legal entities and individuals of foreign states in the territory of Azerbaijan to the competent authorities of those countries approved by the Cabinet of Ministers in the decision No. 211 as amended on 22 June, 2018, 15 September, 2021 and 31 January 2023; and
- made reference to the Law of the Republic of Azerbaijan on the Prevention of the Legalisation of Criminally Obtained Funds or Other Property and the Financing of Terrorism (AML law), for the purposes of the identification of Controlling Persons under the AEOI Standard.

Under this framework Reporting Financial Institutions were required to commence the due diligence procedures in relation to New Accounts from 1 July 2017. Reporting Financial Institutions were required to complete the due diligence procedures on all Preexisting Accounts by 30 June 2018.

Following the initial Global Forum peer review, Azerbaijan amended its legislative framework to address issues identified, the last of which was effective from 31 January 2023.

With respect to the exchange of information under the AEOI Standard, Azerbaijan is a Party to the Convention on Mutual Administrative Assistance in Tax Matters and activated the associated CRS Multilateral Competent Authority Agreement in time for exchanges in 2018.

Detailed findings

The detailed findings for Azerbaijan are below, organised per Core Requirement (CR) and sub-requirement (SR), as extracted from the AEOI Terms of Reference (see Annex B).

CR1 Domestic legal framework: Jurisdictions should have a domestic legislative framework in place that requires all Reporting Financial Institutions to conduct the due diligence and reporting procedures in the CRS, and that provides for the effective implementation of the CRS as set out therein.

Determination: In Place But **Needs Improvement**

Azerbaijan's domestic legislative framework is in place and contains many of the key aspects of the CRS and the Commentary requiring Reporting Financial Institutions to conduct the due diligence and reporting procedures, but it needs improvement in relation to the framework to enforce the requirements (SR 1.4). More specifically, Azerbaijan's legislative framework does not impose sanctions on Account Holders and Controlling Persons for providing a false self-certification, and it does not include an explicit legal basis to enforce a sanction where a Reporting Financial Institution is a legal arrangement.

SR 1.1 Jurisdictions should define the scope of Reporting Financial Institutions consistently with the CRS.

Azerbaijan has defined the scope of Reporting Financial Institutions in its domestic legislative framework in accordance with the CRS and its Commentary.

Recommendations:

No recommendations made.

SR 1.2 Jurisdictions should define the scope of Financial Accounts and Reportable Accounts consistently with the CRS and incorporate the due diligence procedures to identify them.

Azerbaijan has defined the scope of the Financial Accounts that are required to be reported in its domestic legislative framework and incorporated the due diligence procedures that must be applied to identify them in accordance with the CRS and its Commentary.

Recommendations:

No recommendations made.

SR 1.3 Jurisdictions should incorporate the reporting requirements contained in Section I of the CRS into their domestic legislative framework.

Azerbaijan has incorporated the reporting requirements in its domestic legislative framework in accordance with the CRS and its Commentary.

Recommendations:

No recommendations made.

SR 1.4 Jurisdictions should have a legislative framework in place that allows for the enforcement of the requirements of the CRS in practice.

Azerbaijan has a legislative framework in place to enforce the requirements in a manner that is largely consistent with the CRS and its Commentary. However, deficiencies have been identified. More specifically, Azerbaijan's legislative framework does not impose sanctions on Account Holders and Controlling Persons for the provision of a false self-certification, and it does not include an explicit legal basis to enforce a sanction where a Reporting Financial Institution is a legal arrangement. These are key elements of the required enforcement framework and are therefore material to the proper functioning of the AEOI Standard.

Recommendations:

Azerbaijan should amend its domestic legislative framework to include sanctions on Account Holders and Controlling Persons for the provision of a false self-certification.

Azerbaijan should amend its legislative framework to ensure that there is an explicit legal basis to enforce a sanction when there is non-compliance by a Reporting Financial Institution that is a legal arrangement.

CR2 International legal framework: Jurisdictions should have exchange relationships in effect with all Interested Appropriate Partners as committed to and that provide for the exchange of information in accordance with the Model CAA.

Determination: In Place

Azerbaijan's international legal framework to exchange the information is in place, is consistent with the Model CAA and its Commentary and provides for exchange with all of Azerbaijan's Interested Appropriate Partners (i.e. all jurisdictions that are interested in receiving information from Azerbaijan and that meet the required standard in relation to confidentiality and data safeguards) (SRs 2.1 – 2.3).

SR 2.1 Jurisdictions should have exchange agreements in effect with all Interested Appropriate Partners that permit the automatic exchange of CRS information.

Azerbaijan has exchange agreements that permit the automatic exchange of CRS information in effect with all its Interested Appropriate Partners.

Recommendations:

No recommendations made.

SR 2.2 Such an exchange agreement should be put in place without undue delay, following the receipt of an expression of interest from an Interested Appropriate Partner.

Azerbaijan put in place its exchange agreements without undue delay.

Recommendations:

No recommendations made.

SR 2.3 Jurisdictions should ensure that the exchange agreements in effect provide for the exchange of information in accordance with the requirements of the Model CAA.

Azerbaijan's exchange agreements provide for the exchange of information in accordance with the requirements of the Model CAA.

Recommendations:

No recommendations made.

Comments by the assessed jurisdiction

No comments made.

The Bahamas

Overall findings

The Bahamas' legal framework implementing the AEOI Standard is in place but needs improvement in order to be fully consistent with the requirements of the AEOI Terms of Reference. While The Bahamas' international legal framework to exchange the information with all of The Bahamas' Interested Appropriate Partners (CR2) is consistent with the requirements, its domestic legislative framework requiring Reporting Financial Institutions to conduct the due diligence and reporting procedures (CR1) has deficiencies significant to the proper functioning of elements of the AEOI Standard. More specifically, the rules in The Bahamas' legislative framework to prevent the adoption of practices intended to circumvent the reporting and due diligence procedures are insufficient in scope.

The methodology used for the peer reviews and that therefore underpins this report is outlined in Chapter 2.

Overall determination on the legal framework: In Place But **Needs Improvement**

Conclusions on the legal framework

General context

The Bahamas commenced exchanges under the AEOI Standard in 2018.

In order to provide for Reporting Financial Institutions to collect and report the information to be exchanged, The Bahamas:

- enacted the Automatic Exchange of Financial Account Information Act 2016 (amended in 2017, 2019, 2022 and 2024);
- introduced the Automatic Exchange of Financial Account Information Regulations 2017 (amended in 2017, 2019, 2020 and 2024); and
- issued further guidance, which is not legally binding.

Under this framework Reporting Financial Institutions were required to commence the due diligence procedures in relation to New Accounts from 1 July 2017. With respect to Preexisting Accounts, Reporting Financial Institutions were required to complete the due diligence procedures on High Value Individual Accounts by 31 December 2017 and on Lower Value Individual Accounts and Entity Accounts by 31 December 2018.

Following the initial Global Forum peer review, The Bahamas made various amendments to its legislative framework to address issues identified, the last of which was effective from 11 July 2024.

With respect to the exchange of information under the AEOI Standard, The Bahamas is a Party to the Convention on Mutual Administrative Assistance in Tax Matters and activated the associated CRS Multilateral Competent Authority Agreement in time for exchanges in 2018.

Detailed findings

The detailed findings for The Bahamas are below, organised per Core Requirement (CR) and sub-requirement (SR), as extracted from the AEOI Terms of Reference (see Annex B).

CR1 Domestic legal framework: Jurisdictions should have a domestic legislative framework in place that requires all Reporting Financial Institutions to conduct the due diligence and reporting procedures in the CRS, and that provides for the effective implementation of the CRS as set out therein.

Determination: In Place But **Needs Improvement**

The Bahamas' domestic legislative framework is in place and contains many of the key aspects of the CRS and its Commentary requiring Reporting Financial Institutions to conduct the due diligence and reporting procedures, but it needs improvement in one area relating to the framework to enforce the requirements (SR 1.4). More specifically, the rules in The Bahamas' legislative framework to prevent persons from adopting practices intended to circumvent the reporting and due diligence procedures are insufficient in scope as they do not cover all relevant persons and circumstances.

SR 1.1 Jurisdictions should define the scope of Reporting Financial Institutions consistently with the CRS.

The Bahamas has defined the scope of Reporting Financial Institutions in accordance with the CRS and its Commentary.

Recommendations:

No recommendations made.

SR 1.2 Jurisdictions should define the scope of Financial Accounts and Reportable Accounts consistently with the CRS and incorporate the due diligence procedures to identify them.

The Bahamas has defined the scope of the Financial Accounts that are required to be reported in its domestic legislative framework and incorporated the due diligence procedures that must be applied to identify them in accordance with the CRS and its Commentary.

Recommendations:

No recommendations made.

SR 1.3 Jurisdictions should incorporate the reporting requirements contained in Section I of the CRS into their domestic legislative framework.

The Bahamas has incorporated the reporting requirements in its domestic legislative framework in accordance with the CRS and its Commentary.

Recommendations:

No recommendations made.

SR 1.4 Jurisdictions should have a legislative framework in place that allows for the enforcement of the requirements of the CRS in practice.

The Bahamas has a legislative framework in place to enforce the requirements in a manner that is largely consistent with the CRS and its Commentary. However, a deficiency has been identified. More specifically, The Bahamas' legislative framework has an anti-circumvention rule that does not cover all relevant persons that may engage in practices to avoid due diligence and reporting. This is a key element of the required enforcement framework and is therefore material to the proper functioning of the AEOI Standard.

Recommendations:

The Bahamas should ensure that its anti-avoidance rule covers avoidance of the reporting and due diligence requirements when entered into by Account Holders or intermediaries, not just by Financial Institutions.

CR2 International legal framework: Jurisdictions should have exchange relationships in effect with all Interested Appropriate Partners as committed to and that provide for the exchange of information in accordance with the Model CAA.

Determination: In Place

The Bahamas' international legal framework to exchange the information is in place, is consistent with the Model CAA and its Commentary and provides for exchange with all of The Bahamas' Interested Appropriate Partners (i.e. all jurisdictions that are interested in receiving information from The Bahamas and that meet the required standard in relation to confidentiality and data safeguards) (SRs 2.1 – 2.3).

SR 2.1 Jurisdictions should have exchange agreements in effect with all Interested Appropriate Partners that permit the automatic exchange of CRS information.

The Bahamas has exchange agreements that permit the automatic exchange of CRS information in effect with all its Interested Appropriate Partners.

Recommendations:

No recommendations made.

SR 2.2 Such an exchange agreement should be put in place without undue delay, following the receipt of an expression of interest from an Interested Appropriate Partner.

The Bahamas put in place its exchange agreements without undue delay.

Recommendations:

No recommendations made.

SR 2.3 Jurisdictions should ensure that the exchange agreements in effect provide for the exchange of information in accordance with the requirements of the Model CAA.

The Bahamas' exchange agreements provide for the exchange of information in accordance with the requirements of the Model CAA.

Recommendations:

No recommendations made.

Comments by the assessed jurisdiction

No comments made.

Barbados

Overall findings

Barbados' legal framework implementing the AEOI Standard is in place and is consistent with the requirements of the AEOI Terms of Reference. This includes Barbados' domestic legislative framework requiring Reporting Financial Institutions to conduct the due diligence and reporting procedures (CR1) and its international legal framework to exchange the information with all of Barbados' Interested Appropriate Partners (CR2).

The methodology used for the peer reviews and that therefore underpins this report is outlined in Chapter 2.

Overall determination on the legal framework: In Place

Conclusions on the legal framework

General context

Barbados commenced exchanges under the AEOI Standard in 2018.

In order to provide for Reporting Financial Institutions to collect and report the information to be exchanged, Barbados:

- enacted Section 83 of the Income Tax Act of Barbados; and
- introduced the Income Tax (Automatic Exchange of Information) Regulations 2017.

Under this framework Reporting Financial Institutions were required to commence the due diligence procedures in relation to New Accounts from 1 July 2017. With respect to Preexisting Accounts, Reporting Financial Institutions were required to complete the due diligence procedures on High Value Individual Accounts by 31 December 2017 and on Lower Value Individual Accounts and Entity Accounts by 31 December 2018.

Following the initial Global Forum review, Barbados amended its legislative framework to address issues identified, effective from 11 August 2024.

With respect to the exchange of information under the AEOI Standard, Barbados is a Party to the Convention on Mutual Administrative Assistance in Tax Matters and activated the associated CRS Multilateral Competent Authority Agreement in time for exchanges in 2018.

Detailed findings

The detailed findings for Barbados are below, organised per Core Requirement (CR) and sub-requirement (SR), as extracted from the AEOI Terms of Reference (see Annex B).

CR1 Domestic legal framework: Jurisdictions should have a domestic legislative framework in place that requires all Reporting Financial Institutions to conduct the due diligence and reporting procedures in the CRS, and that provides for the effective implementation of the CRS as set out therein.

Determination: In Place

Barbados' domestic legislative framework is in place and contains all of the key aspects of the CRS and its Commentary requiring Reporting Financial Institutions to conduct the due diligence and reporting procedures (SRs 1.1 – 1.3). It also provides for a framework to enforce the requirements (SR 1.4).

SR 1.1 Jurisdictions should define the scope of Reporting Financial Institutions consistently with the CRS.

Barbados has defined the scope of Reporting Financial Institutions in its domestic legislative framework in accordance with the CRS and its Commentary.

Recommendations:

No recommendations made.

SR 1.2 Jurisdictions should define the scope of Financial Accounts and Reportable Accounts consistently with the CRS and incorporate the due diligence procedures to identify them.

Barbados has defined the scope of the Financial Accounts that are required to be reported in its domestic legislative framework and incorporated the due diligence procedures that must be applied to identify them in accordance with the CRS and its Commentary.

Recommendations:

No recommendations made.

SR 1.3 Jurisdictions should incorporate the reporting requirements contained in Section I of the CRS into their domestic legislative framework.

Barbados has incorporated the reporting requirements in its domestic legislative framework in accordance with the CRS and its Commentary.

Recommendations:

No recommendations made.

SR 1.4 Jurisdictions should have a legislative framework in place that allows for the enforcement of the requirements of the CRS in practice.

Barbados has a legislative framework in place to enforce the requirements in accordance with the CRS and its Commentary.

Recommendations:

No recommendations made.

CR2 International legal framework: Jurisdictions should have exchange relationships in effect with all Interested Appropriate Partners as committed to and that provide for the exchange of information in accordance with the Model CAA.

Determination: In Place

Barbados' international legal framework to exchange the information is in place, is consistent with the Model CAA and its Commentary and provides for exchange with all of Barbados' Interested Appropriate Partners (i.e. all jurisdictions that are interested in receiving information from Barbados and that meet the required standard in relation to confidentiality and data safeguards) (SRs 2.1 – 2.3).

SR 2.1 Jurisdictions should have exchange agreements in effect with all Interested Appropriate Partners that permit the automatic exchange of CRS information.

Barbados has exchange agreements that permit the automatic exchange of CRS information in effect with all its Interested Appropriate Partners.

Recommendations:

No recommendations made.

SR 2.2 Such an exchange agreement should be put in place without undue delay, following the receipt of an expression of interest from an Interested Appropriate Partner.

Barbados put in place its exchange agreements without undue delay.

Recommendations:

No recommendations made.

SR 2.3 Jurisdictions should ensure that the exchange agreements in effect provide for the exchange of information in accordance with the requirements of the Model CAA.

Barbados' exchange agreements provide for the exchange of information in accordance with the requirements of the Model CAA.

Recommendations:

No recommendations made.

Comments by the assessed jurisdiction

No comments made.

British Virgin Islands

Overall findings

The British Virgin Islands' legal framework implementing the AEOI Standard is in place but needs improvement in order to be fully consistent with the requirements of the AEOI Terms of Reference. While the British Virgin Islands' international legal framework to exchange the information with all of the British Virgin Islands' Interested Appropriate Partners (CR2) is consistent with the requirements, its domestic legislative framework requiring Reporting Financial Institutions to conduct the due diligence and reporting procedures (CR1) has a deficiency significant to the proper functioning of elements of the AEOI Standard. More specifically, a deficiency has been identified in relation to the British Virgin Islands' enforcement framework.

The methodology used for the peer reviews and that therefore underpins this report is outlined in Chapter 2.

Overall determination on the legal framework: In Place But **Needs Improvement**

Conclusions on the legal framework

General context

The British Virgin Islands commenced exchanges under the AEOI Standard on a non-reciprocal basis in 2017 (i.e. it sends but it does not receive information).

In order to provide for Reporting Financial Institutions to collect and report the information to be exchanged, the British Virgin Islands:

- enacted the Mutual Legal Assistance (Tax Matters) (Amendment) (No.2) Act, 2015, as amended in 2018 and in 2022; and
- issued further guidance, which is not legally binding.

Under this framework Reporting Financial Institutions were required to commence the due diligence procedures in relation to New Accounts from 1 January 2016. With respect to Preexisting Accounts, Reporting Financial Institutions were required to complete the due diligence procedures on High Value Individual Accounts by 31 December 2016 and on Lower Value Individual Accounts and Entity Accounts by 31 December 2017.

Following the initial Global Forum peer review, the British Virgin Islands made various amendments to its legislative framework to address issues identified, the last of which was effective from 1 June 2022.

With respect to the exchange of information under the AEOI Standard, the British Virgin Islands:

- has the Convention on Mutual Administrative Assistance in Tax Matters in place[1] and activated the associated CRS Multilateral Competent Authority Agreement in time for exchanges in 2017; and
- put in place three bilateral agreements.[2]

Detailed findings

The detailed findings for the British Virgin Islands are below, organised per Core Requirement (CR) and sub-requirement (SR), as extracted from the AEOI Terms of Reference (see Annex B).

CR1 Domestic legal framework: Jurisdictions should have a domestic legislative framework in place that requires all Reporting Financial Institutions to conduct the due diligence and reporting procedures in the CRS, and that provides for the effective implementation of the CRS as set out therein.

Determination: In Place But **Needs Improvement**

The British Virgin Islands' domestic legislative framework is in place and contains most of the key aspects of the CRS and its Commentary requiring Reporting Financial Institutions to conduct the due diligence and reporting procedures, but it needs improvement in relation to the framework to enforce the requirements (SR 1.4). More specifically, the British Virgin Islands' legislative framework does not have an explicit legal basis to enforce a sanction for non-compliance if the Reporting Financial Institution is a legal arrangement.

SR 1.1 Jurisdictions should define the scope of Reporting Financial Institutions consistently with the CRS.

Findings:

The British Virgin Islands has defined the scope of Reporting Financial Institutions in its domestic legislative framework in accordance with the CRS and its Commentary.

Recommendations:

No recommendations made.

SR 1.2 Jurisdictions should define the scope of Financial Accounts and Reportable Accounts consistently with the CRS and incorporate the due diligence procedures to identify them.

Findings:

The British Virgin Islands has defined the scope of the Financial Accounts that are required to be reported in its domestic legislative framework and incorporated the due diligence procedures that must be applied to identify them in accordance with the CRS and its Commentary.

Recommendations:

No recommendations made.

SR 1.3 Jurisdictions should incorporate the reporting requirements contained in Section I of the CRS into their domestic legislative framework.

Findings:

The British Virgin Islands has incorporated the reporting requirements in its domestic legislative framework in accordance with the CRS and its Commentary.

Recommendations:

No recommendations made.

SR 1.4 Jurisdictions should have a legislative framework in place that allows for the enforcement of the requirements of the CRS in practice.

Findings:

The British Virgin Islands has a legislative framework in place to enforce the requirements in a manner that is largely consistent with the CRS and its Commentary. However, a deficiency has been identified. More specifically, the British Virgin Islands' legislative framework does not include an explicit legal basis to enforce a sanction where a Reporting Financial Institution is a legal arrangement. This deficiency relates to a key element of the AEOI Standard and is therefore material to the proper functioning of the AEOI Standard.

Recommendations:

The British Virgin Islands should amend its legislative framework to ensure that there is an explicit legal basis to enforce a sanction when there is non-compliance by a Reporting Financial Institution that is a legal arrangement.

CR2 International legal framework: Jurisdictions should have exchange relationships in effect with all Interested Appropriate Partners as committed to and that provide for the exchange of information in accordance with the Model CAA.

Determination: In Place

The British Virgin Islands' international legal framework to exchange the information is in place, is consistent with the Model CAA and its Commentary and provides for exchanges with all of the British Virgin Islands' Interested Appropriate Partners (i.e. all jurisdictions that are interested in receiving information from the British Virgin Islands and that meet the required standard in relation to confidentiality and data safeguards) (SRs 2.1 – 2.3).

SR 2.1 Jurisdictions should have exchange agreements in effect with all Interested Appropriate Partners that permit the automatic exchange of CRS information.

Findings:

The British Virgin Islands has exchange agreements that permit the automatic exchange of CRS information in effect with all its Interested Appropriate Partners.

Recommendations:

No recommendations made.

SR 2.2 Such an exchange agreement should be put in place without undue delay, following the receipt of an expression of interest from an Interested Appropriate Partner.

Findings:

The British Virgin Islands put in place its exchange agreements without undue delay.

Recommendations:

No recommendations made.

SR 2.3 Jurisdictions should ensure that the exchange agreements in effect provide for the exchange of information in accordance with the requirements of the Model CAA.

Findings:

The British Virgin Islands' exchange agreements provide for the exchange of information in accordance with the requirements of the Model CAA.

Recommendations:

No recommendations made.

Comments by the assessed jurisdiction

No comments made.

Note

[1] Through a territorial extension by the United Kingdom.

[2] With Guernsey, the Isle of Man and the United Kingdom.

Brunei Darussalam

Overall findings

Brunei Darussalam's legal framework implementing the AEOI Standard is in place but needs improvement in order to be fully consistent with the requirements of the AEOI Terms of Reference. While Brunei Darussalam's international legal framework to exchange the information with all of Brunei Darussalam's Interested Appropriate Partners (CR2) is consistent with the requirements, its domestic legislative framework requiring Reporting Financial Institutions to conduct the due diligence and reporting procedures (CR1) has deficiencies significant to the proper functioning of elements of the AEOI Standard. More specifically, deficiencies have been identified in relation to the Brunei Darussalam's enforcement framework.

The methodology used for the peer reviews and that therefore underpins this report is outlined in Chapter 2.

Overall determination on the legal framework: In Place But **Needs Improvement**

Conclusions on the legal framework

General context

Brunei Darussalam commenced exchanges under the AEOI Standard in 2018.

In order to provide for Reporting Financial Institutions to collect and report the information to be exchanged, Brunei Darussalam:

- enacted Income Tax Act (Amendment) No. 3 Order, 2017;
- issued Income Tax (International Tax Compliance Agreements) (Common Reporting Standard) Regulations 2017; and
- published further guidance, which is not legally binding.

Under this framework Reporting Financial Institutions were required to commence the due diligence procedures in relation to New Accounts from 1 January 2017. With respect to Preexisting Accounts, Reporting Financial Institutions were required to complete the due diligence procedures on High Value Individual Accounts by 31 December 2017 and on Lower Value Individual Accounts and Entity Accounts by 31 December 2018.

With respect to the exchange of information under the AEOI Standard, Brunei Darussalam is a Party to the Convention on Mutual Administrative Assistance in Tax Matters and activated the associated CRS Multilateral Competent Authority Agreement in time for exchanges in 2018.

Detailed findings

The detailed findings for Brunei Darussalam are below, organised per Core Requirement (CR) and sub-requirement (SR), as extracted from the AEOI Terms of Reference (see Annex B).

CR1 Domestic legal framework: Jurisdictions should have a domestic legislative framework in place that requires all Reporting Financial Institutions to conduct the due diligence and reporting procedures in the CRS, and that provides for the effective implementation of the CRS as set out therein.

Determination: In Place But **Needs Improvement**

Brunei Darussalam's domestic legislative framework is in place and contains most of the key aspects of the CRS and its Commentary requiring Reporting Financial Institutions to conduct the due diligence and reporting procedures, but it needs improvement in relation to the framework to enforce the requirements (SR 1.4). Most significantly, Brunei Darussalam's legislative framework only allows for sanctioning a Reporting Financial Institution for failing to file or filing incorrect information after a further failure to comply with a warning notice.

SR 1.1 Jurisdictions should define the scope of Reporting Financial Institutions consistently with the CRS.

Brunei Darussalam has defined the scope of Reporting Financial Institutions in its domestic legislative framework in accordance with the CRS and its Commentary.

Recommendations:

No recommendations made.

SR 1.2 Jurisdictions should define the scope of Financial Accounts and Reportable Accounts consistently with the CRS and incorporate the due diligence procedures to identify them.

Brunei Darussalam has defined the scope of the Financial Accounts that are required to be reported in its domestic legislative framework and incorporated the due diligence procedures that must be applied to identify them in accordance with the CRS and its Commentary.

Recommendations:

No recommendations made.

SR 1.3 Jurisdictions should incorporate the reporting requirements contained in Section I of the CRS into their domestic legislative framework.

Brunei Darussalam has incorporated the reporting requirements in its domestic legislative framework in accordance with the CRS and its Commentary.

Recommendations:

No recommendations made.

SR 1.4 Jurisdictions should have a legislative framework in place that allows for the enforcement of the requirements of the CRS in practice.

Brunei Darussalam has a legislative framework in place to enforce the requirements in a manner that is largely consistent with the CRS and its Commentary. However, deficiencies have been identified. Most significantly, Brunei Darussalam's legislative framework has sanctions on Reporting Financial Institution for failing to file or filing incorrect information that have a limited deterrent effect, as they depend on a warning notice being issued and are not applicable if the notice is complied with. This deficiency relates to a key element of the AEOI Standard and is therefore material to its proper functioning.

Recommendations:

Brunei Darussalam should ensure that sanctions for failing to report information or filing incorrect information are capable of being applied even where the noncompliance is corrected.

Brunei Darussalam should amend its legislative framework to ensure that there is an explicit legal basis to enforce a sanction when there is non-compliance by a Reporting Financial Institution that is a legal arrangement.

CR2 International legal framework: Jurisdictions should have exchange relationships in effect with all Interested Appropriate Partners as committed to and that provide for the exchange of information in accordance with the Model CAA.

Determination: In Place

Brunei Darussalam's international legal framework to exchange the information is in place, is consistent with the Model CAA and its Commentary and provides for exchange with all of Brunei Darussalam's Interested Appropriate Partners (i.e. all jurisdictions that are interested in receiving information from Brunei Darussalam and that meet the required standard in relation to confidentiality and data safeguards) (SRs 2.1 – 2.3).

SR 2.1 Jurisdictions should have exchange agreements in effect with all Interested Appropriate Partners that permit the automatic exchange of CRS information.

Brunei Darussalam has exchange agreements that permit the automatic exchange of CRS information in effect with all its Interested Appropriate Partners.

Recommendations:

No recommendations made.

SR 2.2 Such an exchange agreement should be put in place without undue delay, following the receipt of an expression of interest from an Interested Appropriate Partner.

Brunei Darussalam put in place its exchange agreements without undue delay.

Recommendations:

No recommendations made.

SR 2.3 Jurisdictions should ensure that the exchange agreements in effect provide for the exchange of information in accordance with the requirements of the Model CAA.

Brunei Darussalam's exchange agreements provide for the exchange of information in accordance with the requirements of the Model CAA.

Recommendations:

No recommendations made.

Comments by the assessed jurisdiction

No comments made.

Bulgaria

Overall findings

Bulgaria's legal framework implementing the AEOI Standard is in place but needs improvement in order to be fully consistent with the requirements of the AEOI Terms of Reference. While Bulgaria's international legal framework to exchange the information with all of Bulgaria's Interested Appropriate Partners (CR2) is consistent with the requirements, its domestic legislative framework requiring Reporting Financial Institutions to conduct the due diligence and reporting procedures (CR1) has a deficiency significant to the proper functioning of elements of the AEOI Standard. More specifically, a deficiency has been identified in relation to Bulgaria's enforcement framework.

The methodology used for the peer reviews and that therefore underpins this report is outlined in Chapter 2.

Overall determination on the legal framework: In Place But **Needs Improvement**

Conclusions on the legal framework

General context

Bulgaria commenced exchanges under the AEOI Standard in 2017.

In order to provide for Reporting Financial Institutions to collect and report the information to be exchanged, Bulgaria:

- enacted Art. 142a to Art. 142y of the Tax and Social Security Procedure Code (TSSPC), §1a of the Additional Provisions of the TSSPC;
- enacted Order ZCU-1576/18.12.2015 of the Executive Director of the National Revenue Agency as amended by Order № ZCU-720/22.05.2018 of the Executive Director of the National Revenue Agency;
- introduced § 55 - § 66 of the Transitional and Concluding Provisions; and
- made reference to §2 of the Supplementary Provisions of the Measures Against Money Laundering Act implementing the FATF Recommendations for the purposes of the identification of Controlling Persons under the AEOI Standard.

Under this framework Reporting Financial Institutions were required to commence the due diligence procedures in relation to New Accounts from 1 January 2016. With respect to Preexisting Accounts, Reporting Financial Institutions were required to complete the due diligence procedures on High Value Individual Accounts by 31 December 2016 and on Lower Value Individual Accounts and Entity Accounts by 31 December 2017.

Following the initial Global Forum peer review, Bulgaria amended its legislative framework to address an issue identified, effective from 22 May 2018.

With respect to the exchange of information under the AEOI Standard, Bulgaria:

- is a Party to the Convention on Mutual Administrative Assistance in Tax Matters and activated the associated CRS Multilateral Competent Authority Agreement in time for exchanges in 2017;
- has in place European Directive 2011/16/EU on Administrative Cooperation in the Field of Taxation as amended by Directive 2014/107/EU; and

- has in place European Union agreements with five European third countries.[1]

Detailed findings

The detailed findings for Bulgaria are below, organised per Core Requirement (CR) and sub-requirement (SR), as extracted from the AEOI Terms of Reference (see Annex B).

CR1 Domestic legal framework: Jurisdictions should have a domestic legislative framework in place that requires all Reporting Financial Institutions to conduct the due diligence and reporting procedures in the CRS, and that provides for the effective implementation of the CRS as set out therein.

Determination: In Place But **Needs Improvement**

Bulgaria's domestic legislative framework is in place and contains all of the key aspects of the CRS and its Commentary requiring Reporting Financial Institutions to conduct the due diligence and reporting procedures but it needs improvement in relation to the framework to enforce the requirements (SR 1.4). More specifically, Bulgaria's legislative framework does not have an explicit legal basis to enforce a sanction for non-compliance if the Reporting Financial Institution is a legal arrangement.

SR 1.1 Jurisdictions should define the scope of Reporting Financial Institutions consistently with the CRS.

Bulgaria has defined the scope of Reporting Financial Institutions in its domestic legislative framework in accordance with the CRS and its Commentary.

Recommendations:

No recommendations made.

SR 1.2 Jurisdictions should define the scope of Financial Accounts and Reportable Accounts consistently with the CRS and incorporate the due diligence procedures to identify them.

Bulgaria has defined the scope of the Financial Accounts that are required to be reported in its domestic legislative framework and incorporated the due diligence procedures that must be applied to identify them in accordance with the CRS and its Commentary.

Recommendations:

No recommendations made.

SR 1.3 Jurisdictions should incorporate the reporting requirements contained in Section I of the CRS into their domestic legislative framework.

Bulgaria has incorporated the reporting requirements in its domestic legislative framework in accordance with the CRS and its Commentary.

Recommendations:

No recommendations made.

SR 1.4 Jurisdictions should have a legislative framework in place that allows for the enforcement of the requirements of the CRS in practice.

Bulgaria has a legislative framework in place to enforce the requirements in a manner that is largely consistent with the CRS and its Commentary. However, deficiencies have been identified. Most significantly, Bulgaria's legislative framework does not include an explicit legal basis to enforce a sanction where a Reporting Financial Institution is a legal arrangement. This deficiency relates to a key element of the AEOI Standard and is therefore material to the proper functioning of the AEOI Standard. A deficiency has also been identified with respect to the retention period for records in relation to closed accounts, it is considered relatively minor and does not materially undermine the implementation of SR 1.4. This is because the deficiency is only with respect to closed accounts and Bulgarian Financial Institutions are still required to keep records of the steps taken and evidence relied upon in relation to such accounts for five years after the account is closed.

Recommendations:

Bulgaria should amend its domestic legislative framework to require Reporting Financial Institutions to maintain records for at least five years from the deadline to report the information, even when the account is closed.

Bulgaria should amend its domestic legislative framework to ensure that there is an explicit legal basis to enforce a sanction when there is noncompliance by a Reporting Financial Institution that is a legal arrangement.

CR2 International legal framework: Jurisdictions should have exchange relationships in effect with all Interested Appropriate Partners as committed to and that provide for the exchange of information in accordance with the Model CAA.

Determination: In Place

Bulgaria's international legal framework to exchange the information is in place, is consistent with the Model CAA and its Commentary and provides for exchange with all of Bulgaria's Interested Appropriate Partners (i.e. all jurisdictions that are interested in receiving information from Bulgaria and that meet the required standard in relation to confidentiality and data safeguards) (SRs 2.1 – 2.3).

SR 2.1 Jurisdictions should have exchange agreements in effect with all Interested Appropriate Partners that permit the automatic exchange of CRS information.

Bulgaria has exchange agreements that permit the automatic exchange of CRS information in effect with all its Interested Appropriate Partners.

Recommendations:

No recommendations made.

SR 2.2 Such an exchange agreement should be put in place without undue delay, following the receipt of an expression of interest from an Interested Appropriate Partner.

Bulgaria put in place its exchange agreements without undue delay.

Recommendations:

No recommendations made.

SR 2.3 Jurisdictions should ensure that the exchange agreements in effect provide for the exchange of information in accordance with the requirements of the Model CAA.

Bulgaria's exchange agreements provide for the exchange of information in accordance with the requirements of the Model CAA.

Recommendations:

No recommendations made.

Comments by the assessed jurisdiction

Bulgaria acknowledges the recommendations made and confirms that it has already taken steps to change its legislation and address the deficiencies identified.

Note

[1] Andorra, Liechtenstein, Monaco, San Marino and Switzerland.

Canada

Overall findings

Canada's legal framework implementing the AEOI Standard is in place but needs improvement in order to be fully consistent with the requirements of the AEOI Terms of Reference. While Canada's international legal framework to exchange the information with all of Canada's Interested Appropriate Partners (CR2) is consistent with the requirements, its domestic legislative framework requiring Reporting Financial Institutions to conduct the due diligence and reporting procedures (CR1) has deficiencies significant to the proper functioning of elements of the AEOI Standard. Most significantly, Canada's legislative framework does not incorporate the definition of Investment Entity in line with the requirements and provides for a jurisdiction-specific Non-Reporting Financial Institution that does not meet the requirements.

The methodology used for the peer reviews and that therefore underpins this report is outlined in Chapter 2.

Overall determination on the legal framework: In Place But **Needs Improvement**

Conclusions on the legal framework

General context

Canada commenced exchanges under the AEOI Standard in 2018.

In order to provide for Reporting Financial Institutions to collect and report the information to be exchanged, Canada:

- enacted Part XIX of the Income Tax Act (ITA);
- Introduced Sections 9005 and 9006 of the Income Tax Regulations; and
- issued further guidance, which is not legally binding.

Under this framework Reporting Financial Institutions were required to commence the due diligence procedures in relation to New Accounts from 1 July 2017. With respect to Preexisting Accounts, Reporting Financial Institutions were required to complete due diligence procedures on High Value Individual Accounts by 31 December 2018 and on Lower Value Individual Accounts and Entity Accounts by 31 December 2019.

Following the initial Global Forum peer review, Canada amended its legislative framework to address issues identified, effective from 10 July 2020.

With respect to the exchange of information under the AEOI Standard, Canada:

- is a Party to the Convention on Mutual Administrative Assistance in Tax Matters and activated the associated CRS Multilateral Competent Authority Agreement in time for exchanges in 2018; and
- put in place two bilateral agreements.[1]

Detailed findings

The detailed findings for Canada are below, organised per Core Requirement (CR) and sub-requirement (SR), as extracted from the AEOI Terms of Reference (see Annex B).

CR1 Domestic legal framework: Jurisdictions should have a domestic legislative framework in place that requires all Reporting Financial Institutions to conduct the due diligence and reporting procedures in the CRS, and that provides for the effective implementation of the CRS as set out therein.

Determination: In Place But **Needs Improvement**

Canada's domestic legislative framework is in place and contains most of the key aspects of the CRS and its Commentary requiring Reporting Financial Institutions to conduct the due diligence and reporting procedures, but it needs improvement in relation to the scope of Reporting Financial Institutions required to report information (SR 1.1) and in relation to the framework to enforce the requirements (SR 1.4). Most significantly, Canada's legislative framework does not incorporate the definition of Investment Entity in line with the requirements, and provides for a jurisdiction-specific Non-Reporting Financial Institution that does not meet the requirements.

SR 1.1 Jurisdictions should define the scope of Reporting Financial Institutions consistently with the CRS.

Canada has defined the scope of Reporting Financial Institutions in its domestic legislative framework in a manner that is largely consistent with the CRS and its Commentary. However, deficiencies have been identified. More specifically, Canada's legislative framework does not fully incorporate the definition of Investment Entity in line with the requirements. In addition, Canada's legislative framework provides for a jurisdiction-specific Non-Reporting Financial Institution that does not meet the requirements. The definition of Reporting Financial Institutions, including the provision of Non-Reporting Financial Institutions, is material to the proper functioning of the AEOI Standard.

Recommendations:

Canada should amend its domestic legislative framework to ensure that its definition of Investment Entity includes all relevant Entities, not only those promoting or representing themselves to the public as an investment vehicle.

Canada should amend its domestic legislative framework to remove Labour Sponsored Venture Capital Corporations (LSVCCs) from its jurisdiction-specific list of Non-Reporting Financial Institutions as they do not meet the requirements, including not being established to provide benefits upon retirement, disability or death and not having limits on the contributions as required.

SR 1.2 Jurisdictions should define the scope of Financial Accounts and Reportable Accounts consistently with the CRS and incorporate the due diligence procedures to identify them.

Canada has defined the scope of the Financial Accounts that are required to be reported in its domestic legislative framework and incorporated the due diligence procedures that must be applied to identify them in accordance with the CRS and its Commentary.

Recommendations:

No recommendations made.

SR 1.3 Jurisdictions should incorporate the reporting requirements contained in Section I of the CRS into their domestic legislative framework.

Canada has incorporated the reporting requirements in its domestic legislative framework in accordance with the CRS and its Commentary.

Recommendations:

No recommendations made.

SR 1.4 Jurisdictions should have a legislative framework in place that allows for the enforcement of the requirements of the CRS in practice.

Canada has a legislative framework in place to enforce the requirements in a manner that is largely consistent with the CRS and its Commentary. However, a deficiency has been identified. More specifically, Canada's legislative framework has an anti-circumvention rule that does not explicitly cover all relevant persons that may engage in practices to avoid due diligence and reporting. This is a key element of the required enforcement framework and is material to the proper functioning of the AEOI Standard.

Recommendations:

Canada should ensure that its anti-avoidance rule covers avoidance of CRS reporting and due diligence when entered into by intermediaries, not just by Financial Institutions and Account Holders.

CR2 International legal framework: Jurisdictions should have exchange relationships in effect with all Interested Appropriate Partners as committed to and that provide for the exchange of information in accordance with the Model CAA.

Determination: In Place

Canada's international legal framework to exchange the information is in place, is consistent with the Model CAA and its Commentary and provides for exchange with all of Canada's Interested Appropriate Partners (i.e. all jurisdictions that are interested in receiving information from Canada and that meet the required standard in relation to confidentiality and data safeguards) (SRs 2.1 – 2.3).

SR 2.1 Jurisdictions should have exchange agreements in effect with all Interested Appropriate Partners that permit the automatic exchange of CRS information.

Canada has exchange agreements that permit the automatic exchange of CRS information in effect with all its Interested Appropriate Partners.

Recommendations:

No recommendations made.

SR 2.2 Such an exchange agreement should be put in place without undue delay, following the receipt of an expression of interest from an Interested Appropriate Partner.

Canada put in place its exchange agreements without undue delay.

Recommendations:

No recommendations made.

SR 2.3 Jurisdictions should ensure that the exchange agreements in effect provide for the exchange of information in accordance with the requirements of the Model CAA.

Canada's exchange agreements provide for the exchange of information in accordance with the requirements of the Model CAA.

Recommendations:

No recommendations made.

Comments by the assessed jurisdiction

Canada would like to reiterate its commitment to the work of the Global Forum on Transparency and Exchange of Information for Tax Purposes (Global Forum) in promoting and monitoring the effective implementation of the international standards of transparency and exchange of information for tax purposes. Canada would also like to express its appreciation for the work of the Assessment Panel, the Global Forum Secretariat and the Automatic Exchange of Information (AEOI) Peer Review Group (APRG) for their work on the review of the implementation of the AEOI legal frameworks.

Canada takes its commitment to the AEOI Standard very seriously, and is making every effort to implement it in an effective manner, in terms of both its legislative framework and in practice.

Regarding the recommendation concerning investment entities, Canada believes that its legislative framework is consistent with the AEOI Standard regarding the definition of investment entities, when taking into account the last part of the definition of investment entities that says the definition of the term "Investment Entity" shall be interpreted in a manner consistent with similar language set forth in the definition of "financial institution" in the Financial Action Task Force Recommendations.

Further, Canada is concerned that treating closely-held professionally-managed entities that hold passive assets as investment entities, where the "account holders" are the same as the people responsible for conducting due diligence and reporting on non-resident account holders, risks weakening the integrity of the AEOI Standard. It is generally a better approach to treat such an entity as a passive Non-Financial Entity, so that the custodial institution where the entity holds its assets is responsible for due diligence and reporting.

Regarding the recommendation concerning LSVCCs, Canada believes that the unique features of LSVCCs mean that they present a low risk of being used by non-residents to evade taxes or hide assets. Nonetheless, the federal government announced in its 2024 Budget its intention to remove LSVCCs from the list of non-reporting financial institutions and treat a non-registered account held in an LSVCC as an excluded account provided that annual contributions to the account do not exceed US$50,000. It is intended that these changes would apply as of 2026.

Regarding the recommendation concerning Canada's anti-avoidance provision, this provision is broadly worded and is interpreted to include intermediaries that are engaged in circumvention of the CRS rules. Nonetheless, the federal government is proposing to amend the rule to clarify its intended scope. Specifically, the government proposed in its 2024 Budget that the anti-avoidance provision of the CRS would be amended to clarify that it applies when an individual or any entity enters into an arrangement or engages in a practice, if it can reasonably be considered that the primary purpose is to avoid an obligation of any person under the CRS. It is intended that the amendment would come into force for 2026.

Note

[1] With Hong Kong (China) and Singapore. Canada has also activated a relationship under the CRS MCAA with Singapore.

Cayman Islands

Overall findings

The Cayman Islands' legal framework implementing the AEOI Standard is in place and is consistent with the requirements of the AEOI Terms of Reference. This includes the Cayman Islands' domestic legislative framework requiring Reporting Financial Institutions to conduct the due diligence and reporting procedures (CR1) and its international legal framework to exchange the information with all of the Cayman Islands' Interested Appropriate Partners (CR2).

The methodology used for the peer reviews and that therefore underpins this report is outlined in Chapter 2.

Overall determination on the legal framework: In Place

Conclusions on the legal framework

General context

The Cayman Islands commenced exchanges under the AEOI Standard in 2017.

In order to provide for Reporting Financial Institutions to collect and report the information to be exchanged, the Cayman Islands:

- enacted the Tax Information Authority Law (2017 Revision);
- introduced the Tax Information Authority (International Tax Compliance) (Common Reporting Standard) Regulations, (2018 Revision), further amended in 2020;
- published further guidance, most recently revised March 2018, which is not legally binding.

Under this framework Reporting Financial Institutions were required to commence the due diligence procedures in relation to New Accounts from 1 January 2016. With respect to Preexisting Accounts, Reporting Financial Institutions were required to complete the due diligence procedures on High Value Individual Accounts by 31 December 2016 and on Lower Value Individual Accounts and Entity Accounts by 31 December 2017.

Following the initial Global Forum peer review, the Cayman Islands amended its legislative framework to address an issue identified, effective from 15 March 2018.

With respect to the exchange of information under the AEOI Standard, the Cayman Islands:

- has the Convention on Mutual Administrative Assistance in Tax Matters in place[1] and activated the associated CRS Multilateral Competent Authority Agreement in time for exchanges in 2017; and
- put in place three bilateral agreements.[2]

Detailed findings

The detailed findings for the Cayman Islands are below, organised per Core Requirement (CR) and sub-requirement (SR), as extracted from the AEOI Terms of Reference (see Annex B).

CR1 Domestic legal framework: Jurisdictions should have a domestic legislative framework in place that requires all Reporting Financial Institutions to conduct the due diligence and reporting procedures in the CRS, and that provides for the effective implementation of the CRS as set out therein.

Determination: In Place

The Cayman Islands' domestic legislative framework is in place and contains all of the key aspects of the CRS and its Commentary requiring Reporting Financial Institutions to conduct the due diligence and reporting procedures (SRs 1.1 – 1.3). It also provides for a framework to enforce the requirements (SR 1.4).

SR 1.1 Jurisdictions should define the scope of Reporting Financial Institutions consistently with the CRS.

The Cayman Islands has defined the scope of Reporting Financial Institutions in its domestic legislative framework in accordance with the CRS and its Commentary.

Recommendations:

No recommendations made.

SR 1.2 Jurisdictions should define the scope of Financial Accounts and Reportable Accounts consistently with the CRS and incorporate the due diligence procedures to identify them.

The Cayman Islands has defined the scope of the Financial Accounts that are required to be reported in its domestic legislative framework and incorporated the due diligence procedures that must be applied to identify them in a manner that is largely consistent with the CRS and its Commentary. While a deficiency has been identified with respect to defining the term Participating Jurisdiction, it is considered relatively minor and does not materially undermine the implementation of SR 1.2. The Cayman Islands has taken all necessary steps to ensure relevant agreements are in place.

Recommendations:

The Cayman Islands should amend its legislative framework to ensure that the approach taken with respect to the one jurisdiction defined as a Participating Jurisdiction and with which the Cayman Islands does not have an agreement to exchange CRS information with, is in accordance with the AEOI Standard.

SR 1.3 Jurisdictions should incorporate the reporting requirements contained in Section I of the CRS into their domestic legislative framework.

The Cayman Islands has incorporated the reporting requirements in its domestic legislative framework in accordance with the CRS and its Commentary.

Recommendations:

No recommendations made.

SR 1.4 Jurisdictions should have a legislative framework in place that allows for the enforcement of the requirements of the CRS in practice.

The Cayman Islands has a legislative framework in place to enforce the requirements in accordance with the CRS and its Commentary.

Recommendations:

No recommendations made.

CR2 International legal framework: Jurisdictions should have exchange relationships in effect with all Interested Appropriate Partners as committed to and that provide for the exchange of information in accordance with the Model CAA.

Determination: In Place

The Cayman Islands' international legal framework to exchange the information is in place, is consistent with the Model CAA and its Commentary and provides for exchange with all of the Cayman Islands' Interested Appropriate Partners (i.e. all jurisdictions that are interested in receiving information from the Cayman Islands and that meet the required standard in relation to confidentiality and data safeguards) (SRs 2.1 – 2.3).

SR 2.1 Jurisdictions should have exchange agreements in effect with all Interested Appropriate Partners that permit the automatic exchange of CRS information.

The Cayman Islands has exchange agreements that permit the automatic exchange of CRS information in effect with all its Interested Appropriate Partners.

Recommendations:

No recommendations made.

SR 2.2 Such an exchange agreement should be put in place without undue delay, following the receipt of an expression of interest from an Interested Appropriate Partner.

The Cayman Islands put in place its exchange agreements without undue delay.

Recommendations:

No recommendations made.

SR 2.3 Jurisdictions should ensure that the exchange agreements in effect provide for the exchange of information in accordance with the requirements of the Model CAA.

The Cayman Islands' exchange agreements provide for the exchange of information in accordance with the requirements of the Model CAA.

Recommendations:

No recommendations made.

Comments by the assessed jurisdiction

No comments made.

Notes

[1] Through a territorial extension by the United Kingdom.

[2] With Guernsey, the Isle of Man and the United Kingdom.

Cook Islands

Overall findings

The Cook Islands' legal framework implementing the AEOI Standard is in place but needs improvement in order to be fully consistent with the requirements of the AEOI Terms of Reference. While the Cook Islands' international legal framework to exchange the information with all of the Cook Islands' Interested Appropriate Partners (CR2) is consistent with the requirements, its domestic legislative framework requiring Reporting Financial Institutions to conduct the due diligence and reporting procedures (CR1) has deficiencies significant to the proper functioning of elements of the AEOI Standard. Most significantly, deficiencies have been identified in relation to the Cook Islands' enforcement framework.

The methodology used for the peer reviews and that therefore underpins this report is outlined in Chapter 2.

Overall determination on the legal framework: In Place But **Needs Improvement**

Conclusions on the legal framework

General context

The Cook Islands commenced exchanges under the AEOI Standard in 2018.

In order to provide for Reporting Financial Institutions to collect and report the information to be exchanged, the Cook Islands:

- enacted amendments to the Income Tax Act 1997;
- issued the Income Tax (Automatic Exchange of Financial Account Information) Regulations 2017; and
- published guidance, which is not legally binding.

Under this framework Reporting Financial Institutions were required to commence the due diligence procedures in relation to New Accounts from 1 January 2017. With respect to Preexisting Accounts, Reporting Financial Institutions were required to complete the due diligence procedures on High Value Individual Accounts by 31 December 2017 and on Lower Value Individual Accounts and Entity Accounts by 31 December 2018.

Following the initial Global Forum peer review, the Cook Islands amended its legislative framework to address an issue identified, effective from 4 December 2019.

With respect to the exchange of information under the AEOI Standard, the Cook Islands is a Party to the Convention on Mutual Administrative Assistance in Tax Matters and activated the associated CRS Multilateral Competent Authority Agreement in time for exchanges in 2018.

Detailed findings

The detailed findings for the Cook Islands are below, organised per Core Requirement (CR) and sub-requirement (SR), as extracted from the AEOI Terms of Reference (see Annex B).

CR1 Domestic legal framework: Jurisdictions should have a domestic legislative framework in place that requires all Reporting Financial Institutions to conduct the due diligence and reporting procedures in the CRS, and that provides for the effective implementation of the CRS as set out therein.

Determination: In Place But **Needs Improvement**

The Cook Islands' domestic legislative framework is in place and contains most of the key aspects of the CRS and its Commentary requiring Reporting Financial Institutions to conduct the due diligence and reporting procedures but it needs improvement in relation to the scope of Financial Accounts required to be reported and the due diligence procedures to identify them (SR 1.2) and the framework to enforce the requirements (SR 1.4). Most significantly, the Cook Islands does not require records to be kept in accordance with the requirements and it does not have an explicit legal basis to impose or enforce a sanction for non-compliance if the Reporting Financial Institution is a legal arrangement.

SR 1.1 Jurisdictions should define the scope of Reporting Financial Institutions consistently with the CRS.

The Cook Islands has defined the scope of Reporting Financial Institutions in its domestic legislative framework in accordance with the CRS and its Commentary.

Recommendations:

No recommendations made.

SR 1.2 Jurisdictions should define the scope of Financial Accounts and Reportable Accounts consistently with the CRS and incorporate the due diligence procedures to identify them.

The Cook Islands has defined the scope of the Financial Accounts that are required to be reported in its domestic legislative framework and incorporated the due diligence procedures that must be applied to identify them in a manner that is largely consistent with the CRS and its Commentary. However, a deficiency has been identified. More specifically, the Cook Islands' legislative framework does not incorporate the requirements in relation to certain Entities not located in Participating Jurisdictions in line with the AEOI Standard. This deficiency is material to the proper functioning of the AEOI Standard as it does not ensure that all Investment Entities that are not in Participating Jurisdictions are subject to the "look-through" approach to identify their Controlling Persons.

Recommendations:

The Cook Islands should amend its domestic legislative framework to ensure that the approach taken with respect to the two jurisdictions defined as Participating Jurisdictions and with which the Cook Islands does not have an agreement to exchange CRS information with (one of which has not implemented the AEOI Standard), is in accordance with the AEOI Standard.

SR 1.3 Jurisdictions should incorporate the reporting requirements contained in Section I of the CRS into their domestic legislative framework.

The Cook Islands has incorporated the reporting requirements in its domestic legislative framework in accordance with the CRS and its Commentary.

Recommendations:

No recommendations made.

SR 1.4 Jurisdictions should have a legislative framework in place that allows for the enforcement of the requirements of the CRS in practice.

The Cook Islands has a legislative framework in place to enforce the requirements in a manner that is largely consistent with the CRS and its Commentary. However, deficiencies have been identified. More specifically, the Cook Islands' legislative framework:

- has an anti-circumvention rule that does not cover all relevant persons that may engage in practices to avoid due diligence and reporting;
- does not include an explicit legal basis to impose or enforce a sanction where a Reporting Financial Institution is a legal arrangement;
- does not include rules requiring Reporting Financial Institutions to keep records in accordance with the requirements; and
- has limited sanctions for filing incorrect information as the incorrect filing must be shown to have been either intentional or due to a failure to carry out due diligence.

These deficiencies relate to key elements of the AEOI Standard and are therefore material to its proper functioning.

Recommendations:

The Cook Islands should ensure that its anti-avoidance rule covers avoidance of CRS reporting and due diligence when entered into by Account Holders or intermediaries, not just by Financial Institutions.

The Cook Islands should amend its domestic legislative framework to require Reporting Financial Institutions to keep records of the steps taken and evidence relied upon for the performance of the procedures, rather than permitting either to be kept.

The Cook Islands should amend its domestic legislative framework to ensure that it is able to sanction noncompliance by a Reporting Financial Institution that is a legal arrangement.

The Cook Islands should amend its domestic legislative framework to ensure that sanctions for filing incorrect information are not limited only to intentional reporting of incorrect information or are due to a failure to carry out due diligence.

CR2 International legal framework: Jurisdictions should have exchange relationships in effect with all Interested Appropriate Partners as committed to and that provide for the exchange of information in accordance with the Model CAA.

Determination: In Place

The Cook Islands' international legal framework to exchange the information is in place, is consistent with the Model CAA and its Commentary and provides for exchange with all of the Cook Islands' Interested Appropriate Partners (i.e. all jurisdictions that are interested in receiving information from the Cook Islands and that meet the required standard in relation to confidentiality and data safeguards) (SRs 2.1 – 2.3).

SR 2.1 Jurisdictions should have exchange agreements in effect with all Interested Appropriate Partners that permit the automatic exchange of CRS information.

The Cook Islands has exchange agreements that permit the automatic exchange of CRS information in effect with all its Interested Appropriate Partners.

Recommendations:

No recommendations made.

SR 2.2 Such an exchange agreement should be put in place without undue delay, following the receipt of an expression of interest from an Interested Appropriate Partner.

The Cook Islands put in place its exchange agreements without undue delay.

Recommendations:

No recommendations made.

SR 2.3 Jurisdictions should ensure that the exchange agreements in effect provide for the exchange of information in accordance with the requirements of the Model CAA.

The Cook Islands' exchange agreements provide for the exchange of information in accordance with the requirements of the Model CAA.

Recommendations:

No recommendations made.

Comments by the assessed jurisdiction

No comments made.

Costa Rica

Overall findings

Costa Rica's legal framework implementing the AEOI Standard is in place and is consistent with the requirements of the AEOI Terms of Reference. This includes Costa Rica's domestic legislative framework requiring Reporting Financial Institutions to conduct the due diligence and reporting procedures (CR1) and its international legal framework to exchange the information with all of Costa Rica's Interested Appropriate Partners (CR2).

The methodology used for the peer reviews and that therefore underpins this report is outlined in Chapter 2.

Overall determination on the legal framework: In Place

Conclusions on the legal framework

General context

Costa Rica commenced exchanges under the AEOI Standard in 2018.

In order to provide for Reporting Financial Institutions to collect and report the information to be exchanged, Costa Rica:

- enacted Article 106 quárter of the General Tax Code Law No. 4755; and
- introduced the Resolution No. DGT-R-006-2017, Resolution No. DGT-R-006-2018, Resolution No. DGT-R-16-2020, Resolution No. DGT-R-27-2021 and Resolution No. DGT-R-23-2022.

Under this framework Reporting Financial Institutions were required to commence the due diligence procedures in relation to New Accounts from 1 January 2017. With respect to Preexisting Accounts, Reporting Financial Institutions were required to complete the due diligence procedures on High Value Individual Accounts and on Lower Value Individual Accounts and Entity Accounts by 31 December 2017.

Following the initial Global Forum review, Costa Rica amended its legislative framework to address issues identified, the last of which was effective from 7 May 2024.

With respect to the exchange of information under the AEOI Standard, Costa Rica is a Party to the Convention on Mutual Administrative Assistance in Tax Matters and activated the associated CRS Multilateral Competent Authority Agreement in time for exchanges in 2018.

Detailed findings

The detailed findings for Costa Rica are below, organised per Core Requirement (CR) and sub-requirement (SR), as extracted from the AEOI Terms of Reference (see Annex B).

CR1 Domestic legal framework: Jurisdictions should have a domestic legislative framework in place that requires all Reporting Financial Institutions to conduct the due diligence and reporting procedures in the CRS, and that provides for the effective implementation of the CRS as set out therein.

Determination: In Place

Costa Rica's domestic legislative framework is in place and contains all of the key aspects of the CRS and its Commentary requiring Reporting Financial Institutions to conduct the due diligence and reporting procedures (SRs 1.1 – 1.3). It also provides for a framework to enforce the requirements (SR 1.4).

SR 1.1 Jurisdictions should define the scope of Reporting Financial Institutions consistently with the CRS.

Costa Rica has defined the scope of Reporting Financial Institutions in its domestic legislative framework in accordance with the CRS and its Commentary.

Recommendations:

No recommendations made.

SR 1.2 Jurisdictions should define the scope of Financial Accounts and Reportable Accounts consistently with the CRS and incorporate the due diligence procedures to identify them.

Costa Rica has defined the scope of the Financial Accounts that are required to be reported in its domestic legislative framework and incorporated the due diligence procedures that must be applied to identify them in accordance with the CRS and its Commentary.

Recommendations:

No recommendations made.

SR 1.3 Jurisdictions should incorporate the reporting requirements contained in Section I of the CRS into their domestic legislative framework.

Costa Rica has incorporated the reporting requirements in its domestic legislative framework in accordance with the CRS and its Commentary.

Recommendations:

No recommendations made.

SR 1.4 Jurisdictions should have a legislative framework in place that allows for the enforcement of the requirements of the CRS in practice.

Costa Rica has a legislative framework in place to enforce the requirements in a manner that is consistent with the CRS and its Commentary.

Recommendations:

No recommendations made.

CR2 International legal framework: Jurisdictions should have exchange relationships in effect with all Interested Appropriate Partners as committed to and that provide for the exchange of information in accordance with the Model CAA.

Determination: In Place

Costa Rica's international legal framework to exchange the information is in place, is consistent with the Model CAA and its Commentary and provides for exchange with all of Costa Rica's Interested Appropriate Partners (i.e. all jurisdictions that are interested in receiving information from Costa Rica and that meet the required standard in relation to confidentiality and data safeguards) (SRs 2.1 – 2.3).

SR 2.1 Jurisdictions should have exchange agreements in effect with all Interested Appropriate Partners that permit the automatic exchange of CRS information.

Costa Rica has exchange agreements that permit the automatic exchange of CRS information in effect with all its Interested Appropriate Partners.

Recommendations:

No recommendations made.

SR 2.2 Such an exchange agreement should be put in place without undue delay, following the receipt of an expression of interest from an Interested Appropriate Partner.

Costa Rica put in place its exchange agreements without undue delay.

Recommendations:

No recommendations made.

SR 2.3 Jurisdictions should ensure that the exchange agreements in effect provide for the exchange of information in accordance with the requirements of the Model CAA.

Costa Rica's exchange agreements provide for the exchange of information in accordance with the requirements of the Model CAA.

Recommendations:

No recommendations made.

Comments by the assessed jurisdiction

No comments made.

Curaçao

Overall findings

Curaçao's legal framework implementing the AEOI Standard is in place and is consistent with the requirements of the AEOI Terms of Reference. This includes Curaçao's domestic legislative framework requiring Reporting Financial Institutions to conduct the due diligence and reporting procedures (CR1) and its international legal framework to exchange the information with all of Curacao's Interested Appropriate Partners (CR2.

The methodology used for the peer reviews and that therefore underpins this report is outlined in Chapter 2.

Overall determination on the legal framework: In Place

Conclusions on the legal framework

General context

Curaçao commenced exchanges under the AEOI Standard in 2018.

In order to provide for Reporting Financial Institutions to collect and report the information to be exchanged, Curaçao:

- enacted National Ordinance International Assistance Taxation;
- introduced National Decree International Assistance Taxation; and
- issued further guidance, which is not legally binding.

Under this framework Reporting Financial Institutions were required to commence the due diligence procedures in relation to New Accounts from 1 January 2017. With respect to Preexisting Accounts, Reporting Financial Institutions were required to complete the due diligence procedures on High Value Individual Accounts by 31 December 2017 and on Lower Value Individual Accounts and Entity Accounts by 31 December 2018.

Following the initial Global Forum review, Curacao amended its legislative framework to address issues identified, the last of which was effective from 25 June 2024.

With respect to the exchange of information under the AEOI Standard, Curaçao has the Convention on Mutual Administrative Assistance in Tax Matters in place[1] and activated the associated CRS Multilateral Competent Authority Agreement in time for exchanges in 2018.

Detailed findings

The detailed findings for Curaçao are below, organised per Core Requirement (CR) and sub-requirement (SR), as extracted from the AEOI Terms of (see Annex B).

CR1 Domestic legal framework: Jurisdictions should have a domestic legislative framework in place that requires all Reporting Financial Institutions to conduct the due diligence and reporting procedures in the CRS, and that provides for the effective implementation of the CRS as set out therein.

Determination: In Place

Curaçao's domestic legislative framework is inin place and contains all of the key aspects of the CRS and its Commentary requiring Reporting Financial Institutions to conduct the due diligence and reporting procedures (SRs 1.1 – 1.3). their also provides for a framework to enforce the requirements (SR 1.4).

SR 1.1 Jurisdictions should define the scope of Reporting Financial Institutions consistently with the CRS.

Curaçao has defined the scope of Reporting Financial Institutions in its domestic legislative framework in accordance with the CRS and its Commentary.

Recommendations:

No recommendations made..

SR 1.2 Jurisdictions should define the scope of Financial Accounts and Reportable Accounts consistently with the CRS and incorporate the due diligence procedures to identify them.

Curaçao has defined the scope of the Financial Accounts that are required to be reported in its domestic legislative framework and has incorporated the due diligence procedures that must be applied to identify them in accordance with the CRS and its Commentary.

Recommendations:

No recommendations made.

SR 1.3 Jurisdictions should incorporate the reporting requirements contained in Section I of the CRS into their domestic legislative framework.

Curaçao has incorporated the reporting requirements in its domestic legislative framework in accordance with the CRS and its Commentary.

Recommendations:

No recommendations made.

SR 1.4 Jurisdictions should have a legislative framework in place that allows for the enforcement of the requirements of the CRS in practice.

Curaçao has a legislative framework in place to enforce the requirements in a manner that is consistent with the CRS and its Commentary.

Recommendations:

No recommendations made.

CR2 International legal framework: Jurisdictions should have exchange relationships in effect with all Interested Appropriate Partners as committed to and that provide for the exchange of information in accordance with the Model CAA.

Determination: In Place

Curaçao's international legal framework to exchange the information is in place, is consistent with the Model CAA and its Commentary and provides for exchange with all of Curaçao's Interested Appropriate

Partners (i.e. all jurisdictions that are interested in receiving information from Curaçao and that meet the required standard in relation to confidentiality and data safeguards) (SRs 2.1 – 2.3).

SR 2.1 Jurisdictions should have exchange agreements in effect with all Interested Appropriate Partners that permit the automatic exchange of CRS information.

Curaçao has exchange agreements that permit the automatic exchange of CRS information in effect with all its Interested Appropriate Partners.

Recommendations:

No recommendations made.

SR 2.2 Such an exchange agreement should be put in place without undue delay, following the receipt of an expression of interest from an Interested Appropriate Partner.

Curaçao put in place its exchange agreements without undue delay.

Recommendations:

No recommendations made.

SR 2.3 Jurisdictions should ensure that the exchange agreements in effect provide for the exchange of information in accordance with the requirements of the Model CAA.

Curaçao's exchange agreements provide for the exchange of information in accordance with the requirements of the Model CAA.

Recommendations:

No recommendations made.

Comments by the assessed jurisdiction

No comments made.

Note

[1] Through a territorial extension by the Netherlands.

Ecuador

Overall findings

Ecuador's legal framework implementing the AEOI Standard is in place and is consistent with the requirements of the AEOI Terms of Reference. This includes Ecuador's domestic legislative framework requiring Reporting Financial Institutions to conduct the due diligence and reporting procedures (CR1) and its international legal framework to exchange the information with all of Ecuador's Interested Appropriate Partners (CR2).

The methodology used for the peer reviews and that therefore underpins this report is outlined in Chapter 2.

Overall determination on the legal framework: In Place

Conclusions on the legal framework

General context

Ecuador commenced exchanges under the AEOI Standard in 2021.

In order to provide for Reporting Financial Institutions to collect and report the information to be exchanged, Ecuador:

- relies on the Tax Code;
- issued SRI Resolution No. NAC-DGERCGC19-000000045 in 2019, amended by SRI Resolution No. NAC-DGERCGC21-00000006 in 2021 and further amended by Resolution No. NAC-DGERCGC23-00000007 in 2023; and
- issued SRI Resolution No. NAC-DGERCGC19-000000062 in 2019, and SRI Resolution No. NAC-DGERCGC23-00000031 in 2023, which was amended by Resolution No. NAC-DGERCGC24-00000031 in 2024.

Under this framework Reporting Financial Institutions were required to commence the due diligence procedures in relation to New Accounts from 1 October 2019. With respect to Preexisting Accounts, Reporting Financial Institutions were required to complete the due diligence procedures on High Value Individual Accounts by 31 December 2019 and on Lower Value Individual Accounts and Entity Accounts by 31 December 2020.

Following the initial Global Forum review, Ecuador amended its legislative framework to address issues identified, the last of which was effective from 29 August 2024.

With respect to the exchange of information under the AEOI Standard, Ecuador is a Party to the Convention on Mutual Administrative Assistance in Tax Matters and activated the associated CRS Multilateral Competent Authority Agreement in time for exchanges in 2021.

Detailed findings

The detailed findings for Ecuador are below, organised per Core Requirement (CR) and sub-requirement (SR), as extracted from the AEOI Terms of Reference (see Annex B).

CR1 Domestic legal framework: Jurisdictions should have a domestic legislative framework in place that requires all Reporting Financial Institutions to conduct the due diligence and reporting procedures in the CRS, and that provides for the effective implementation of the CRS as set out therein.

Determination: In Place

Ecuador's domestic legislative framework is in place and contains all of the key aspects of the CRS and the Commentary requiring Reporting Financial Institutions to conduct the due diligence and reporting procedures (SRs 1.1 – 1.3). It also provides a framework to enforce the requirements (SR 1.4).

SR 1.1 Jurisdictions should define the scope of Reporting Financial Institutions consistently with the CRS.

Ecuador has defined the scope of Reporting Financial Institutions in its domestic legislative framework in accordance with the CRS and its Commentary.

Recommendations:

No recommendations made.

SR 1.2 Jurisdictions should define the scope of Financial Accounts and Reportable Accounts consistently with the CRS and incorporate the due diligence procedures to identify them.

Ecuador has defined the scope of the Financial Accounts that are required to be reported in its domestic legislative framework and incorporated the due diligence procedures that must be applied to identify them in accordance with the CRS and its Commentary.

Recommendations:

No recommendations made.

SR 1.3 Jurisdictions should incorporate the reporting requirements contained in Section I of the CRS into their domestic legislative framework.

Ecuador has incorporated the reporting requirements in its domestic legislative framework in accordance with the CRS and its Commentary.

Recommendations:

No recommendations made.

SR 1.4 Jurisdictions should have a legislative framework in place that allows for the enforcement of the requirements of the CRS in practice.

Ecuador has a legislative framework in place to enforce the requirements in a manner that is consistent with the CRS and its Commentary.

Recommendations:

No recommendations made.

CR2 International legal framework: Jurisdictions should have exchange relationships in effect with all Interested Appropriate Partners as committed to and that provide for the exchange of information in accordance with the Model CAA.

Determination: In Place

Ecuador's international legal framework to exchange the information is in place, is consistent with the Model CAA and its Commentary and provides for exchange with all of Ecuador's Interested Appropriate

Partners (i.e. all jurisdictions that are interested in receiving information from Ecuador and that meet the required standard in relation to confidentiality and data safeguards) (SRs 2.1 – 2.3).

SR 2.1 Jurisdictions should have exchange agreements in effect with all Interested Appropriate Partners that permit the automatic exchange of CRS information.

Ecuador has exchange agreements that permit the automatic exchange of CRS information in effect with all its Interested Appropriate Partners.

Recommendations:

No recommendations made.

SR 2.2 Such an exchange agreement should be put in place without undue delay, following the receipt of an expression of interest from an Interested Appropriate Partner.

Ecuador put in place its exchange agreements without undue delay.

Recommendations:

No recommendations made.

SR 2.3 Jurisdictions should ensure that the exchange agreements in effect provide for the exchange of information in accordance with the requirements of the Model CAA.

Ecuador's exchange agreements provide for the exchange of information in accordance with the requirements of the Model CAA.

Recommendations:

No recommendations made.

Comments by the assessed jurisdiction

No comments made.

Faroe Islands

Overall findings

The Faroe Islands' legal framework implementing the AEOI Standard is in place and is consistent with the requirements of the AEOI Terms of Reference. This includes the Faroe Islands' domestic legislative framework requiring Reporting Financial Institutions to conduct the due diligence and reporting procedures (CR1) and its international legal framework to exchange the information with all of the Faroe Islands' Interested Appropriate Partners (CR2).

The methodology used for the peer reviews and that therefore underpins this report is outlined in Chapter 2.

Overall determination on the legal framework: In Place

Conclusions on the legal framework

General context

The Faroe Islands commenced exchanges under the AEOI Standard in 2017.

In order to provide for Reporting Financial Institutions to collect and report the information to be exchanged, the Faroe Islands:

- amended the Faroese Tax Act No. 86 of 1 September 1983 (by Act No. 50 of 6 May 2016) and Act No. 39 of 16 May 2024; and
- introduced the Regulation No. 11 of 19 February 2016, as amended in 2017, 2018, 2019 and 2021.

Under this framework Reporting Financial Institutions were required to commence the due diligence procedures in relation to New Accounts from 1 January 2016. With respect to Preexisting Accounts, Reporting Financial Institutions were required to complete the due diligence procedures on High Value Individual Accounts by 31 December 2016 and on Lower Value Individual Accounts and Entity Accounts by 31 December 2017.

Following the initial Global Forum peer review, the Faroe Islands made various amendments to its legislative framework to address issues identified, the last of which was effective from 17 May 2024.

With respect to the exchange of information under the AEOI Standard, the Faroe Islands:

- has the Convention on Mutual Administrative Assistance in Tax Matters in place,[1] and activated the associated CRS Multilateral Competent Authority Agreement in time for exchanges in 2017; and
- put in place two bilateral agreements.[2]

Detailed findings

The detailed findings for the Faroe Islands are below, organised per Core Requirement (CR) and sub-requirement (SR), as extracted from the AEOI Terms of Reference (see Annex B).

CR1 Domestic legal framework: Jurisdictions should have a domestic legislative framework in place that requires all Reporting Financial Institutions to conduct the due diligence and reporting procedures in the CRS, and that provides for the effective implementation of the CRS as set out therein.

Determination: In Place

The Faroe Islands' domestic legislative framework is in place and contains all of the key aspects of the CRS and its Commentary requiring Reporting Financial Institutions to conduct the due diligence and reporting procedures (SRs 1.1 – 1.3). It also provides for a framework to enforce the requirements (SR 1.4).

SR 1.1 Jurisdictions should define the scope of Reporting Financial Institutions consistently with the CRS.

The Faroe Islands has defined the scope of Reporting Financial Institutions in its domestic legislative framework in accordance with the CRS and its Commentary.

Recommendations:

No recommendations made.

SR 1.2 Jurisdictions should define the scope of Financial Accounts and Reportable Accounts consistently with the CRS and incorporate the due diligence procedures to identify them.

The Faroe Islands has defined the scope of the Financial Accounts that are required to be reported in its domestic legislative framework and incorporated the due diligence procedures that must be applied to identify them in accordance with the CRS and its Commentary.

Recommendations:

No recommendations made.

SR 1.3 Jurisdictions should incorporate the reporting requirements contained in Section I of the CRS into their domestic legislative framework.

The Faroe Islands has incorporated the reporting requirements in its domestic legislative framework in accordance with the CRS and its Commentary.

Recommendations:

No recommendations made.

SR 1.4 Jurisdictions should have a legislative framework in place that allows for the enforcement of the requirements of the CRS in practice.

The Faroe Islands has a legislative framework in place to enforce the requirements in a manner that is in accordance with the CRS and its Commentary. While a deficiency has been identified with respect to a lack of an explicit legal basis to enforce a sanction where a Reporting Financial Institution is a legal arrangement, it is considered relatively minor and does not materially undermine the implementation of SR 1.4. This is because such Reporting Financial Institutions have so far not been known to exist in the Faroe Islands and are considered unlikely to exist under the Faroe Islands' financial and legal frameworks.

Recommendations:

The Faroe Islands should amend its legislative framework to ensure that there is an explicit legal basis to enforce a sanction when there is non-compliance by a Reporting Financial Institution that is a legal arrangement.

CR2 International legal framework: Jurisdictions should have exchange relationships in effect with all Interested Appropriate Partners as committed to and that provide for the exchange of information in accordance with the Model CAA.

Determination: In Place

The Faroe Islands' international legal framework to exchange the information is in place, is consistent with the Model CAA and its Commentary and provides for exchange with all of the Faroe Islands' Interested Appropriate Partners (i.e. all jurisdictions that are interested in receiving information from The Faroe Islands and that meet the required standard in relation to confidentiality and data safeguards) (SRs 2.1 – 2.3).

SR 2.1 Jurisdictions should have exchange agreements in effect with all Interested Appropriate Partners that permit the automatic exchange of CRS information.

The Faroe Islands has exchange agreements that permit the automatic exchange of CRS information in effect with all its Interested Appropriate Partners.

Recommendations:

No recommendations made.

SR 2.2 Such an exchange agreement should be put in place without undue delay, following the receipt of an expression of interest from an Interested Appropriate Partner.

The Faroe Islands put in place its exchange agreements without undue delay.

Recommendations:

No recommendations made.

SR 2.3 Jurisdictions should ensure that the exchange agreements in effect provide for the exchange of information in accordance with the requirements of the Model CAA.

The Faroe Islands' exchange agreements provide for the exchange of information in accordance with the requirements of the Model CAA.

Recommendations:

No recommendations made.

Comments by the assessed jurisdiction

No comments made.

Notes

[1] Through a territorial extension by Denmark.

[2] With Denmark and Greenland.

France

Overall findings

France's legal framework implementing the AEOI Standard is in place but needs improvement in order to be fully consistent with the requirements of the AEOI Terms of Reference. While France's international legal framework to exchange the information with all of France's Interested Appropriate Partners (CR2) is consistent with the requirements, its domestic legislative framework requiring Reporting Financial Institutions to conduct the due diligence and reporting procedures (CR1) has deficiencies significant to the proper functioning of elements of the AEOI Standard. More specifically, deficiencies have been identified in relation to France's enforcement framework.

The methodology used for the peer reviews and that therefore underpins this report is outlined in Chapter 2.

Overall determination on the legal framework: In Place But **Needs Improvement**

Conclusions on the legal framework

General context

France commenced exchanges under the AEOI Standard in 2017.

In order to provide for Reporting Financial Institutions to collect and report the information to be exchanged, France:

- enacted *Code général des impôts (CGI), art. 1649AC, and CGI, art. 1736,I 5°, Décret n° 2016-1683 du 5 décembre 2016 fixant les règles et procédures concernant l'échange automatique de renseignements relatifs aux comptes financiers, dites « norme commune de déclaration »*;
- introduced the *Arrêté du 9 décembre 2016 précisant le décret n° 2016-1683 du 5 décembre 2016 fixant les règles et procédures concernant l'échange automatique de renseignements relatifs aux comptes financiers, dites « norme commune de déclaration* »; as amended by the *Arrêté du 10 février 2020*;
- issued further guidance, which is legally binding; and
- made reference to the *Code monétaire et financier* for the purposes of the identification of Controlling Persons under the AEOI Standard.

Under this framework Reporting Financial Institutions were required to commence the due diligence procedures in relation to New Accounts from 1 January 2016. With respect to Preexisting Accounts, Reporting Financial Institutions were required to complete the due diligence procedures on High Value Individual Accounts by 31 December 2016 and on Lower Value Individual Accounts and on Entity Accounts by 31 December 2017.

Following the initial Global Forum peer review, France amended its legislative framework to address issues identified, effective from 16 February 2020.

With respect to the exchange of information under the AEOI Standard, France:

- is a Party to the Convention on Mutual Administrative Assistance in Tax Matters and activated the associated CRS Multilateral Competent Authority Agreement in time for exchanges in 2017;
- has in place European Directive 2011/16/EU on Administrative Cooperation in the Field of Taxation as amended by Directive 2014/107/EU; and

- has in place European Union agreements with five European third countries.[1]

Detailed findings

The detailed findings for France are below, organised per Core Requirement (CR) and sub-requirement (SR), as extracted from the AEOI Terms of Reference (see Annex B).

CR1 Domestic legal framework: Jurisdictions should have a domestic legislative framework in place that requires all Reporting Financial Institutions to conduct the due diligence and reporting procedures in the CRS, and that provides for the effective implementation of the CRS as set out therein.

Determination: In Place But **Needs Improvement**

France's domestic legislative framework is in place and contains most of the key aspects of the CRS and its Commentary requiring Reporting Financial Institutions to conduct the due diligence and reporting procedures, but it needs improvement in relation to the framework to enforce the requirements (SR 1.4). More specifically, France's legislative framework for sanctioning due diligence and record keeping failures and providing authorities access to such records relevant to the AEOI Standard does not fully cover all Reporting Financial Institutions.

SR 1.1 Jurisdictions should define the scope of Reporting Financial Institutions consistently with the CRS.

France has defined the scope of Reporting Financial Institutions in its domestic legislative framework in accordance with the CRS and its Commentary.

Recommendations:

No recommendations made.

SR 1.2 Jurisdictions should define the scope of Financial Accounts and Reportable Accounts consistently with the CRS and incorporate the due diligence procedures to identify them.

France has defined the scope of the Financial Accounts that are required to be reported in its domestic legislative framework and incorporated the due diligence procedures that must be applied to identify them in accordance with the CRS and its Commentary.

Recommendations:

No recommendations made.

SR 1.3 Jurisdictions should incorporate the reporting requirements contained in Section I of the CRS into their domestic legislative framework.

France has incorporated the reporting requirements in its domestic legislative framework in accordance with the CRS and its Commentary.

Recommendations:

No recommendations made.

SR 1.4 Jurisdictions should have a legislative framework in place that allows for the enforcement of the requirements of the CRS in practice.

France has a legislative framework in place to enforce the requirements in a manner that is largely consistent with the CRS and its Commentary. However, deficiencies have been identified. More specifically, while France's legislative framework provides for sanctions that cover most Reporting Financial Institutions that fail to conduct due diligence or fail to keep records relevant to the AEOI Standard, and also provide relevant authorities access to such records, there are a small number of Reporting Financial Institutions falling out of scope of these provisions. These deficiencies relate to key elements of the AEOI Standard and are therefore material to its proper functioning.

Recommendations:

France should amend its domestic legislative framework to provide the appropriate authorities with the power to access the records and evidence relevant for verifying and enforcing the AEOI Standard for all Reporting Financial Institutions.

France should ensure that it has sanction provisions applicable to all Reporting Financial Institutions that fail to conduct the due diligence requirements or fail to keep records in accordance with the AEOI Standard, regardless of the impact on reporting.

CR2 International legal framework: Jurisdictions should have exchange relationships in effect with all Interested Appropriate Partners as committed to and that provide for the exchange of information in accordance with the Model CAA.

Determination: In Place

France's international legal framework to exchange the information is in place, is consistent with the Model CAA and its Commentary and provides for exchange with all of France's Interested Appropriate Partners (i.e. all jurisdictions that are interested in receiving information from France and that meet the required standard in relation to confidentiality and data safeguards) (SRs 2.1 – 2.3).

SR 2.1 Jurisdictions should have exchange agreements in effect with all Interested Appropriate Partners that permit the automatic exchange of CRS information.

France has exchange agreements that permit the automatic exchange of CRS information in effect with all its Interested Appropriate Partners.

Recommendations:

No recommendations made.

SR 2.2 Such an exchange agreement should be put in place without undue delay, following the receipt of an expression of interest from an Interested Appropriate Partner.

France put in place its exchange agreements without undue delay.

Recommendations:

No recommendations made.

SR 2.3 Jurisdictions should ensure that the exchange agreements in effect provide for the exchange of information in accordance with the requirements of the Model CAA.

France's exchange agreements provide for the exchange of information in accordance with the requirements of the Model CAA.

Recommendations:

No recommendations made.

Comments by the assessed jurisdiction

La France a pris note des recommandations formulées sur son cadre juridique et souhaite préciser qu'elle a introduit dans le projet de loi de finances pour 2025, actuellement en cours d'examen par le Parlement, des dispositions permettant d'y remédier. Sous réserve de l'adoption du texte par le Parlement, ces dispositions entreront en vigueur au 1er janvier 2025.

Translation: *France has taken note of the recommendations made regarding its legal framework and would like to point out that it has introduced provisions to remedy the situation in the Finance Bill for 2025, which is currently being examined by Parliament. Subject to the adoption of the text by Parliament, these provisions will come into force on 1 January 2025.*

Note

[1] Andorra, Liechtenstein, Monaco, San Marino and Switzerland.

Germany

Overall findings

Germany's legal framework implementing the AEOI Standard is in place but needs improvement in order to be fully consistent with the requirements of the AEOI Terms of Reference. While Germany's international legal framework to exchange the information with all of Germany's Interested Appropriate Partners (CR2) is consistent with the requirements, its domestic legislative framework requiring Reporting Financial Institutions to conduct the due diligence and reporting procedures (CR1) has deficiencies significant to the proper functioning of elements of the AEOI Standard. More specifically, deficiencies have been identified in relation to Germany's enforcement framework.

The methodology used for the peer reviews and that therefore underpins this report is outlined in Chapter 2.

Overall determination on the legal framework: In Place But **Needs Improvement**

Conclusions on the legal framework

General context

Germany commenced exchanges under the AEOI Standard in 2017.

In order to provide for Reporting Financial Institutions to collect and report the information to be exchanged, Germany:

- enacted the Law of December 21, 2015; announced in the Bundesgesetzblatt Part II, No. 35, December 29, 2015, page 1630 and Law of December 21, 2015; announced in Bundesgesetzblatt Part I, No. 55, December 30, 2015, page 2531; and
- issued further guidance, which is legally binding.

Under this framework Reporting Financial Institutions were required to commence the due diligence procedures in relation to New Accounts from 1 January 2016. With respect to Preexisting Accounts, Reporting Financial Institutions were required to complete the due diligence procedures on High Value Individual Accounts by 31 December 2016 and on Lower Value Individual Accounts and Entity Accounts by 31 December 2017.

Following the initial Global Forum peer review, Germany made various amendments to its legislative framework to address issues identified, the last of which is effective from 1 January 2023.

With respect to the exchange of information under the AEOI Standard, Germany:

- is a Party to the Convention on Mutual Administrative Assistance in Tax Matters and activated the associated CRS Multilateral Competent Authority Agreement in time for exchanges in 2017;
- has in place European Directive 2011/16/EU on Administrative Cooperation in the Field of Taxation as amended by Directive 2014/107/EU; and
- has in place European Union agreements with five European third countries.[1]

Detailed findings

The detailed findings for Germany are below, organised per Core Requirement (CR) and sub-requirement (SR), as extracted from the AEOI Terms of Reference (see Annex B).

CR1 Domestic legal framework: Jurisdictions should have a domestic legislative framework in place that requires all Reporting Financial Institutions to conduct the due diligence and reporting procedures in the CRS, and that provides for the effective implementation of the CRS as set out therein.

Determination: In Place But **Needs Improvement**

Germany's domestic legislative framework is in place and contains all of the key aspects of the CRS and its Commentary requiring Reporting Financial Institutions to conduct the due diligence and reporting procedures but it needs improvement in relation to the framework to enforce the requirements (SR 1.4). Most significantly, Germany's legislative framework does not fully provide for sanctions on Reporting Financial Institutions for failing to keep records.

SR 1.1 Jurisdictions should define the scope of Reporting Financial Institutions consistently with the CRS.

Germany has defined the scope of Reporting Financial Institutions in its domestic legislative framework in accordance with the CRS and its Commentary.

Recommendations:

No recommendations made.

SR 1.2 Jurisdictions should define the scope of Financial Accounts and Reportable Accounts consistently with the CRS and incorporate the due diligence procedures to identify them.

Germany has defined scope of the Financial Accounts that are required to be reported in its domestic legislative framework and incorporated the due diligence procedures that must be applied to identify them in accordance with the CRS and its Commentary.

Recommendations:

No recommendations made.

SR 1.3 Jurisdictions should incorporate the reporting requirements contained in Section I of the CRS into their domestic legislative framework.

Germany has incorporated the reporting requirements in its domestic legislative framework in accordance with the CRS and its Commentary.

Recommendations:

No recommendations made.

SR 1.4 Jurisdictions should have a legislative framework in place that allows for the enforcement of the requirements of the CRS in practice.

Germany has a legislative framework in place to enforce the requirements in a manner that is largely consistent with the CRS and its Commentary. However, deficiencies have been identified. More specifically, Germany's domestic legislative framework does not include rules to prevent Financial Institutions, persons or intermediaries from adopting practices to circumvent the reporting and due diligence procedures, and does not in all cases provide for sanctions on Reporting Financial Institutions for failing to keep records. These are key elements of the required enforcement framework and are therefore material to its proper functioning.

Recommendations:

Germany should amend its legislative framework introduce an anti-avoidance provision in accordance with the Standard.

While Germany is able to impose penalties for failing to report, reporting incorrect information and failing to carry out due diligence, it is recommended to amend its legislative framework to ensure it is able to also impose penalties for any failure to maintain records in accordance with the AEOI Standard.

CR2 International legal framework: Jurisdictions should have exchange relationships in effect with all Interested Appropriate Partners as committed to and that provide for the exchange of information in accordance with the Model CAA.

Determination: In Place

Germany's international legal framework to exchange the information is in place, is consistent with the Model CAA and its Commentary and provides for exchange with all of Germany's Interested Appropriate Partners (i.e. all jurisdictions that are interested in receiving information from Germany and that meet the required standard in relation to confidentiality and data safeguards) (SRs 2.1 – 2.3).

SR 2.1 Jurisdictions should have exchange agreements in effect with all Interested Appropriate Partners that permit the automatic exchange of CRS information.

Germany has exchange agreements that permit the automatic exchange of CRS information in effect with all its Interested Appropriate Partners.

Recommendations:

No recommendations made.

SR 2.2 Such an exchange agreement should be put in place without undue delay, following the receipt of an expression of interest from an Interested Appropriate Partner.

Germany put in place its exchange agreements without undue delay.

Recommendations:

No recommendations made.

SR 2.3 Jurisdictions should ensure that the exchange agreements in effect provide for the exchange of information in accordance with the requirements of the Model CAA.

Germany's exchange agreements provide for the exchange of information in accordance with the requirements of the Model CAA.

Recommendations:

No recommendations made.

Comments by the assessed jurisdiction

No comments made.

Note

[1] Andorra, Liechtenstein, Monaco, San Marino and Switzerland.

Greece

Overall findings

Greece's legal framework implementing the AEOI Standard is in place and is consistent with the requirements of the AEOI Terms of Reference. This includes Greece's domestic legislative framework requiring Reporting Financial Institutions to conduct the due diligence and reporting procedures (CR1) and its international legal framework to exchange the information with all of Greece's Interested Appropriate Partners (CR2).

The methodology used for the peer reviews and that therefore underpins this report is outlined in Chapter 2.

Overall determination on the legal framework: In Place

Conclusions on the legal framework

General context

Greece commenced exchanges under the AEOI Standard in 2017.

In order to provide for Reporting Financial Institutions to collect and report the information to be exchanged Greece:

- enacted Law 4428/2016, "Ratification of Multilateral Competent Authority Agreement on Automatic Exchange of Financial Account Information and implementing provisions";
- made reference to Law 4174/2013 "Tax Procedure Code and other provisions";
- issued the following Decisions from the Governor of the Independent Authority for Public Revenue: No. 1130/2017 as amended, No. 1133/2017 as amended and No. 1137/2017 as amended;
- issued the Joint Decision No. 1157/2018 of the Governor of the Independent Authority for Public Revenue and the Minister of Finance; and
- made reference to Law 4557/2018, "Prevention and suppression of money laundering and terrorist financing (transposition of Directive 2015/849/EU) and other provisions" for the purposes of the identification of Controlling Persons under the AEOI Standard.

Under this framework Reporting Financial Institutions were required to commence the due diligence procedures in relation to New Accounts from 1 January 2016. With respect to Preexisting Accounts, Reporting Financial Institutions were required to complete the due diligence procedures on High Value Individual Accounts by 31 December 2016 and on Lower Value Individual Accounts and Entity Accounts by 31 December 2017.

Following the initial Global Forum peer review, Greece made several amendments to its legislative framework to address issues identified, the last of which was effective from 9 July 2018.

With respect to the exchange of information under the AEOI Standard, Greece:

- Is a Party to the Convention on Mutual Administrative Assistance in Tax Matters and activated the associated CRS Multilateral Competent Authority Agreement in time for exchanges in 2017;
- has in place European Directive 2011/16/EU on Administrative Cooperation in the Field of Taxation, as amended by Directive 2014/107/EU; and

- has in place European Union agreements with five European third countries.[1]

Detailed findings

The detailed findings for Greece are below, organised per Core Requirement (CR) and sub-requirement (SR), as extracted from the AEOI Terms of Reference (see Annex B).

CR1 Domestic legal framework: Jurisdictions should have a domestic legislative framework in place that requires all Reporting Financial Institutions to conduct the due diligence and reporting procedures in the CRS, and that provides for the effective implementation of the CRS as set out therein.

Determination: In Place

Greece's domestic legislative framework is in place and contains all of the key aspects of the CRS and its Commentary requiring Reporting Financial Institutions to conduct the due diligence and reporting procedures (SRs 1.1 – 1.3). It also provides for a framework to enforce the requirements (SR 1.4).

SR 1.1 Jurisdictions should define the scope of Reporting Financial Institutions consistently with the CRS.

Greece has defined the scope of Reporting Financial Institutions in its domestic legislative framework in accordance with the CRS and its Commentary.

Recommendations:

No recommendations made.

SR 1.2 Jurisdictions should define the scope of Financial Accounts and Reportable Accounts consistently with the CRS and incorporate the due diligence procedures to identify them.

Greece has defined the scope of the Financial Accounts that are required to be reported in its domestic legislative framework and incorporated the due diligence procedures that must be applied to identify them in accordance with the CRS and its Commentary.

Recommendations:

No recommendations made.

SR 1.3 Jurisdictions should incorporate the reporting requirements contained in Section I of the CRS into their domestic legislative framework.

Greece has incorporated the reporting requirements in its domestic legislative framework in accordance with the CRS and its Commentary.

Recommendations:

No recommendations made.

SR 1.4 Jurisdictions should have a legislative framework in place that allows for the enforcement of the requirements of the CRS in practice.

Greece has a legislative framework in place to enforce the requirements in accordance with the CRS and its Commentary. While a deficiency has been identified with respect to a lack of an explicit legal basis to enforce a sanction where a Reporting Financial Institution is a legal arrangement, it is considered relatively minor and does not materially undermine the implementation of SR 1.4. This is because such Reporting Financial Institutions have so far not been known to exist in Greece and are considered unlikely to exist under Greece's financial and legal frameworks.

Recommendations:

Greece should amend its legislative framework to ensure that there is an explicit legal basis to enforce a sanction when there is non-compliance by a Reporting Financial Institution that is a legal arrangement.

CR2 International legal framework: Jurisdictions should have exchange relationships in effect with all Interested Appropriate Partners as committed to and that provide for the exchange of information in accordance with the Model CAA.

Determination: In Place

Greece's international legal framework to exchange the information is in place, is consistent with the Model CAA and its Commentary and provides for exchange with all of Greece's Interested Appropriate Partners (i.e. all jurisdictions that are interested in receiving information from Greece and that meet the required standard in relation to confidentiality and data safeguards) (SRs 2.1 – 2.3).

SR 2.1 Jurisdictions should have exchange agreements in effect with all Interested Appropriate Partners that permit the automatic exchange of CRS information.

Greece has exchange agreements that permit the automatic exchange of CRS information in effect with all its Interested Appropriate Partners.

Recommendations:

No recommendations made.

SR 2.2 Such an exchange agreement should be put in place without undue delay, following the receipt of an expression of interest from an Interested Appropriate Partner.

Greece put in place its exchange agreements without undue delay.

Recommendations:

No recommendations made.

SR 2.3 Jurisdictions should ensure that the exchange agreements in effect provide for the exchange of information in accordance with the requirements of the Model CAA.

Greece's exchange agreements provide for the exchange of information in accordance with the requirements of the Model CAA.

Recommendations:

No recommendations made.

Comments by the assessed jurisdiction

No comments made.

Note

[1] Andorra, Liechtenstein, Monaco, San Marino and Switzerland.

Greenland

Overall findings

Greenland's legal framework implementing the AEOI Standard is in place and is consistent with the requirements of the AEOI Terms of Reference. This includes Greenland's domestic legislative framework requiring Reporting Financial Institutions to conduct the due diligence and reporting procedures (CR1) and its international legal framework to exchange the information with all of Greenland's Interested Appropriate Partners (CR2).

The methodology used for the peer reviews and that therefore underpins this report is outlined in Chapter 2.

Overall determination on the legal framework: In Place

Conclusions on the legal framework

General context

Greenland commenced exchanges under the AEOI Standard in 2018.

In order to provide for Reporting Financial Institutions to collect and report the information to be exchanged, Greenland enacted the Government of Greenland Executive Order No. 13 of 30 August 2017 on Identification of and Reporting on Foreign Financial Accounts, pursuant to Section 35 of Greenland Landsting's Act No. 11 of 2 November of 2016 on administration of taxes. The Government of Greenland Executive Order No. 13 was later amended through the Government of Greenland Executive Order No. 15 of 24 October 2019.

Under this framework Reporting Financial Institutions were required to commence the due diligence procedures in relation to New Accounts from 1 January 2016. With respect to Preexisting Accounts, Reporting Financial Institutions were required to complete the due diligence procedures on High Value Individual Accounts by 1 August 2017 and on Lower Value Individual Accounts and Entity Accounts by 31 December 2017.

Following the initial Global Forum peer review, Greenland amended its legislative framework to address issues identified, effective from 1 January 2020.

With respect to the exchange of information under the AEOI Standard, Greenland:

- has the Convention on Mutual Administrative Assistance in Tax Matters in place[1] and activated the associated CRS Multilateral Competent Authority Agreement in time for exchanges in 2018; and
- put in place two bilateral agreements.[2]

Detailed findings

The detailed findings for Greenland are below, organised per Core Requirement (CR) and sub-requirement (SR), as extracted from the AEOI Terms of Reference (see Annex B).

CR1 Domestic legal framework: Jurisdictions should have a domestic legislative framework in place that requires all Reporting Financial Institutions to conduct the due diligence and reporting procedures in the CRS, and that provides for the effective implementation of the CRS as set out therein.

Determination: In Place

Greenland's domestic legislative framework is in place and contains all of the key aspects of the CRS and its Commentary requiring Reporting Financial Institutions to conduct the due diligence and reporting procedures (SRs 1.1 – 1.3). It also provides for a framework to enforce the requirements (SR 1.4).

SR 1.1 Jurisdictions should define the scope of Reporting Financial Institutions consistently with the CRS.

Greenland has defined the scope of Reporting Financial Institutions in its domestic legislative framework in accordance with the CRS and its Commentary.

Recommendations:

No recommendations made.

SR 1.2 Jurisdictions should define the scope of Financial Accounts and Reportable Accounts consistently with the CRS and incorporate the due diligence procedures to identify them.

Greenland has defined the scope of the Financial Accounts that are required to be reported in its domestic legislative framework and incorporated the due diligence procedures that must be applied to identify them in accordance with the CRS and its Commentary.

Recommendations:

No recommendations made.

SR 1.3 Jurisdictions should incorporate the reporting requirements contained in Section I of the CRS into their domestic legislative framework.

Greenland has incorporated the reporting requirements in its domestic legislative framework in accordance with the CRS and its Commentary.

Recommendations:

No recommendations made.

SR 1.4 Jurisdictions should have a legislative framework in place that allows for the enforcement of the requirements of the CRS in practice.

Greenland has a legislative framework in place to enforce the requirements in accordance with the CRS and its Commentary. While a deficiency has been identified with respect to a lack of an explicit legal basis to enforce a sanction where a Reporting Financial Institution is a legal arrangement, it is considered relatively minor and does not materially undermine the implementation of SR 1.4. This is because such Reporting Financial Institutions have so far not been known to exist in Greenland and are considered unlikely to exist under Greenland's financial and legal frameworks.

Recommendations:

Greenland should amend its legislative framework to ensure that there is an explicit legal basis to enforce a sanction when there is non-compliance by a Reporting Financial Institution that is a legal arrangement.

CR2 International legal framework: Jurisdictions should have exchange relationships in effect with all Interested Appropriate Partners as committed to and that provide for the exchange of information in accordance with the Model CAA.

Determination: In Place

Greenland's international legal framework to exchange the information is in place, is consistent with the Model CAA and its Commentary and provides for exchange with all of Greenland's Interested Appropriate Partners (i.e. all jurisdictions that are interested in receiving information from Greenland and that meet the required standard in relation to confidentiality and data safeguards) (SRs 2.1 – 2.3).

SR 2.1 Jurisdictions should have exchange agreements in effect with all Interested Appropriate Partners that permit the automatic exchange of CRS information.

Greenland has exchange agreements that permit the automatic exchange of CRS information in effect with all its Interested Appropriate Partners.

Recommendations:

No recommendations made.

SR 2.2 Such an exchange agreement should be put in place without undue delay, following the receipt of an expression of interest from an Interested Appropriate Partner.

Greenland put in place its exchange agreements without undue delay.

Recommendations:

No recommendations made.

SR 2.3 Jurisdictions should ensure that the exchange agreements in effect provide for the exchange of information in accordance with the requirements of the Model CAA.

Greenland's exchange agreements provide for the exchange of information in accordance with the requirements of the Model CAA.

Recommendations:

No recommendations made.

Comments by the assessed jurisdiction

No comments made.

Notes

[1] Through a territorial extension by Denmark.

[2] With Denmark and the Faroe Islands.

Jamaica

Overall findings

Jamaica's legal framework implementing the AEOI Standard is in place but needs improvement in order to be fully consistent with the requirements of the AEOI Terms of Reference. While Jamaica's international legal framework to exchange the information with all of Jamaica's Interested Appropriate Partners (CR2) is consistent with the requirements, its domestic legislative framework requiring Reporting Financial Institutions to conduct the due diligence and reporting procedures (CR1) has deficiencies significant to the proper functioning of elements of the AEOI Standard. More specifically, the deficiencies relate to defining certain Entities subject to due diligence and the enforcement framework.

The methodology used for the peer reviews and that therefore underpins this report is outlined in Chapter 2.

Overall determination on the legal framework: In Place **But Needs Improvement**

Conclusions on the legal framework

General context

Jamaica commenced exchanges under the AEOI Standard in 2022.

In order to provide for Reporting Financial Institutions to collect and report the information to be exchanged, Jamaica relies on:

- the Revenue Administration Act 1985, as amended; and
- the Revenue Administration (Convention on Mutual Administrative Assistance in Tax Matters) Regulations, 2020.

Under this framework Reporting Financial Institutions were required to commence the due diligence procedures in relation to New Accounts from 1 January 2021. With respect to Preexisting Accounts, Reporting Financial Institutions were required to complete due diligence procedures on High Value Individual Accounts by 31 December 2021 and on Lower Value Individual Accounts and Entity Accounts by 31 December 2022.

With respect to the exchange of information under the AEOI Standard, Jamaica is a Party to the Convention on Mutual Administrative Assistance in Tax Matters and activated the associated CRS Multilateral Competent Authority Agreement in time for exchanges in 2022.

Detailed findings

The detailed findings for Jamaica are below, organised per Core Requirement (CR) and sub-requirement (SR), as extracted from the AEOI Terms of Reference (see Annex B).

CR1 Domestic legal framework: Jurisdictions should have a domestic legislative framework in place that requires all Reporting Financial Institutions to conduct the due diligence and reporting procedures in the CRS, and that provides for the effective implementation of the CRS as set out therein.

Overall determination on the legal framework: In Place **But Needs Improvement**

Jamaica's domestic legislative framework is in place and contains many of the key aspects of CRS and its Commentary requiring Reporting Financial Institutions to conduct the due diligence and reporting procedures, but it needs improvement in relation to the scope of Reporting Financial Institutions required to report information (SR 1.1), the due diligence procedures that must be applied to Financial Accounts (SR 1.2) and the framework to enforce the requirements (SR 1.4). Most significantly, Jamaica's domestic legislative framework does not define the terms Investment Entity and Controlling Persons in accordance with the requirements and there are deficiencies in Jamaica's enforcement framework.

SR 1.1 Jurisdictions should define the scope of Reporting Financial Institutions consistently with the CRS.

Jamaica has defined the scope of Reporting Financial Institutions in its domestic legislative framework in a manner that is largely consistent with the CRS and its Commentary. However, deficiencies have been identified. More specifically, Jamaica's legislative framework does not define Investment Entity in accordance with the requirements. The definition of Investment Entity is a key element of the AEOI Standard and is therefore material to its proper functioning.

Recommendations:

Jamaica should amend its definition of Investment Entity to exclude certain categories of Active NFE, as required by the AEOI Standard.

Jamaica should ensure that the interpretation of Investment Entity is consistent with similar language defining "Financial Institution" in the Financial Action Task Force Recommendations.

SR 1.2 Jurisdictions should define the scope of Financial Accounts and Reportable Accounts consistently with the CRS and incorporate the due diligence procedures to identify them.

Jamaica has defined the scope of the Financial Accounts that are required to be reported in its domestic legislative framework and has incorporated the due diligence procedures that must be applied to identify them in a manner that is largely consistent with the CRS and its Commentary. However, a deficiency has been identified. More specifically, Jamaica's legislative framework does not define Controlling Persons in accordance with the requirements.

Recommendation:

Jamaica should amend its domestic legislative framework to ensure that "Controlling Person" is defined in accordance with the AEOI Standard.

SR 1.3 Jurisdictions should incorporate the reporting requirements contained in Section I of the CRS into their domestic legislative framework.

Jamaica has incorporated the reporting requirements in its domestic legislative framework in accordance with the CRS and its Commentary.

Recommendations:

No recommendations made.

SR 1.4 Jurisdictions should have a legislative framework in place that allows for the enforcement of the requirements of the CRS in practice.

Jamaica has a legislative framework in place to enforce the requirements in a manner that is largely consistent with the CRS and its Commentary. However, deficiencies have been identified. More specifically, Jamaica's legislative framework has an anti-circumvention rule that does not cover all relevant persons that may engage in practices to avoid due diligence and reporting, and Jamaica does not include an explicit basis to impose or enforce a sanction where a Reporting Financial Institution is a legal arrangement. These are the key elements of the required enforcement framework and are therefore material to the proper functioning of the AEOI Standard.

Recommendations:

Jamaica should ensure that its anti-avoidance rule covers avoidance of CRS reporting and due diligence when entered into by Account Holders or intermediaries, not just by Financial Institutions.

Jamaica should amend its legislative framework to ensure there is an explicit legal basis to enforce a sanction when there is non-compliance by a Reporting Financial Institution that is a legal arrangement.

CR2 International legal framework: Jurisdictions should have exchange relationships in effect with all Interested Appropriate Partners as committed to and that provide for the exchange of information in accordance with the Model CAA.

Determination: In Place

Jamaica's international legal framework to exchange the information is in place, is consistent with the Model CAA and its Commentary and provides for exchange with all of Jamaica's Interested Appropriate Partners (i.e. all jurisdictions that are interested in receiving information from Jamaica and that meet the required standard in relation to confidentiality and data safeguards) (SRs 2.1 – 2.3).

SR 2.1 Jurisdictions should have exchange agreements in effect with all Interested Appropriate Partners that permit the automatic exchange of CRS information.

Jamaica has exchange agreements that permit the automatic exchange of CRS information in effect with all its Interested Appropriate Partners.

Recommendations:

No recommendations made.

SR 2.2 Such an exchange agreement should be put in place without undue delay, following the receipt of an expression of interest from an Interested Appropriate Partner.

Jamaica put in place its exchange agreements without undue delay.

Recommendations:

No recommendations made.

SR 2.3 Jurisdictions should ensure that the exchange agreements in effect provide for the exchange of information in accordance with the requirements of the Model CAA.

Jamaica's exchange agreements provide for the exchange of information in accordance with the requirements of the Model CAA.

Recommendations:

No recommendations made.

Comments by the assessed jurisdiction

No comments made.

Japan

Overall findings

Japan's legal framework implementing the AEOI Standard is in place but needs improvement in order to be fully consistent with the requirements of the AEOI Terms of Reference. While Japan's international legal framework to exchange the information with all of Japan's Interested Appropriate Partners (CR2) is consistent with the requirements, its domestic legislative framework requiring Reporting Financial Institutions to conduct the due diligence and reporting procedures (CR1) has deficiencies significant to the proper functioning of elements of the AEOI Standard. Most significantly, Japan's legislative framework is deficient as far as the definition and identification process for Controlling Persons is concerned.

The methodology used for the peer reviews and that therefore underpins this report is outlined in Chapter 2.

Overall determination on the legal framework: In Place But **Needs Improvement**

Conclusions on the legal framework

General context

Japan commenced exchanges under the AEOI Standard in 2018.

In order to provide for Reporting Financial Institutions to collect and report the information to be exchanged, Japan:

- enacted the Act on Special Provisions of the Income Tax Act, the Corporation Tax Act and the Local Tax Act Incidental to Enforcement of Tax Treaties (CRS Act), as amended;
- introduced the Order for the Enforcement of the Act on Special Provisions of the Income Tax Act, the Corporation Tax Act and the Local Tax Act Incidental to Enforcement of Tax Treaties (CRS Order), as amended;
- introduced the Ordinance for the Enforcement of the Act on Special Provisions of the Income Tax Act, the Corporation Tax Act and the Local Tax Act Incidental to Enforcement of Tax Treaties (CRS Ordinance), as amended; and
- made reference to the Order for Enforcement of the Act on Prevention of Transfer of Criminal Proceeds as well as the Ordinance for Enforcement of the Act on Prevention of Transfer of Criminal Proceeds for the purposes of implementing the FATF Recommendations for the purposes of the identification of Controlling Persons under the AEOI Standard.

Under this framework Reporting Financial Institutions were required to commence the due diligence procedures in relation to New Accounts from 1 January 2017. With respect to Preexisting Accounts, Reporting Financial Institutions were required to complete the due diligence procedures on High Value Individual Accounts by 31 December 2017 and on Lower Value Individual Accounts and Entity Accounts by 31 December 2018.

Following the initial Global Forum peer review, Japan amended its legislative framework to address issues identified, effective from 1 April 2020.

With respect to the exchange of information under the AEOI Standard, Japan:

- is a Party to the Convention on Mutual Administrative Assistance in Tax Matters and activated the associated CRS Multilateral Competent Authority Agreement in time for exchanges in 2018; and
- put in place two bilateral agreements.[1]

Detailed findings

The detailed findings for Japan are below, organised per Core Requirement (CR) and sub-requirement (SR), as extracted from the AEOI Terms of Reference (see Annex B).

CR1 Domestic legal framework: Jurisdictions should have a domestic legislative framework in place that requires all Reporting Financial Institutions to conduct the due diligence and reporting procedures in the CRS, and that provides for the effective implementation of the CRS as set out therein.

Determination: In Place But **Needs Improvement**

Japan's domestic legislative framework is in place and contains most of the key aspects of the CRS and its Commentary requiring Reporting Financial Institutions to conduct the due diligence and reporting procedures, but it needs improvement in relation to the scope of Financial Accounts required to be reported (SR 1.2). Most significantly, Japan's legislative framework does not fully incorporate the definitions and processes related to the identification of Controlling Persons of trusts and similar legal arrangements.

SR 1.1 Jurisdictions should define the scope of Reporting Financial Institutions consistently with the CRS.

Japan has defined the scope of Reporting Financial Institutions in its domestic legislative framework in accordance with the CRS and its Commentary.

Recommendations:

No recommendations made.

SR 1.2 Jurisdictions should define the scope of Financial Accounts and Reportable Accounts consistently with the CRS and incorporate the due diligence procedures to identify them.

Japan has defined the scope of the Financial Accounts that are required to be reported in its domestic legislative framework and incorporated the due diligence procedures that must be applied to identify them in a manner that is largely consistent with the CRS and its Commentary. However, deficiencies have been identified. Most significantly, Japan's legislative framework does not fully incorporate the definition of Controlling Persons as required and does not fully incorporate the due diligence procedures to identify Controlling Persons. The definition and identification of Controlling Persons is material to the proper functioning of the AEOI Standard.

Recommendations:

Japan should amend its domestic legislative framework to require Reporting Financial Institutions to always identify and determine the reportable status of the Controlling Persons of trusts and similar legal arrangements in accordance with the AEOI Standard.

Japan should amend its domestic legislative framework to fully incorporate the definition of Controlling Persons in accordance with the AEOI Standard by including all natural persons required to be identified with respect to trusts and similar legal arrangements.

Japan should amend its domestic legislative framework to ensure that the approach taken with respect to the five jurisdictions defined as Participating Jurisdictions and with which Japan does not have an agreement to exchange CRS information with (including four that have not implemented the AEOI Standard), is in accordance with the AEOI Standard.

SR 1.3 Jurisdictions should incorporate the reporting requirements contained in Section I of the CRS into their domestic legislative framework.

Japan has incorporated the reporting requirements in its domestic legislative framework in accordance with the CRS and its Commentary.

Recommendations:

No recommendations made.

SR 1.4 Jurisdictions should have a legislative framework in place that allows for the enforcement of the requirements of the CRS in practice.

Japan has a legislative framework in place to enforce the requirements in accordance with the CRS and its Commentary.

Recommendations:

No recommendations made.

CR2 International legal framework: Jurisdictions should have exchange relationships in effect with all Interested Appropriate Partners as committed to and that provide for the exchange of information in accordance with the Model CAA.

Determination: In Place

Japan's international legal framework to exchange the information is in place, is consistent with the Model CAA and its Commentary and provides for exchange with all of Japan's Interested Appropriate Partners (i.e. all jurisdictions that are interested in receiving information from Japan and that meet the required standard in relation to confidentiality and data safeguards) (SRs 2.1 – 2.3).

SR 2.1 Jurisdictions should have exchange agreements in effect with all Interested Appropriate Partners that permit the automatic exchange of CRS information.

Japan has exchange agreements that permit the automatic exchange of CRS information in effect with all its Interested Appropriate Partners.

Recommendations:

No recommendations made.

SR 2.2 Such an exchange agreement should be put in place without undue delay, following the receipt of an expression of interest from an Interested Appropriate Partner.

Japan put in place its exchange agreements without undue delay.

Recommendations:

No recommendations made.

SR 2.3 Jurisdictions should ensure that the exchange agreements in effect provide for the exchange of information in accordance with the requirements of the Model CAA.

Japan's exchange agreements provide for the exchange of information in accordance with the requirements of the Model CAA.

Recommendations:

No recommendations made.

Comments by the assessed jurisdiction

No comments made.

Note

[1] With Hong Kong (China) and Singapore. Japan has also activated a relationship under the CRS MCAA with Singapore.

Jersey

Overall findings

Jersey's legal framework implementing the AEOI Standard is in place and is consistent with the requirements of the AEOI Terms of Reference. This includes Jersey's domestic legislative framework requiring Reporting Financial Institutions to conduct the due diligence and reporting procedures (CR1) and its international legal framework to exchange the information with all of Jersey's Interested Appropriate Partners (CR2).

The methodology used for the peer reviews and that therefore underpins this report is outlined in Chapter 2.

Overall determination on the legal framework: In Place

Conclusions on the legal framework

General context

Jersey commenced exchanges under the AEOI Standard in 2017.

In order to provide for Reporting Financial Institutions to collect and report the information to be exchanged, Jersey:

- relies on the Taxation (Implementation) (Jersey) Law 2004;
- introduced the Taxation (Implementation) (International Tax Compliance) (Common Reporting Standard) (Jersey) Regulations in 2015; and
- issued further guidance, which is not legally binding.

Under this framework Reporting Financial Institutions were required to commence the due diligence procedures in relation to New Accounts from 1 January 2016. With respect to Preexisting Accounts, Reporting Financial Institutions were required to complete the due diligence procedures on High Value Individual Accounts by 31 December 2016 and on Lower Value Individual Accounts and Entity Accounts by 31 December 2017.

Following the initial Global Forum peer review, Jersey made various amendments to its legislative framework to address issues identified, the last of which was effective from 11 June 2024.

With respect to the exchange of information under the AEOI Standard, Jersey:

- has the Convention on Mutual Administrative Assistance in Tax Matters in place[1] and activated the associated CRS Multilateral Competent Authority Agreement in time for exchanges in 2017; and
- put in place three bilateral agreements.[2]

Detailed findings

The detailed findings for Jersey are below, organised per Core Requirement (CR) and sub-requirement (SR), as extracted from the AEOI Terms of Reference (see Annex B).

CR1 Domestic legal framework: Jurisdictions should have a domestic legislative framework in place that requires all Reporting Financial Institutions to conduct the due diligence and reporting procedures in the CRS, and that provides for the effective implementation of the CRS as set out therein.

Determination: In Place

Jersey's domestic legislative framework is in place and contains all of the key aspects of the CRS and its Commentary requiring Reporting Financial Institutions to conduct the due diligence and reporting procedures (SRs 1.1 – 1.3). It also provides for a framework to enforce the requirements (SR 1.4).

SR 1.1 Jurisdictions should define the scope of Reporting Financial Institutions consistently with the CRS.

Jersey has defined the scope of Reporting Financial Institutions in its domestic legislative framework in accordance with the CRS and its Commentary.

Recommendations:

No recommendations made.

SR 1.2 Jurisdictions should define the scope of Financial Accounts and Reportable Accounts consistently with the CRS and incorporate the due diligence procedures to identify them.

Jersey has defined the scope of the Financial Accounts that are required to be reported in its domestic legislative framework and incorporated the due diligence procedures that must be applied to identify them in a manner that is largely consistent with the CRS and its Commentary. While a deficiency has been identified with respect to defining the term Participating Jurisdiction, it is considered relatively minor and does not materially undermine the implementation of SR 1.2. Jersey has taken all necessary steps to ensure relevant agreements are in place.

Recommendations:

Jersey should amend its legislative framework to ensure that the approach taken with respect to the three jurisdictions defined as a Participating Jurisdiction and with which Jersey does not have agreements to exchange CRS information with, is in accordance with the AEOI Standard.

SR 1.3 Jurisdictions should incorporate the reporting requirements contained in Section I of the CRS into their domestic legislative framework.

Jersey has incorporated the reporting requirements in its domestic legislative framework in accordance with the CRS and its Commentary.

Recommendations:

No recommendations made.

SR 1.4 Jurisdictions should have a legislative framework in place that allows for the enforcement of the requirements of the CRS in practice.

Jersey has a legislative framework in place to enforce the requirements in accordance with the CRS and its Commentary.

Recommendations:

No recommendations made.

CR2 International legal framework: Jurisdictions should have exchange relationships in effect with all Interested Appropriate Partners as committed to and that provide for the exchange of information in accordance with the Model CAA.

Determination: In Place

Jersey's international legal framework to exchange the information is in place, is consistent with the Model CAA and its Commentary and provides for exchange with all of Jersey's Interested Appropriate Partners (i.e. all jurisdictions that are interested in receiving information from Jersey and that meet the required standard in relation to confidentiality and data safeguards) (SRs 2.1 – 2.3).

SR 2.1 Jurisdictions should have exchange agreements in effect with all Interested Appropriate Partners that permit the automatic exchange of CRS information.

Jersey has exchange agreements that permit the automatic exchange of CRS information in effect with all its Interested Appropriate Partners.

Recommendations:

No recommendations made.

SR 2.2 Such an exchange agreement should be put in place without undue delay, following the receipt of an expression of interest from an Interested Appropriate Partner.

Jersey put in place its exchange agreements without undue delay.

Recommendations:

No recommendations made.

SR 2.3 Jurisdictions should ensure that the exchange agreements in effect provide for the exchange of information in accordance with the requirements of the Model CAA.

Jersey's exchange agreements provide for the exchange of information in accordance with the requirements of the Model CAA.

Recommendations:

No recommendations made.

Comments by the assessed jurisdiction

No comments made.

Notes

[1] Through a territorial extension by the United Kingdom.

[2] With Guernsey, the Isle of Man and the United Kingdom.

Jordan

Overall findings

Jordan's legal framework to implement the AEOI Standard is not in place. This is because Jordan has not put in place a domestic legislative framework requiring Reporting Financial Institutions to conduct the due diligence and reporting procedures (CR1) nor an international legal framework to exchange the information with all Interested Appropriate Partners (CR2).

The methodology used for the peer reviews and that therefore underpins this report is outlined in Chapter 2.

Overall determination on the legal framework: Not In Place

Conclusions on the legal framework

General context

Jordan has not yet implemented the necessary legal frameworks.

Detailed findings

The detailed findings for Jordan are below, organised per Core Requirement (CR) and sub-requirement (SR), as extracted from the AEOI Terms of Reference (see Annex B).

CR1 Domestic legal framework: Jurisdictions should have a domestic legislative framework in place that requires all Reporting Financial Institutions to conduct the due diligence and reporting procedures in the CRS, and that provides for the effective implementation of the CRS as set out therein.

Determination: Not In Place

Jordan has not put in place a domestic legislative framework requiring Reporting Financial Institutions to conduct the due diligence and reporting procedures, therefore the CR1 Domestic legal framework is determined to be not in place. As no such framework is in place a detailed analysis in relation to each SR has not been possible.

CR2 International legal framework: Jurisdictions should have exchange relationships in effect with all Interested Appropriate Partners as committed to and that provide for the exchange of information in accordance with the Model CAA.

Determination: Not In Place

Jordan has not put in place the international legal framework to exchange the information with all of Jordan's Interested Appropriate Partners, therefore the CR2 International legal framework is determined to be not in place. As no such framework is in place a detailed analysis in relation to each SR has not been possible.

Comments by the assessed jurisdiction

No comments made.

Kuwait

This report analyses the implementation of the AEOI Standard in Kuwait with respect to the requirements of the AEOI Terms of Reference. It assesses the legal frameworks put in place to implement the AEOI Standard.

The methodology used for the peer reviews and that therefore underpins this report is outlined in Chapter 2.

Overall findings

AEOI legal framework

Kuwait's legal framework implementing the AEOI Standard is not in place in accordance with the requirements of the AEOI Terms of Reference. While Kuwait's international legal framework to exchange the information with all of Kuwait's Interested Appropriate Partners (CR2) is consistent with the requirements, the domestic legislative framework requiring Reporting Financial Institutions to conduct the due diligence and reporting procedures (CR1) has significant deficiencies in areas that are fundamental to the proper functioning of the AEOI Standard. More specifically, deficiencies have been identified in Kuwait's enforcement framework.

Overall determination on the legal framework: Not In Place

General context

Kuwait commenced exchanges under the AEOI Standard in 2019, when it exchanged information relating to both 2017 and 2018.

In order to provide for Reporting Financial Institutions to collect and report the information to be exchanged, Kuwait issued Ministerial Decision No. (36) for the year 2017.

Under this framework Reporting Financial Institutions were required to commence the due diligence procedures in relation to New Accounts from 1 April 2017. With respect to Preexisting Accounts, Reporting Financial Institutions were required to complete the due diligence procedures on High Value Individual Accounts by 31 December 2017 and on Lower Value Individual Accounts and Entity Accounts by 31 December 2018.

With respect to the exchange of information under the AEOI Standard, Kuwait is a Party to the Convention on Mutual Administrative Assistance in Tax Matters and activated the associated CRS Multilateral Competent Authority Agreement in time for exchanges in 2019.

Findings and conclusions on the legal frameworks

The detailed findings and conclusions on the AEOI legal frameworks for Kuwait are below, organised per Core Requirement (CR) and then per sub-requirement (SR) as extracted from the AEOI Terms of Reference (see Annex B).

CR1 Domestic legal framework: Jurisdictions should have a domestic legislative framework in place that requires all Reporting Financial Institutions to conduct the due diligence and reporting procedures in the CRS, and that provides for the effective implementation of the CRS as set out therein.

Determination: Not In Place

Kuwait's domestic legislative framework is not in place as required as it does not contain several key aspects of the CRS and the Commentary. Significant deficiencies have been identified in relation to the framework to enforce the requirements (SR 1.4). Most significantly, Kuwait's domestic legislative framework does not provide relevant authorities access to records kept by Financial Institutions, does not incorporate a framework for enforcement to address non-compliance, and does not include strong measures to ensure that valid self-certifications are always obtained for New Accounts.

SR 1.1 Jurisdictions should define the scope of Reporting Financial Institutions consistently with the CRS.

Findings:

Kuwait has defined the scope of Reporting Financial Institutions in its domestic legislative framework in accordance with the CRS and its Commentary.

Recommendations:

No recommendations made.

SR 1.2 Jurisdictions should define the scope of Financial Accounts and Reportable Accounts consistently with the CRS and incorporate the due diligence procedures to identify them.

Findings:

Kuwait has defined the scope of the Financial Accounts that are required to be reported in its domestic legislative framework and incorporated the due diligence procedures that must be applied to identify them in accordance with the CRS and its Commentary.

Recommendations:

No recommendations made.

SR 1.3 Jurisdictions should incorporate the reporting requirements contained in Section I of the CRS into their domestic legislative framework.

Findings:

Kuwait has incorporated the reporting requirements in its domestic legislative framework in accordance with the CRS and its Commentary.

Recommendations:

No recommendations made.

SR 1.4 Jurisdictions should have a legislative framework in place that allows for the enforcement of the requirements of the CRS in practice.

Findings:

Kuwait does not have a legislative framework in place to enforce the requirements in a manner that is consistent with the CRS and its Commentary as significant deficiencies have been identified. More specifically, Kuwait's legislative framework:

- includes a rule to address Reporting Financial Institutions engaging in practices intended to circumvent the reporting and due diligence procedures, however it will not cover circumstances where other persons such as Account Holders or intermediaries engage in such practices;
- does not include sanctions on Account Holders and Controlling Persons for the provision of a false self-certification;
- does not provide the relevant authorities with the power to access the records held by Reporting Financial Institutions in relation to the due diligence procedures applied;
- does not provide for sanctions on Reporting Financial Institutions for failing to carry out the due diligence procedures; and
- does not incorporate measures to ensure that self-certifications are always obtained and validated for New Accounts as is required.

These are key elements of the required enforcement framework and are therefore material to the proper functioning of the AEOI Standard.

Recommendations:

Kuwait should amend its domestic legislative framework to ensure that its anti-circumvention rule covers avoidance of reporting and due diligence in all cases, including when entered into by Account Holders or intermediaries, not just by Financial Institutions.

Kuwait should amend its domestic legislative framework to include sanctions on Account Holders and Controlling Persons for the provision of a false self-certification.

Kuwait should amend its domestic legislative framework to provide the appropriate authorities with access to the records required to be kept by Reporting Financial Institutions.

Kuwait should amend its domestic legislative framework to include sanctions for failure to comply with the due diligence and reporting procedures.

Kuwait should amend its domestic legislative framework to include strong measures to ensure that valid self-certifications are always obtained for New Accounts in accordance with the requirements.

CR2 International legal framework: Jurisdictions should have exchange relationships in effect with all Interested Appropriate Partners as committed to and that provide for the exchange of information in accordance with the Model CAA.

Determination: In Place

Kuwait's international legal framework to exchange the information is in place, is consistent with the Model CAA and its Commentary and provides for exchange with all of Kuwait's Interested Appropriate Partners (i.e. all jurisdictions that are interested in receiving information from Kuwait and that meet the required standard in relation to confidentiality and data safeguards) (SRs 2.1 – 2.3).

SR 2.1 Jurisdictions should have exchange agreements in effect with all Interested Appropriate Partners that permit the automatic exchange of CRS information.

Findings::

Kuwait has exchange agreements that permit the automatic exchange of CRS information in effect with all its Interested Appropriate Partners.

Recommendations:

No recommendations made.

SR 2.2 Such an exchange agreement should be put in place without undue delay, following the receipt of an expression of interest from an Interested Appropriate Partner.

Findings::

Kuwait put in place its exchange agreements without undue delay.

Recommendations:

No recommendations made.

SR 2.3 Jurisdictions should ensure that the exchange agreements in effect provide for the exchange of information in accordance with the requirements of the Model CAA.

Findings::

Kuwait's exchange agreements provide for the exchange of information in accordance with the requirements of the Model CAA.

Recommendations:

No recommendations made.

Assessed jurisdiction's comments on the assessment of its legal frameworks

Kuwait issued Decree Law No. 4 of 2024 on the Exchange of Information on Tax Matters on 14 July 2024. Kuwait subsequently issued the Executive Regulations of the Decree Law under Ministerial Decision No. 75 of 2024 on 25 September 2024. The Decree and its Executive Regulations came into effect on 29 September 2024 and addresses the recommendations outlined in this report.

Latvia

Overall findings

Latvia's legal framework implementing the AEOI Standard is in place but needs improvement in order to be fully consistent with the requirements of the AEOI Terms of Reference. While Latvia's international legal framework to exchange the information with all of Latvia's Interested Appropriate Partners (CR2) is consistent with the requirements, its domestic legislative framework requiring Reporting Financial Institutions to conduct the due diligence and reporting procedures (CR1) has deficiencies significant to the proper functioning of elements of the AEOI Standard. Most significantly, Financial Institutions are not defined in accordance with the AEOI Standard.

The methodology used for the peer reviews and that therefore underpins this report is outlined in Chapter 2.

Overall determination on the legal framework: In Place But **Needs Improvement**

Conclusions on the legal framework

General context

Latvia commenced exchanges under the AEOI Standard in 2017.

In order to provide for Reporting Financial Institutions to collect and report the information to be exchanged, Latvia:

- amended the Law "On Taxes and Duties", amended it in 2020 and further amended it in 2023;
- introduced Regulation No. 20 "Procedures by which a Financial Institution Implements the Due Diligence Procedures for Financial Accounts and Provides Financial Accounts Information to the State Revenue Service" and amended it in 2021; and
- Relies on Section 275(1) of the Criminal Law.

Under this framework Reporting Financial Institutions were required to commence the due diligence procedures in relation to New Accounts from 1 January 2016. With respect to Preexisting Accounts, Reporting Financial Institutions were required to complete due diligence procedures on High Value Individual Accounts by 31 December 2016 and on Lower Value Individual Accounts and Entity Accounts by 31 December 2017.

Following the initial Global Forum peer review, Latvia made amendments to its legislative framework to address issues identified, the last of which was effective from 4 July 2023.

With respect to the exchange of information under the AEOI Standard, Latvia:

- is a Party to the Convention on Mutual Administrative Assistance in Tax Matters and activated the associated CRS Multilateral Competent Authority Agreement in time for exchanges in 2017;
- has in place European Union Directive 2011/16/EU on Administrative Cooperation in the Field of Taxation, as amended by Directive 2014/107/EU;
- has in place agreements with five European third countries[1]; and
- put in place three bilateral agreements[2].

Detailed findings

The detailed findings for Latvia are below, organised per Core Requirement (CR) and sub-requirement (SR), as extracted from the AEOI Terms of Reference (see Annex B).

CR1 Domestic legal framework: Jurisdictions should have a domestic legislative framework in place that requires all Reporting Financial Institutions to conduct the due diligence and reporting procedures in the CRS, and that provides for the effective implementation of the CRS as set out therein.

Determination: In Place But **Needs Improvement**

Latvia's domestic legislative framework is in place and contains most of the key aspects of the CRS and its Commentary requiring Reporting Financial Institutions to conduct the due diligence and reporting procedures, but it needs improvement in relation to the scope of Reporting Financial Institutions (SR 1.1), defining the term Participating Jurisdiction (SR 1.2) and the framework to enforce the requirements (SR 1.4). More specifically, Latvia's domestic legislative framework does not define the term Investment Entity in accordance with the requirements and broadly allows self-certifications to be obtained after account opening.

SR 1.1 Jurisdictions should define the scope of Reporting Financial Institutions consistently with the CRS.

Latvia has defined the scope of Reporting Financial Institutions in its domestic legislative framework in a manner that is largely consistent with the CRS and its Commentary. However, a deficiency has been identified. More specifically, the definition of Investment Entity is not in accordance with the requirements. The scope of Reporting Financial Institutions is material to the proper functioning of the AEOI Standard.

Recommendations:

Latvia should amend its domestic legislative framework to require the term Investment Entity to be interpreted consistently with similar language defining "financial institution" in the Financial Action Task Force Recommendations.

SR 1.2 Jurisdictions should define the scope of Financial Accounts and Reportable Accounts consistently with the CRS and incorporate the due diligence procedures to identify them.

Latvia has defined the scope of the Financial Accounts that are required to be reported in its domestic legislative framework and incorporated the due diligence procedures that must be applied to identify them in a manner that is largely consistent with the CRS and its Commentary. However, a deficiency has been identified. More specifically, Latvia's legislative framework does not incorporate the requirements in relation to certain Entities not located in Participating Jurisdictions in line with the AEOI Standard. This deficiency is material to the proper functioning of the AEOI Standard as it does not ensure that all Investment Entities that are not in Participating Jurisdictions are subject to the "look-through" approach to identify their Controlling Persons.

Recommendations:

Latvia should amend its domestic legislative framework to ensure that the approach taken with respect to the one jurisdiction defined as a Participating Jurisdiction and with which Latvia does not have an agreement to exchange CRS information with (and which has not implemented the AEOI Standard), is in accordance with the AEOI Standard.

SR 1.3 Jurisdictions should incorporate the reporting requirements contained in Section I of the CRS into their domestic legislative framework.

Latvia has incorporated the reporting requirements in its domestic legislative framework in accordance with the CRS and its Commentary.

Recommendations:

No recommendations made.

SR 1.4 Jurisdictions should have a legislative framework in place that allows for the enforcement of the requirements of the CRS in practice.

Latvia has a legislative framework in place to enforce the requirements in a manner that is largely consistent with the CRS and its Commentary. However, a deficiency has been identified. More specifically, Latvia's legislative framework allows self-certifications to be obtained after the opening of the account in circumstances beyond those that are permitted. The deficiency relates to a key element of the AEOI Standard and is therefore material to its proper functioning.

Recommendations:

Latvia should amend its domestic legislative framework to limit the circumstances when it is permissible to obtain a valid self-certification after the opening of a New Account in accordance with the requirements.

CR2 International legal framework: Jurisdictions should have exchange relationships in effect with all Interested Appropriate Partners as committed to and that provide for the exchange of information in accordance with the Model CAA.

Determination: In Place

Latvia's international legal framework to exchange the information is in place, is consistent with the Model CAA and its Commentary and provides for exchange with all of Latvia's Interested Appropriate Partners (i.e. all jurisdictions that are interested in receiving information from Latvia and that meet the required standard in relation to confidentiality and data safeguards) (SRs 2.1 – 2.3).

SR 2.1 Jurisdictions should have exchange agreements in effect with all Interested Appropriate Partners that permit the automatic exchange of CRS information.

Latvia has exchange agreements that permit the automatic exchange of CRS information in effect with all its Interested Appropriate Partners.

Recommendations:

No recommendations made.

SR 2.2 Such an exchange agreement should be put in place without undue delay, following the receipt of an expression of interest from an Interested Appropriate Partner.

Latvia put in place its exchange agreements without undue delay.

Recommendations:

No recommendations made.

SR 2.3 Jurisdictions should ensure that the exchange agreements in effect provide for the exchange of information in accordance with the requirements of the Model CAA.

Latvia's exchange agreements provide for the exchange of information in accordance with the requirements of the Model CAA.

Recommendations:

No recommendations made.

Comments by the assessed jurisdiction

Latvia has been working diligently to address recommendations received and has introduced strong measures to ensure that valid self-certifications are always obtained for new accounts. Although it is allowed to obtain a self-certification after the opening of the account, there are measures in place to ensure that it cannot be used to circumvent CRS requirements (a new account is frozen until a valid self-certification is obtained with few exceptions that are in line with FAQ 22)

Notes

[1] Andorra, Liechtenstein, Monaco, San Marino and Switzerland

[2] With Qatar, Singapore and Türkiye. Latvia has also activated relationships under the CRS MCAA with Qatar and Türkiye

Lithuania

Overall findings

Lithuania's legal framework implementing the AEOI Standard is in place but needs improvement in order to be fully consistent with the requirements of the AEOI Terms of Reference. While Lithuania's international legal framework to exchange the information with all of Lithuania's Interested Appropriate Partners (CR2) is consistent with the requirements, its domestic legislative framework requiring Reporting Financial Institutions to conduct the due diligence and reporting procedures (CR1) has deficiencies significant to the proper functioning of elements of the AEOI Standard. Most significantly, deficiencies have been identified in relation to Lithuania's enforcement framework.

The methodology used for the peer reviews and that therefore underpins this report is outlined in Chapter 2.

Overall determination on the legal framework: In Place But **Needs Improvement**

Conclusions on the legal framework

General context

Lithuania commenced exchanges under the AEOI Standard in 2017.

In order to provide for Reporting Financial Institutions to collect and report the information to be exchanged, Lithuania:

- enacted Article 61-[1] of the Law on Tax Administration, Resolution No. 1017 of 23 September 2015 and Article 198-[1] of the Code of Administrative Offences;
- introduced the Rules for the Provision of Information Necessary for Implementation of the International Cooperation Obligations Concerning Automatic Exchange of Financial Account Information;
- introduced Article 198–[1] of the Code of Administrative Offences of 3 December 2019; and
- issued further guidance, which is legally binding.

Under this framework Reporting Financial Institutions were required to commence the due diligence procedures in relation to New Accounts from 1 January 2016. With respect to Preexisting Accounts, Reporting Financial Institutions were required to complete the due diligence procedures on High Value Individual Accounts by 31 December 2016 and on Lower Value Individual Accounts and Entity Accounts by 31 December 2017.

Following the initial Global Forum peer review, Lithuania amended its legislative framework to address issues identified, most recently with effect from 20 February 2024.

With respect to the exchange of information under the AEOI Standard, Lithuania:

- is a Party to the Convention on Mutual Administrative Assistance in Tax Matters and activated the associated CRS Multilateral Competent Authority Agreement in time for exchanges in 2017;
- has in place the European Directive 2011/16/EU on Administrative Cooperation in the Field of Taxation as amended by Directive 2014/107/EU;
- has in place European Union agreements with five European third countries;[1] and
- put in place a bilateral agreement.[2]

Detailed findings

The detailed findings for Lithuania are below, organised per Core Requirement (CR) and sub-requirement (SR), as extracted from the AEOI Terms of Reference (see Annex B).

CR1 Domestic legal framework: Jurisdictions should have a domestic legislative framework in place that requires all Reporting Financial Institutions to conduct the due diligence and reporting procedures in the CRS, and that provides for the effective implementation of the CRS as set out therein.

Determination: In Place But **Needs Improvement**

Lithuania's domestic legislative framework is in place and contains most of the key aspects of the CRS and its Commentary requiring Reporting Financial Institutions to conduct the due diligence and reporting procedures, but it needs improvement in relation to the due diligence procedures to be applied (SR 1.2) and the framework to enforce the requirements (SR 1.4). Most significantly, Lithuania does not provide for sanctions on Reporting Financial Institutions for failing to carry out the due diligence procedures or failing to keep records in all cases.

SR 1.1 Jurisdictions should define the scope of Reporting Financial Institutions consistently with the CRS.

Lithuania has defined the scope of Reporting Financial Institutions in its domestic legislative framework in accordance with the CRS and its Commentary.

Recommendations:

No recommendations made.

SR 1.2 Jurisdictions should define the scope of Financial Accounts and Reportable Accounts consistently with the CRS and incorporate the due diligence procedures to identify them.

Lithuania has defined the scope of the Financial Accounts that are required to be reported in its domestic legislative framework and incorporated the due diligence procedures that must be applied to identify them in a manner that is largely consistent with the CRS and its Commentary. However, a deficiency has been identified. More specifically, Lithuania's legislative framework does not incorporate the requirements in relation to certain Entities not located in Participating Jurisdictions in line with the AEOI Standard. This deficiency is material to the proper functioning of the AEOI Standard as it does not ensure that all Investment Entities that are not in Participating Jurisdictions are subject to the "look-through" approach to identify their Controlling Persons.

Recommendations:

Lithuania should amend its domestic legislative framework to ensure that the approach taken with respect to the one jurisdiction defined as a Participating Jurisdiction and with which Lithuania does not have an agreement to exchange CRS information with (and which has not implemented the AEOI Standard), is in accordance with the AEOI Standard.

SR 1.3 Jurisdictions should incorporate the reporting requirements contained in Section I of the CRS into their domestic legislative framework.

Lithuania has incorporated the reporting requirements in its domestic legislative framework in accordance with the CRS and its Commentary.

Recommendations:

No recommendations made.

SR 1.4 Jurisdictions should have a legislative framework in place that allows for the enforcement of the requirements of the CRS in practice.

Lithuania has a legislative framework in place to enforce the requirements in a manner that is largely consistent with the CRS and its Commentary. However, a deficiency has been identified. More specifically, Lithuania's legislative framework does not impose sanctions for failing to carry out the due diligence procedures or failing to keep records required under the AEOI Standard where it does not impact reporting. These are key elements of the required enforcement framework and are therefore material to the proper functioning of the AEOI Standard.

Recommendations:

While Lithuania is able to impose penalties for failing to report and for reporting incorrect information, it is recommended to amend its legislative framework to ensure it is able to also impose penalties for failing to carry out due diligence and failing to keep records.

CR2 International legal framework: Jurisdictions should have exchange relationships in effect with all Interested Appropriate Partners as committed to and that provide for the exchange of information in accordance with the Model CAA.

Determination: In Place

Lithuania's international legal framework to exchange the information is in place, is consistent with the Model CAA and its Commentary and provides for exchange with all of Lithuania's Interested Appropriate Partners (i.e. all jurisdictions that are interested in receiving information from Lithuania and that meet the required standard in relation to confidentiality and data safeguards) (SRs 2.1 – 2.3).

SR 2.1 Jurisdictions should have exchange agreements in effect with all Interested Appropriate Partners that permit the automatic exchange of CRS information.

Lithuania has exchange agreements that permit the automatic exchange of CRS information in effect with all its Interested Appropriate Partners.

Recommendations:

No recommendations made.

SR 2.2 Such an exchange agreement should be put in place without undue delay, following the receipt of an expression of interest from an Interested Appropriate Partner.

Lithuania put in place its exchange agreements without undue delay.

Recommendations:

No recommendations made.

SR 2.3 Jurisdictions should ensure that the exchange agreements in effect provide for the exchange of information in accordance with the requirements of the Model CAA.

Lithuania's exchange agreements provide for the exchange of information in accordance with the requirements of the Model CAA.

Recommendations:

No recommendations made.

Comments by the assessed jurisdiction

No comments made.

Notes

[1] Andorra, Liechtenstein, Monaco, San Marino and Switzerland.

[2] With Singapore.

Maldives

Overall findings

The Maldives' legal framework implementing the AEOI Standard is not in place in accordance with the requirements of the AEOI Terms of Reference. While the Maldives' international legal framework to exchange the information with all of the Maldives' Interested Appropriate Partners (CR2) is consistent with the requirements, its domestic legislative framework requiring Reporting Financial Institutions to conduct the due diligence and reporting procedures (CR1) has significant deficiencies in areas that are fundamental to the proper functioning of the AEOI Standard. Most significantly, the Maldives' legislative framework does not define some categories of Financial Institutions in line with the AEOI Standard, does not define some terms that are essential to the due diligence requirements and has an incomplete enforcement framework.

The methodology used for the peer reviews and that therefore underpins this report is outlined in Chapter 2.

Overall determination on the legal framework: Not In Place

Conclusions on the legal framework

General context

The Maldives commenced exchanges under the AEOI Standard in 2022.

In order to provide for Reporting Financial Institutions to collect and report the information to be exchanged, the Maldives relies on:

- Sections 51-2, 51-3 of the Tax Administration Act; and
- Chapter 14 of the Tax Administration Regulations as of 9 March 2023.

Under this framework Reporting Financial Institutions were instructed to commence the due diligence procedures in relation to New Accounts by 1 January 2021. With respect to Preexisting Accounts, Reporting Financial Institutions were required to complete due diligence procedures on High Value Individual Accounts and on Lower Value Individual Accounts and Entity Accounts by 31 December 2021.

With respect to the exchange of information under the AEOI Standard, the Maldives has the Convention on Mutual Administrative Assistance in Tax Matters in place and activated the associated CRS Multilateral Competent Authority Agreement in time for exchanges in 2022.

Detailed findings

The detailed findings for the Maldives are below, organised per Core Requirement (CR) and sub-requirement (SR), as extracted from the AEOI Terms of Reference (www.oecd.org/tax/transparency/documents/aeoi-terms-of-reference.pdf).

CR1 Domestic legal framework: Jurisdictions should have a domestic legislative framework in place that requires all Reporting Financial Institutions to conduct the due diligence and reporting procedures in the CRS, and that provides for the effective implementation of the CRS as set out therein.

Determination: Not In Place

The Maldives' domestic legislative framework is not in place as required as it does not contain several key aspects of the CRS and its Commentary. Significant deficiencies have been identified in relation to the scope of Reporting Financial Institutions required to report information (SR 1.1), the scope of Financial Accounts required to be reported and the due diligence procedures to be applied (SR 1.2), the information required to be reported (SR 1.3) and the framework to enforce the requirements (SR 1.4). Most significantly, the Maldives' legislative framework does contain some of the key due diligence timelines, does not fully define some categories of Financial Institutions, does not define some terms that are essential to the due diligence requirements in a manner that is binding on Financial Institutions and has incomplete sanctions as part of its enforcement framework.

SR 1.1 Jurisdictions should define the scope of Reporting Financial Institutions consistently with the CRS.

The Maldives has not defined the scope of Reporting Financial Institutions in its domestic legislative framework in a manner that is consistent with the AEOI Standard and its Commentary as significant deficiencies have been identified. Most significantly, the Maldives' legislative framework:

- does not provide for the definitions of Investment Entity and the term "managed by" in accordance with the requirements; and
- does not contain rules for determining the residency of a trust that is a Financial Institution and of a fiscally transparent Financial Institution (other than a trust).

The scope of Reporting Financial Institutions is material to the proper functioning of the AEOI Standard.

Recommendations:

The Maldives should amend its domestic legislative framework to ensure that the residency of (i) a trust that is a Financial Institution and (ii) a fiscally transparent Financial Institution (other than a trust) is determined in accordance with the AEOI Standard.

The Maldives should amend its legislative framework to ensure that the term Investment Entity is defined in accordance with the AEOI Standard.

The Maldives should ensure that the interpretation of Investment Entity is required to be consistent with similar language defining "Financial Institution" in the FATF Recommendations.

The Maldives should amend its domestic legislative framework to include the definition of "managed by" in relation to the definition of Investment Entity.

SR 1.2 Jurisdictions should define the scope of Financial Accounts and Reportable Accounts consistently with the CRS and incorporate the due diligence procedures to identify them.

The Maldives has defined the scope of the Financial Accounts that are required to be reported in its domestic legislative framework and incorporated the due diligence procedures that must be applied to identify them in a manner that is largely consistent with the CRS and its Commentary. However, deficiencies have been identified. Most significantly, the Maldives' legislative framework:

- does not provide for the terms "current" and "change of circumstances" in accordance with the requirements;
- does not include definitions of the terms "Controlling Persons", "NFE", "Active NFE", "Passive NFE" and "Related Entity" as required;
- does not align with the definition of Financial Account in the AEOI Standard and does not incorporate the further definitions for Depository Account, Custodial Account, Equity Interest, Insurance Contract, Cash Value Insurance Contract and Cash Value; and
- does not incorporate the definitions of "Related Entity" and "Documentary Evidence" as required.

The scope of Financial Accounts and the due diligence procedures to identify them are material to the proper functioning of the AEOI Standard.

Recommendations:

The Maldives should ensure that the whole of the definition of the term "current", as set out in the Commentary to the AEOI Standard, is incorporated into its domestic AEOI framework.

The Maldives should ensure that the term "change of circumstances" is defined and applied in line with the Commentary.

The Maldives should amend its domestic legislative framework to ensure that Financial Institutions always collect, review and report information on Controlling Persons in accordance with the definition in the AEOI Standard.

The Maldives should amend its domestic legislative framework to ensure that all terms relevant to identifying Financial Accounts, including "Depository Account", "Custodial Account", "Equity Interest", "Insurance Contract", "Annuity Contract", "Cash Value Insurance Contract" and "Cash Value", are incorporated in accordance with the AEOI Standard.

The Maldives should amend its domestic legislative framework to ensure that "Reportable Jurisdiction Person" and "Participating Jurisdiction" are defined in accordance with the AEOI Standard.

The Maldives should amend its domestic legislative framework to ensure that the definition of "Controlling Person" is incorporated in accordance with the AEOI Standard and its Commentary.

The Maldives should amend its domestic legislative framework to include the definitions of (i) "NFE", (ii) "Active NFE" and (iii) "Passive NFE" as required by the AEOI Standard.

The Maldives should amend its domestic legislative framework to include the definition of "Related Entity" as required by the AEOI Standard.

The Maldives should amend its domestic legislative framework to include the definition of "Documentary Evidence" as required by the AEOI Standard.

SR 1.3 Jurisdictions should incorporate the reporting requirements contained in Section I of the CRS into their domestic legislative framework.

The Maldives has incorporated the reporting requirements in its domestic legislative framework in accordance with the CRS and its Commentary.

Recommendations:

No recommendations made.

SR 1.4 Jurisdictions should have a legislative framework in place that allows for the enforcement of the requirements of the CRS in practice.

The Maldives does not have a legislative framework in place to enforce the requirements in a manner that is consistent with the CRS and its Commentary as significant deficiencies have been identified. More specifically, the Maldives' legislative framework:

- does not include rules to prevent Financial Institutions, persons or intermediaries from adopting practices intended to circumvent the due diligence and reporting procedures;
- does not contain provisions imposing sanctions on Account Holders and Controlling Persons for the provision of a false self-certification;
- does not include rules requiring Reporting Financial Institutions to maintain records in accordance with the AEOI Standard;
- does not provide the relevant authorities with the power to access the records and evidence relied upon held by Reporting Financial Institutions in relation to the due diligence procedures applied;

- does not impose sanctions for failing to carry out the due diligence procedures required by the AEOI Standard,
- does not provide for an explicit basis to enforce sanctions for non-compliance by any legal arrangement that is a Reporting Financial Institution;
- includes sanctions for failing to report, incorrect reporting and failing to keep records but which are calculated with reference to tax payable by the person for a tax period, which may not be applicable in all relevant cases; and
- does not include measures to ensure that valid self-certifications are always obtained and validated for New Accounts.

These are key elements of the required enforcement framework and are therefore material to the proper functioning of the AEOI Standard.

Recommendations:

The Maldives should amend its legislative framework to introduce an anti-avoidance provision in accordance with the Standard.

The Maldives should ensure that it has rules in its domestic legislative framework that impose sanctions on Account Holders and Controlling Persons for providing false self-certifications.

The Maldives should amend its domestic legislative framework to provide the appropriate authorities with the power to access to records and evidence relevant to verifying and enforcing the AEOI Standard.

The Maldives should ensure that it has rules in its domestic legislative framework to require relevant records to be kept for at least 5 years after the end of the period within which the Reporting Financial Institution must report the information required to be reported, rather than 5 years after the end of the calendar year to which the records relate.

While the Maldives is able to impose penalties for failing to report, for reporting incorrect information and for failing to keep the required records, it is recommended to amend its legislative framework to ensure it is able to also impose penalties for failing to carry out due diligence.

The Maldives should amend its legislative framework to ensure that it is able to sanction non-compliance by any Reporting Financial Institution, including those that are legal arrangements or have no tax liability for the period of non-compliance.

The Maldives should introduce measures to ensure that valid self-certifications are always obtained and validated for New Accounts.

CR2 International legal framework: Jurisdictions should have exchange relationships in effect with all Interested Appropriate Partners as committed to and that provide for the exchange of information in accordance with the Model CAA.

Determination: In Place

The Maldives' international legal framework to exchange the information is in place, is consistent with the Model CAA and its Commentary and provides for exchange with all of The Maldives' Interested Appropriate Partners (i.e. all jurisdictions that are interested in receiving information from The Maldives and that meet the required standard in relation to confidentiality and data safeguards) (SRs 2.1 – 2.3).

SR 2.1 Jurisdictions should have exchange agreements in effect with all Interested Appropriate Partners that permit the automatic exchange of CRS information.

The Maldives has exchange agreements that permit the automatic exchange of CRS information in effect with all its Interested Appropriate Partners.

Recommendations:

No recommendations made.

SR 2.2 Such an exchange agreement should be put in place without undue delay, following the receipt of an expression of interest from an Interested Appropriate Partner.

The Maldives put in place its exchange agreements without undue delay.

Recommendations:

No recommendations made.

SR 2.3 Jurisdictions should ensure that the exchange agreements in effect provide for the exchange of information in accordance with the requirements of the Model CAA.

The Maldives' exchange agreements provide for the exchange of information in accordance with the requirements of the Model CAA.

Recommendations:

No recommendations made.

Comments by the assessed jurisdiction

No comments made.

Montenegro

Overall findings

Montenegro's legal framework to implement the AEOI Standard is not in place. This is because Montenegro does not have a domestic legislative framework in effect requiring Reporting Financial Institutions to conduct the due diligence and reporting procedures (CR1) nor an international legal framework in place to exchange the information with all Interested Appropriate Partners (CR2).

The methodology used for the peer reviews and that therefore underpins this report is outlined in Chapter 2.

Overall determination on the legal framework: Not In Place

Conclusions on the legal framework

General context

Montenegro has not yet implemented the necessary legal frameworks. It has introduced due diligence and reporting obligations but has not brought them into effect to ensure Reporting Financial Institutions apply them from a set date.

Detailed findings

The detailed findings for Montenegro are below, organised per Core Requirement (CR) and sub-requirement (SR), as extracted from the AEOI Terms of Reference (see Annex B).

CR1 Domestic legal framework: Jurisdictions should have a domestic legislative framework in place that requires all Reporting Financial Institutions to conduct the due diligence and reporting procedures in the CRS, and that provides for the effective implementation of the CRS as set out therein.

Determination: Not In Place

Montenegro has not brought into effect a domestic legislative framework requiring Reporting Financial Institutions to conduct the due diligence and reporting procedures, therefore the CR1 Domestic legal framework is determined to be not in place. As no such framework is in place a detailed analysis in relation to each SR is not necessary.

CR2 International legal framework: Jurisdictions should have exchange relationships in effect with all Interested Appropriate Partners as committed to and that provide for the exchange of information in accordance with the Model CAA.

Determination: Not In Place

Montenegro has not put in place the international legal framework to exchange the information with all of Montenegro's Interested Appropriate Partners, therefore the CR2 International legal framework is determined to be not in place. As no such framework is in place a detailed analysis in relation to each SR has not been possible.

Comments by the assessed jurisdiction

No comments made.

Montserrat

Overall findings

Montserrat's legal framework implementing the AEOI Standard is in place but needs improvement in order to be fully consistent with the requirements of the AEOI Terms of Reference. While Montserrat's international legal framework to exchange the information with all of Montserrat's Interested Appropriate Partners (CR2) is consistent with the requirements, its domestic legislative framework requiring Reporting Financial Institutions to conduct the due diligence and reporting procedures (CR1) has deficiencies significant to the proper functioning of elements of the AEOI Standard. More specifically, a deficiency has been identified in relation to Montserrat's enforcement framework.

The methodology used for the peer reviews and that therefore underpins this report is outlined in Chapter 2.

Overall determination on the legal framework: In Place But **Needs Improvement**

Conclusions on the legal framework

General context

Montserrat commenced exchanges under the AEOI Standard in 2017.

In order to provide for Reporting Financial Institutions to collect and report the information to be exchanged, Montserrat:

- enacted the Tax Information Exchange Act; and
- introduced the Tax Information Exchange (FATCA Agreement) (UK IGA) (CRS) (Montserrat) (Implementation) Regulations 2016, as amended in 2019.

Under this framework Reporting Financial Institutions were required to commence the due diligence procedures in relation to New Accounts from 1 January 2016. With respect to Preexisting Accounts, Reporting Financial Institutions were required to complete the due diligence procedures on High Value Individual Accounts by 31 December 2016 and on Lower Value Individual Accounts and Entity Accounts by 31 December 2017.

Following the initial Global Forum peer review, Montserrat amended its legislative framework to address issues identified, effective from 5 July 2019.

With respect to the exchange of information under the AEOI Standard, Montserrat:

- has the Convention on Mutual Administrative Assistance in Tax Matters in place[1] and activated the associated CRS Multilateral Competent Authority Agreement in time for exchanges in 2017; and
- put in place a bilateral agreement.[2]

Detailed findings

The detailed findings for Montserrat are below, organised per Core Requirement (CR) and sub-requirement (SR), as extracted from the AEOI Terms of Reference (www.oecd.org/tax/transparency/documents/aeoi-terms-of-reference.pdf).

CR1 Domestic legal framework: Jurisdictions should have a domestic legislative framework in place that requires all Reporting Financial Institutions to conduct the due diligence and reporting procedures in the CRS, and that provides for the effective implementation of the CRS as set out therein.

Determination: In Place But **Needs Improvement**

Montserrat's domestic legislative framework is in place and contains most of the key aspects of the CRS and its Commentary requiring Reporting Financial Institutions to conduct the due diligence and reporting procedures but it needs improvement in relation to the framework to enforce the requirements (SR 1.4). More specifically, Montserrat's legislative framework does not have an explicit legal basis to enforce a sanction for non-compliance if the Reporting Financial Institution is a legal arrangement.

SR 1.1 Jurisdictions should define the scope of Reporting Financial Institutions consistently with the CRS.

Montserrat has defined the scope of Reporting Financial Institutions in its domestic legislative framework in accordance with the CRS and its Commentary.

Recommendations:

No recommendations made.

SR 1.2 Jurisdictions should define the scope of Financial Accounts and Reportable Accounts consistently with the CRS and incorporate the due diligence procedures to identify them.

Montserrat has defined the scope of the Financial Accounts that are required to be reported in its domestic legislative framework and incorporated the due diligence procedures that must be applied to identify them in accordance with the CRS and its Commentary.

Recommendations:

No recommendations made.

SR 1.3 Jurisdictions should incorporate the reporting requirements contained in Section I of the CRS into their domestic legislative framework.

Montserrat has incorporated the reporting requirements in its domestic legislative framework in accordance with the CRS and its Commentary.

Recommendations:

No recommendations made.

SR 1.4 Jurisdictions should have a legislative framework in place that allows for the enforcement of the requirements of the CRS in practice.

Montserrat has a legislative framework in place to enforce the requirements in a manner that is largely consistent with the CRS and its Commentary. However, a deficiency has been identified. More specifically, Montserrat's legislative framework does not include an explicit legal basis to enforce a sanction where a Reporting Financial Institution is a legal arrangement. This deficiency relates to a key element of the required enforcement framework and is therefore material to the proper functioning of the AEOI Standard.

Recommendations:

Montserrat should amend its legislative framework to ensure that there is an explicit legal basis to enforce a sanction when there is non-compliance by a Reporting Financial Institution that is a legal arrangement.

CR2 International legal framework: Jurisdictions should have exchange relationships in effect with all Interested Appropriate Partners as committed to and that provide for the exchange of information in accordance with the Model CAA.

Determination: In Place

Montserrat's international legal framework to exchange the information is in place, is consistent with the Model CAA and its Commentary and provides for exchange with all of Montserrat's Interested Appropriate Partners (i.e. all jurisdictions that are interested in receiving information from Montserrat and that meet the required standard in relation to confidentiality and data safeguards) (SRs 2.1 – 2.3).

SR 2.1 Jurisdictions should have exchange agreements in effect with all Interested Appropriate Partners that permit the automatic exchange of CRS information.

Montserrat has exchange agreements that permit the automatic exchange of CRS information in effect with all its Interested Appropriate Partners.

Recommendations:

No recommendations made.

SR 2.2 Such an exchange agreement should be put in place without undue delay, following the receipt of an expression of interest from an Interested Appropriate Partner.

Montserrat put in place its exchange agreements without undue delay.

Recommendations:

No recommendations made.

SR 2.3 Jurisdictions should ensure that the exchange agreements in effect provide for the exchange of information in accordance with the requirements of the Model CAA.

Montserrat's exchange agreements provide for the exchange of information in accordance with the requirements of the Model CAA.

Recommendations:

No recommendations made.

Comments by the assessed jurisdiction

No comments made.

Notes

[1] Through a territorial extension by the United Kingdom.

[2] With the United Kingdom.

Nauru

Overall findings

Nauru's legal framework implementing the AEOI Standard is in place but needs improvement in order to be fully consistent with the requirements of the AEOI Terms of Reference. While Nauru's international legal framework to exchange the information with all of Nauru's Interested Appropriate Partners (CR2) is consistent with the requirements, its domestic legislative framework requiring Reporting Financial Institutions to conduct the due diligence and reporting procedures (CR1) has deficiencies significant to the proper functioning of elements of the AEOI Standard. More specifically, the deficiencies relates to the approach to non-Participating Jurisdictions and the enforcement framework.

The methodology used for the peer reviews and that therefore underpins this report is outlined in Chapter 2.

Overall determination on the legal framework: In Place But **Needs Improvement**

Conclusions on the legal framework

General context

Nauru commenced exchanges under the AEOI Standard in 2018.

In order to provide for Reporting Financial Institutions to collect and report the information to be exchanged, Nauru:

- enacted the Automatic Exchange of Financial Account Information Act 2016; and
- introduced the Automatic Exchange of Financial Account Information Regulations 2017.

Under this framework Reporting Financial Institutions were required to commence the due diligence procedures in relation to New Accounts from 1 January 2017. With respect to Preexisting Accounts, Reporting Financial Institutions were required to complete the due diligence procedures on High Value Individual Accounts by 31 December 2017 and on Lower Value Individual Accounts and Entity Accounts by 31 December 2018.

With respect to the exchange of information under the AEOI Standard, Nauru is a Party to the Convention on Mutual Administrative Assistance in Tax Matters and activated the associated CRS Multilateral Competent Authority Agreement in time for exchanges in 2017.

Detailed findings

The detailed findings for Nauru are below, organised per Core Requirement (CR) and sub-requirement (SR), as extracted from the AEOI Terms of Reference (www.oecd.org/tax/transparency/documents/aeoi-terms-of-reference.pdf).

CR1 Domestic legal framework: Jurisdictions should have a domestic legislative framework in place that requires all Reporting Financial Institutions to conduct the due diligence and reporting procedures in the CRS, and that provides for the effective implementation of the CRS as set out therein.

Determination: In Place But **Needs Improvement**

Nauru's domestic legislative framework is in place and contains most of the key aspects of the CRS and its Commentary requiring Reporting Financial Institutions to conduct the due diligence and reporting procedures but it needs improvement in relation to the definition of the term Participating Jurisdiction (SR 1.2) and the framework to enforce the requirements (SR 1.4).

SR 1.1 Jurisdictions should define the scope of Reporting Financial Institutions consistently with the CRS.

Nauru has defined the scope of Reporting Financial Institutions in its domestic legislative framework in accordance with the CRS and its Commentary.

Recommendations:

No recommendations made.

SR 1.2 Jurisdictions should define the scope of Financial Accounts and Reportable Accounts consistently with the CRS and incorporate the due diligence procedures to identify them.

Nauru has defined the scope of the Financial Accounts that are required to be reported in its domestic legislative framework and incorporated the due diligence procedures that must be applied to identify them in a manner that is largely consistent with the CRS and its Commentary. However, a deficiency has been identified. More specifically, Nauru's legislative framework does not incorporate the requirements in relation to certain Entities not located in Participating Jurisdictions in line with the AEOI Standard. This deficiency does not ensure that all Investment Entities that are not in Participating Jurisdictions are subject to the "look-through" approach to identify their Controlling Persons.

Recommendations:

Nauru should amend its domestic legislative framework to ensure that the approach taken with respect to the 15 jurisdictions defined as a Participating Jurisdiction and with which Nauru does not have an agreement to exchange CRS information with (one of which has not implemented the AEOI Standard), is in accordance with the AEOI Standard..

SR 1.3 Jurisdictions should incorporate the reporting requirements contained in Section I of the CRS into their domestic legislative framework.

Nauru has incorporated the reporting requirements in its domestic legislative framework in accordance with the CRS and its Commentary.

Recommendations:

No recommendations made.

SR 1.4 Jurisdictions should have a legislative framework in place that allows for the enforcement of the requirements of the CRS in practice.

Nauru has a legislative framework in place to enforce the requirements in accordance with the CRS and its Commentary that is largely consistent with the CRS and its Commentary. However, deficiencies have been identified. Most significantly, Nauru's legislative framework does not include an explicit legal basis to enforce a sanction where a Reporting Financial Institution is a legal arrangement

Recommendations:

Nauru should ensure that its anti-avoidance rule covers avoidance of CRS reporting and due diligence when entered into by Account Holders or intermediaries, not just by Financial Institutions.

Nauru should amend its legislative framework to ensure that there is an explicit legal basis to enforce a sanction when there is non-compliance by a Reporting Financial Institution that is a legal arrangement

CR2 International legal framework: Jurisdictions should have exchange relationships in effect with all Interested Appropriate Partners as committed to and that provide for the exchange of information in accordance with the Model CAA.

Determination: In Place

Nauru's international legal framework to exchange the information is in place, is consistent with the Model CAA and its Commentary and provides for exchange with all of Nauru's Interested Appropriate Partners (i.e. all jurisdictions that are interested in receiving information from Nauru and that meet the required standard in relation to confidentiality and data safeguards) (SRs 2.1 – 2.3).

SR 2.1 Jurisdictions should have exchange agreements in effect with all Interested Appropriate Partners that permit the automatic exchange of CRS information.

Nauru has exchange agreements that permit the automatic exchange of CRS information in effect with all its Interested Appropriate Partners.

Recommendations:

No recommendations made.

SR 2.2 Such an exchange agreement should be put in place without undue delay, following the receipt of an expression of interest from an Interested Appropriate Partner.

Nauru put in place its exchange agreements without undue delay.

Recommendations:

No recommendations made.

SR 2.3 Jurisdictions should ensure that the exchange agreements in effect provide for the exchange of information in accordance with the requirements of the Model CAA.

Nauru's exchange agreements provide for the exchange of information in accordance with the requirements of the Model CAA.

Recommendations:

No recommendations made.

Comments by the assessed jurisdiction

No comments made.

New Caledonia

Overall findings

New Caledonia's legal framework implementing the AEOI Standard is in place but needs improvement in order to be fully consistent with the requirements of the AEOI Terms of Reference. While New Caledonia's international legal framework to exchange the information with all New Caledonia's Interested Appropriate Partners (CR2) is consistent with the requirements, its domestic legislative framework requiring Reporting Financial Institutions to conduct the due diligence and reporting procedures (CR1) has deficiencies significant to the proper functioning of elements of the AEOI Standard. More specifically, deficiencies have been identified in relation to New Caledonia's enforcement framework.

The methodology used for the peer reviews and that therefore underpins this report is outlined in Chapter 2.

Overall determination on the legal framework: In Place But **Needs Improvement**

Conclusions on the legal framework

General context

New Caledonia commenced exchanges under the AEOI Standard in 2020.

In order to provide for Reporting Financial Institutions to collect and report the information to be exchanged, New Caledonia:

- enacted Code des impôts de la Nouvelle-Calédonie Article Lp. 920.9 ; Arrêté n° 2018-3179 du 26 décembre 2018 fixant les règles et procédures concernant l'échange automatique de renseignements relatifs aux comptes financiers, dites « norme commune de déclaration;
- introduced the Arrêté n° 2018-3181 du 26 décembre 2018 précisant les règles et procédures concernant l'échange automatique de renseignements relatifs aux comptes financiers, dites « norme commune de déclaration;
- made reference to the Code monetaire et financier for the purposes of the identification of Controlling Persons under the AEOI Standard; and
- issued further guidance, which is legally binding.

Under this framework Reporting Financial Institutions were required to commence the due diligence procedures in relation to New Accounts from 1 January 2019. With respect to Preexisting Accounts, Reporting Financial Institutions were required to complete the due diligence procedures on High Value Individual Accounts by 31 December 2019 and on Lower Value Individual Accounts and Entity Accounts by 31 December 2020.

With respect to the exchange of the information under the AEOI Standard, New Caledonia has the Convention on Mutual Administrative Assistance in Tax Matters in place[3] and activated the associated CRS Multilateral Competent Authority Agreement in time for exchanges in 2020.

---

[3] Through a territorial extension by France

Detailed findings

The detailed findings for New Caledonia are below, organised per Core Requirement (CR) and sub-requirement (SR), as extracted from the AEOI Terms of Reference (see Annex B).

CR1 Domestic legal framework: Jurisdictions should have a domestic legislative framework in place that requires all Reporting Financial Institutions to conduct the due diligence and reporting procedures in the CRS, and that provides for the effective implementation of the CRS as set out therein.

Determination: In Place But **Needs Improvement**

New Caledonia's domestic legislative framework is in place and contains most of the key aspects of the CRS and its Commentary requiring Reporting Financial Institutions to conduct the due diligence and reporting procedures, but it needs improvement in relation to the framework to enforce the requirements (SR 1.4). More specifically, New Caledonia's legislative framework for sanctioning due diligence and record keeping failures and providing authorities access to such records relevant to the AEOI Standard does not fully cover all Reporting Financial Institutions.

SR 1.1 Jurisdictions should define the scope of Reporting Financial Institutions consistently with the CRS.

New Caledonia has defined the scope of Reporting Financial Institutions in its domestic legislative framework in accordance with the CRS and its Commentary.

Recommendations:

No recommendations made.

SR 1.2 Jurisdictions should define the scope of Financial Accounts and Reportable Accounts consistently with the CRS and incorporate the due diligence procedures to identify them.

New Caledonia has defined the scope of the Financial Accounts that are required to be reported in its domestic legislative framework and incorporated the due diligence procedures that must be applied to identify them in accordance with the CRS and its Commentary.

Recommendations:

No recommendations made.

SR 1.3 Jurisdictions should incorporate the reporting requirements contained in Section I of the CRS into their domestic legislative framework.

New Caledonia has incorporated the reporting requirements in its domestic legislative framework in accordance with the CRS and its Commentary.

Recommendations:

No recommendations made.

SR 1.4 Jurisdictions should have a legislative framework in place that allows for the enforcement of the requirements of the CRS in practice.

New Caledonia has a legislative framework in place to enforce the requirements in a manner that is largely consistent with the CRS and its Commentary. However, deficiencies have been identified. More specifically, while New Caledonia's legislative framework provides for sanctions that cover most Reporting Financial Institutions that fail to conduct due diligence or fail to keep records relevant to the AEOI Standard, and also provide relevant authorities access to such records, there are a small number of Reporting

Financial Institutions falling out of scope of these provisions. These deficiencies relate to key elements of the AEOI Standard and are therefore material to its proper functioning.

Recommendations:

New Caledonia should amend its domestic legislative framework to provide the appropriate authorities with the power to access the records and evidence relevant for verifying and enforcing the AEOI Standard for all Reporting Financial Institutions.

New Caledonia should ensure that it has sanction provisions applicable to all Reporting Financial Institutions that fail to conduct the due diligence requirements or fail to keep records in accordance with the AEOI Standard, regardless of the impact on reporting.

CR2 International legal framework: Jurisdictions should have exchange relationships in effect with all Interested Appropriate Partners as committed to and that provide for the exchange of information in accordance with the Model CAA.

Determination: In Place

New Caledonia's international legal framework to exchange the information is in place, is consistent with the Model CAA and its Commentary and provides for exchange with all of New Caledonia's Interested Appropriate Partners (i.e. all jurisdictions that are interested in receiving information from New Caledonia and that meet the required standard in relation to confidentiality and data safeguards) (SRs 2.1 – 2.3).

SR 2.1 Jurisdictions should have exchange agreements in effect with all Interested Appropriate Partners that permit the automatic exchange of CRS information.

New Caledonia has exchange agreements that permit the automatic exchange of CRS information in effect with all its Interested Appropriate Partners.

Recommendations:

No recommendations made.

SR 2.2 Such an exchange agreement should be put in place without undue delay, following the receipt of an expression of interest from an Interested Appropriate Partner.

New Caledonia put in place its exchange agreements without undue delay.

Recommendations:

No recommendations made.

SR 2.3 Jurisdictions should ensure that the exchange agreements in effect provide for the exchange of information in accordance with the requirements of the Model CAA.

New Caledonia's exchange agreements provide for the exchange of information in accordance with the requirements of the Model CAA.

Recommendations:

No recommendations made.

Comments by the assessed jurisdiction

No comments made.

Nigeria

This report analyses the implementation of the AEOI Standard in Nigeria with respect to the requirements of the AEOI Terms of Reference. It assesses both the legal frameworks put in place to implement the AEOI Standard and the effectiveness of the implementation of the AEOI Standard in practice.

The methodology used for the peer reviews and that therefore underpins this report is outlined in Chapter 2.

Overall findings

AEOI legal framework

Nigeria's legal framework implementing the AEOI Standard is in place but needs improvement in order to be fully consistent with the requirements in the AEOI Terms of Reference. While Nigeria's international legal framework to exchange the information with all of Nigeria's Interested Appropriate Partners (CR2) is consistent with the requirements, its domestic legislative framework requiring Reporting Financial Institutions to conduct the due diligence and reporting procedures (CR1) has deficiencies significant to the proper functioning of elements of the AEOI Standard. More specifically, deficiencies have been identified in relation to Nigeria's enforcement framework.

Overall determination on the legal framework: In Place But **Needs Improvement**

Effectiveness of AEOI in practice

Nigeria's implementation of the AEOI Standard is on track with respect to the requirements of the AEOI Terms of Reference to ensure the effectiveness of the AEOI Standard in practice. This includes ensuring that Reporting Financial Institutions correctly conduct the due diligence and reporting procedures (CR1) and exchanging the information in an effective and timely manner (CR2). Nigeria is encouraged to continue its implementation process accordingly, to ensure its ongoing effectiveness.

Overall rating in relation to the effectiveness in practice: **On Track**

General context

Nigeria commenced exchanges under the AEOI Standard in 2020.

In order to provide for Reporting Financial Institutions to collect and report the information to be exchanged, Nigeria:

- enacted the *Income Tax (Common Reporting Standard) Regulations 2019*;
- introduced *The Income Tax (Common Reporting Standard) Implementation and Compliance Guidelines, 2019*.

Under this framework Reporting Financial Institutions were required to commence the due diligence procedures in relation to New Accounts from 1 July 2019. With respect to Preexisting Accounts, Reporting Financial Institutions were required to complete the due diligence procedures on High-Value Individual Accounts by 31 December 2019 and on Preexisting Lower Value Individual Accounts and Entity Accounts by 31 December 2020.

With respect to the exchange of the information under the AEOI Standard, Nigeria is a Party to the Convention on Mutual Administrative Assistance in Tax Matters and activated the associated CRS Multilateral Competent Authority Agreement in time for exchanges in 2020.

Table 1 sets out the number of Financial Institutions in Nigeria that reported information on Financial Accounts in 2023 as defined in the AEOI Standard essentially because they maintained Financial Accounts for Account Holders, or relating to Controlling Persons, resident in a Reportable Jurisdiction. It also sets out the number of Financial Accounts that they reported in 2023. In this regard, it should be noted that Nigeria requires the reporting of Financial Accounts based on a prescribed list of exchange partners and some accounts may be required to be reported more than once (e.g. jointly held accounts or accounts with multiple related Controlling Persons), which is reflected in the figures below. These figures provide key contextual information to the development and implementation of Nigeria's administrative compliance strategy, which is analysed in the subsequent sections of this report.

Table.1. Number of Financial Institutions reporting and Financial Accounts reported

	Number
Number of Financial Institutions reporting Financial Accounts in 2023	284
Number of Financial Accounts reported in 2023	81 796

Table 2 sets out the number of exchange partners to which information was successfully sent by Nigeria in the past few years (including where the necessary frameworks were in place, containing an obligation on Reporting Financial Institutions to report information, but no relevant Reportable Accounts were identified). These figures provide key contextual information in relation to Nigeria's exchanges in practice, which is also analysed in subsequent sections of this report.

Table.2. Number of exchange partners to which information was successfully sent

	2020	2021	2022	2023
Number of exchange partners to which information was successfully sent	25	63	73	74

In order to provide for the effective implementation of the AEOI Standard, in Nigeria:

- Federal Inland Revenue Service (FIRS) (the tax authority) has the responsibility to ensure the effective implementation of the due diligence and reporting obligations by Reporting Financial Institutions and for exchanging the information with Nigeria's exchange partners, supported by the various financial regulators in Nigeria;
- technical solutions necessary to receive and validate the information reported by Reporting Financial Institutions were put in place through an online portal; and
- the Common Transmission System (CTS) is used for the exchange of the information, along with the associated file preparation and encryption requirements.

It should be noted that the review of Nigeria's legal framework implementing the AEOI Standard concluded with the determination that Nigeria's domestic legal framework is In Place But Needs Improvement and its international legal framework is In Place. This has been taken into account when reviewing the effectiveness of Nigeria's implementation of the AEOI Standard in practice and where particular identified gaps in Nigeria's legal frameworks directly impact its implementation in practice, these are mentioned below.

Findings and conclusions on the legal frameworks

The detailed findings and conclusions on the AEOI legal frameworks for Nigeria are below, organised per Core Requirement (CR) and then per sub-requirement (SR) as extracted from the AEOI Terms of Reference (see Annex B).

CR1 Domestic legal framework: Jurisdictions should have a domestic legislative framework in place that requires all Reporting Financial Institutions to conduct the due diligence and reporting procedures in the CRS, and that provides for the effective implementation of the CRS as set out therein.

Determination: In Place But **Needs Improvement**

Nigeria's domestic legislative framework is in place and contains most of the key aspects of the CRS and its Commentary requiring Reporting Financial Institutions to conduct the due diligence and reporting procedures, but it **needs improvement** in relation to the framework to enforce the requirements (SR 1.4). More specifically, the rules in Nigeria's legislative framework to prevent persons or intermediaries from adopting practices intended to circumvent the reporting and due diligence procedures are insufficient in scope and it does not have an explicit legal basis to enforce a sanction for non-compliance if the Reporting Financial Institution is a legal arrangement.

SR 1.1 Jurisdictions should define the scope of Reporting Financial Institutions consistently with the CRS.

Nigeria has defined the scope of Reporting Financial Institutions in its domestic legislative framework in accordance with the CRS and its Commentary.

Recommendations:

No recommendations made.

SR 1.2 Jurisdictions should define the scope of Financial Accounts and Reportable Accounts consistently with the CRS and incorporate the due diligence procedures to identify them.

Nigeria has defined the scope of the Financial Accounts that are required to be reported in its domestic legislative framework and incorporated the due diligence procedures that must be applied to identify them in accordance with the CRS and its Commentary.

Recommendations:

No recommendations made.

SR 1.3 Jurisdictions should incorporate the reporting requirements contained in Section I of the CRS into their domestic legislative framework.

Nigeria has incorporated the reporting requirements in its domestic legislative framework in accordance with the CRS and its Commentary.

Recommendations:

No recommendations made.

SR 1.4 Jurisdictions should have a legislative framework in place that allows for the enforcement of the requirements of the CRS in practice.

Nigeria has a legislative framework in place to enforce the requirements in a manner that is largely consistent with the CRS and its Commentary. However, a deficiency has been identified. More specifically, Nigeria's legislative framework does not include rules to prevent all relevant persons or intermediaries from adopting practices intended to circumvent the reporting and due diligence procedures as required and it does not include an explicit legal basis to enforce a sanction where a Reporting Financial Institution is a legal arrangement. These deficiencies relate to key elements of the required enforcement framework and are therefore material to the proper functioning of the AEOI Standard.

Recommendations:

Nigeria should amend its domestic legislative framework to include rules to prevent all Financial Institutions, persons and intermediaries from adopting practices intended to circumvent the due diligence and reporting procedures, rather than just those on whom the AEOI Standard imposes an obligation.

Nigeria should amend its legislative framework to ensure that there is an explicit legal basis to enforce a sanction when there is non-compliance by a Reporting Financial Institution that is a legal arrangement.

CR2 International legal framework: Jurisdictions should have exchange relationships in effect with all Interested Appropriate Partners as committed to and that provide for the exchange of information in accordance with the Model CAA.

Determination: In Place

Nigeria's international legal framework to exchange the information is in place, is consistent with the Model CAA and its Commentary and provides for exchange with all of Nigeria's Interested Appropriate Partners (i.e. all jurisdictions that are interested in receiving information from Nigeria and that meet the required standard in relation to confidentiality and data safeguards) (SRs 2.1 – 2.3).

SR 2.1 Jurisdictions should have exchange agreements in effect with all Interested Appropriate Partners that permit the automatic exchange of CRS information.

Nigeria has exchange agreements that permit the automatic exchange of CRS information in effect with all its Interested Appropriate Partners.

Recommendations:

No recommendations made.

SR 2.2 Such an exchange agreement should be put in place without undue delay, following the receipt of an expression of interest from an Interested Appropriate Partner.

Nigeria put in place its exchange agreements without undue delay.

Recommendations:

No recommendations made.

SR 2.3 Jurisdictions should ensure that the exchange agreements in effect provide for the exchange of information in accordance with the requirements of the Model CAA.

Nigeria's exchange agreements provide for the exchange of information in accordance with the requirements of the Model CAA.

Recommendations:

No recommendations made.

Assessed jurisdiction's comments on the assessment of its legal frameworks

Nigeria has observed that under SR.1.4., this Report states that Nigeria's Legislative framework is in place to enforce the requirements in a manner that is Largely consistent with the CRS and its commentary.

However, the Report also highlighted a deficiency – that the Anti-avoidance Rule under Regulation 12 of Nigeria Income Tax (Common Reporting Standard) Regulations 2019 does not prevent ALL relevant persons, including intermediaries from adopting practices intended to circumvent the reporting and due diligence procedures as required.

Nigeria notes the Recommendation to amend its CRS legal framework to address this deficiency, and will take the required steps to update the text of Regulation 12 to meet the Agreed standard.

However, Nigeria hereby places on record that the text of the Nigeria CRS Regulations 2019, including the Anti-avoidance rule, was modelled after the OECD Global Forum CRS Rules that was made available to Nigeria's Legal drafting team in 2018. We are now aware that the Global Forum learning from experience from reviews of CRS legal framework of over 100 jurisdictions, has in recent times issued a new version of CRS Rules, which amongst other things provides an updated text for the Anti-avoidance rule, with a view to ensuring that all persons in scope, are covered.

Nigeria will be guided by text of the latest version of the Global Forum Model CRS Rules, in our efforts to update the Nigeria Income Tax (Common Reporting Standard) Regulations 2019.

Findings and conclusions in relation to effectiveness in practice

The following table contains the detailed findings for Nigeria, organised per Core Requirement (CR) and then per sub-requirement (SR) as extracted from the AEOI Terms of Reference.

CR1 Effectiveness in practice: Jurisdictions should ensure that in practice Reporting Financial Institutions correctly implement the due diligence and reporting procedures, which includes a requirement for jurisdictions to have in place an administrative framework to ensure the effective implementation of the CRS.

Rating: On Track

Nigeria's implementation of the AEOI Standard is on track with respect to ensuring that Reporting Financial Institutions are correctly conducting the due diligence and reporting procedures and are therefore reporting complete and accurate information. This includes ensuring effectiveness in a domestic context, such as through having an effective administrative compliance framework and related procedures (SR 1.5), and collaborating with exchange partners to ensure effectiveness (SR 1.6). Nigeria is encouraged to continue its implementation process accordingly, to ensure its ongoing effectiveness.

SR 1.5 Jurisdictions should ensure that in practice Reporting Financial Institutions identify the Financial Accounts they maintain, identify the Reportable Accounts among those Financial Accounts, as well as their Account Holders, and where relevant Controlling Persons, by correctly conducting the due diligence procedures and collect and report the required information with respect to each Reportable Account. This includes having in place:

- an effective administrative compliance framework to ensure the effective implementation of, and compliance with, the CRS. This framework should:

  i. be based on a strategy that facilitates compliance by Reporting Financial Institutions and which is informed by a risk assessment in respect of the effective implementation of the CRS that takes into account relevant information sources (including third party sources);

  ii. include procedures to ensure that Financial Institutions correctly apply the definitions of Reporting Financial Institutions and Non-Reporting Financial Institutions;

iii. include procedures to periodically verify Reporting Financial Institutions' compliance, conducted by authorities that have adequate powers with respect to the reviewed Reporting Financial Institutions, with procedures to access the records they maintain; and

- effective procedures to ensure that Financial Institutions, persons or intermediaries do not circumvent the due diligence and reporting procedures;
- effective enforcement mechanisms to address non-compliance by Reporting Financial Institutions;
- strong measures to ensure that valid self-certifications are always obtained for New Accounts;
- effective procedures to ensure that each, or each type of, jurisdiction-specific Non-Reporting Financial Institution and Excluded Account continue to present a low risk of being used to evade tax; and
- effective procedures to follow up with a Reporting Financial Institution when undocumented accounts are reported in order to establish the reasons why such information is being reported.

Findings:

In order to ensure that Reporting Financial Institutions correctly conduct the due diligence and reporting procedures, Nigeria implemented all of the requirements in accordance with expectations. The key findings were as follows:

- Nigeria implemented an overarching strategy to ensure compliance with the AEOI Standard developed after conducting a risk assessment that took into account a range of relevant information sources, including the information reported by Reporting Financial Institutions and publicly available information, such as websites of the Reporting Financial Institutions, tax compliance performance and feedback from exchange partners. The FIRS also receives information from the AML authorities regarding their monitoring activities and sanctions imposed on Financial Institutions for non-compliance with AML/KYC obligations upon request. Nigeria's compliance strategy facilitates compliance and incorporates a credible approach to verification and enforcement. Nigeria intends to keep its compliance strategy and risk assessment under review to ensure its effectiveness on an ongoing basis.
- Nigeria maintains a list of regulated Reporting Financial Institutions based on publicly available information, such as websites of Financial Institutions and information from regulatory bodies. Nigeria also follows-up with Reporting Financial Institutions that are identified as possibly incorrectly not reporting to ensure they report as required. With respect to non-regulated Entities that may be Financial Institutions for the purposes of the AEOI Standard, Nigeria checks whether Financial Institutions manage the assets of other Entities during its annual compliance activities and follows up as necessary. Nigeria also plans to request from Reporting Financial Institutions details of their Account Holders that are classified as Financial Institutions and is considering the use of its tax database to further identify such relevant Entities. Nigeria intends to continue to review its Financial Institution population on a routine basis.
- The institution (FIRS) responsible for implementing Nigeria's compliance strategy has the necessary powers and resources to discharge its functions. With respect to resourcing, Nigeria has assigned the equivalent of eight full time staff and two supervisors to monitor and ensure compliance by Reporting Financial Institutions, which have access to IT systems and tools to conduct risk assessments (e.g. SQL, Power BI and Spreadsheets (Excel)). Overall, they appear to have effectively implemented an operational plan to verify compliance with the requirements, incorporating some appropriate compliance activities.
- The FIRS has carried out desk-based reviews of the information reported by Reporting Financial Institutions, using several risk factors, which informed the selection of Reporting Financial Institutions for onsite monitoring visits, designed to understand their processes in place to implement and comply with the AEOI Standard. This includes understanding the frameworks and

procedures in place, as well as some limited spot checks to verify correct reporting. It made such visits to 55 Reporting Financial Institutions in 2021. As a result, some Reporting Financial Institutions that failed to conduct to carry out the required due diligence (including failing to obtain valid self-certifications) or failed to keep the required records were identified. These monitoring visits were primarily used to help improve the Reporting Financial Institutions' understanding of the requirements.

- Building on the onsite monitoring visits, Nigeria conducted onsite audits of 37 Reporting Financial Institutions in 2023 to verify compliance including through the inspection of records held by the Reporting Financial Institutions and to enforce the requirements where appropriate.
- It appears that Nigeria has the ability to effectively enforce the requirements, including through the application of dissuasive penalties and sanctions for non-compliance, although it has not yet done so as its compliance activities and level of financial institution compliance were impacted by the COVID-19 pandemic. Consequently, Nigeria opted not to sanction Reporting Financial Institutions for non-compliance for 2020, 2021 and 2022 but to intensify CRS education and awareness programmes. Nigeria has not yet applied its penalties and sanctions for non-compliance.
- While Nigeria does not have a defined policy in place, it appears ready to take effective action to address circumvention of the requirements if such circumvention is detected. However, it will be somewhat constrained by the scope of its legal power to address circumvention. It also appears that action is being taken to ensure self-certifications are obtained as required and to follow up on undocumented accounts.
- It is noted that Nigeria does not have a jurisdiction-specific list of Non-Reporting Financial Institutions or Excluded Accounts for ongoing monitoring.

Table 3 provides a summary of the specific activities undertaken, or that are planned to be undertaken, in relation to each of the key parts of the framework described above.

Table.3. Activities undertaken

Activity type	Activities undertaken
Communication and outreach	Nigeria has carried out substantial communication and outreach activities, such as through a dedicated channel of communication (mailbox and phone line) for queries, sending regular AEOI-CRS Titbits to Reporting Financial institutions via emails, publishing detailed guidance and user manuals on the FIRS website and organising webinars / workshops with Financial Institutions.
Verifying that Financial Institutions are reporting as required	Nigeria has carried out substantial verification activities to ensure that Financial Institutions are reporting as required, including through contacting Financial Institutions following a comparative analysis of the data reported and collaborating with the financial regulators where reports are unexpectedly not received. Nigeria has developed a process to conduct such activities on a routine basis.
Verifying whether the information reported is complete and accurate	Nigeria has conducted a significant number of desk-based checks to verify whether the information being reported is complete and accurate. It accordingly identified some issues, commonly concerning high number of undocumented accounts, non-reporting, incorrect reporting, missing TINs, etc. It is following up on these issues with a view to ensuring future compliance. Nigeria also conducted monitoring visits of 55 Reporting Financial Institutions based on risk, to review their policies and procedures in 2022. Furthermore, Nigeria has conducted onsite audits of 37 Reporting Financial Institutions in 2023. It accordingly identified some issues, commonly concerning accounts for which information was reported incorrectly. It is following up on these issues with a view to ensure future compliance.
Enforcement	Following the activities mentioned above, Nigeria has not yet imposed penalties and sanctions, but has plans to do so in the near future.

In terms of the Financial Account information collected and sent by Nigeria, while the presence of the key data point of dates of birth and the level of undocumented accounts appeared to be in line with most other jurisdictions, it was found to include a much lower proportion of Tax Identification Numbers with respect to the individuals associated with the accounts when compared to most other jurisdictions. These are key data points for exchange partners to effectively utilise the information. Follow-up discussions confirmed that Nigeria is aware of this issue and is taking steps to address it.

Feedback from Nigeria's exchange partners indicated that, compared to what they generally experience when seeking to match information received from their exchange partners with their taxpayer database, they achieved a much lower level of success when seeking to match information received from Nigeria. Furthermore, 12 exchange partners highlighted issues with respect to the information received such as missing, invalid, or incomplete Tax Identification Numbers, dates of birth and addresses. Follow-up discussions confirmed that Nigeria is aware of some of these issues and is seeking to improve the situation.

Based on these findings it was concluded that, overall, Nigeria is meeting expectations in ensuring that Reporting Financial Institutions correctly conduct the due diligence and reporting procedures, including by having in place the required administrative compliance framework and related procedures. It was also noted that there is room for improvement with respect to implementing a framework to identify non-regulated Entities and put in place a clearly defined policy to address circumvention. Nigeria is therefore encouraged to continue its implementation process accordingly, including in relation to the areas highlighted.

Recommendations:

Nigeria should implement its plans to identify or to follow-up with non-regulated Entities that are Financial Institutions for the purposes of the AEOI Standard.

Nigeria should put in place a clearly defined policy that, where circumvention is identified then action is taken to address it. Reference is made to the recommendation made during the assessment of Nigeria's legal framework.

Nigeria should continue to address the issues raised by its exchange partners.

SR 1.6 Jurisdictions should collaborate on compliance and enforcement. This requires jurisdictions to:

a) use all appropriate measures available under the jurisdiction's domestic law to address errors or non-compliance notified to the jurisdiction by an exchange partner; and

b) have in place effective procedures to notify an exchange partner of errors that may have led to incomplete or incorrect information reporting or non-compliance with the due diligence or reporting procedures by a Reporting Financial Institution in the jurisdiction of the exchange partner.

Findings:

In order to collaborate on compliance and enforcement, it appears that Nigeria implemented all of the requirements in relation to issues notified to them (i.e. under Section 4 of the MCAA or equivalent) in accordance with expectations. While no such notifications have yet been received, Nigeria has the necessary systems and procedures to process them as required. It also appears that Nigeria notifies its partners effectively of errors or suspected non-compliance it identified when utilising the information received.

Based on these findings it was concluded that Nigeria is fully meeting expectations in relation to collaborating with its exchange partners to ensure that Reporting Financial Institutions correctly conduct the due diligence and reporting procedures. Nigeria is encouraged to continue its implementation process accordingly, to ensure its ongoing effectiveness.

Recommendations:

No recommendations made.

CR2 Effectiveness in practice: Jurisdictions should exchange the information effectively in practice, in a timely manner, including by sorting, preparing, validating and transmitting it in accordance with the AEOI Standard

Rating: On Track

Nigeria's implementation of the AEOI Standard is on track with respect to exchanging the information effectively in practice, including in relation to sorting, preparing and validating the information (SR 2.4), correctly transmitting the information in a timely manner (SRs 2.5 – 2.8) and providing corrections, amendments or additions to the information (SR 2.9). Nigeria is encouraged to continue its implementation process accordingly, to ensure its ongoing effectiveness.

SR 2.4 Jurisdictions should sort, prepare and validate the information in accordance with the CRS XML Schema and the associated requirements in the CRS XML Schema User Guide and the File Error and Correction-related validations in the Status Message User Guide (i.e. the 50000 and 80000 range).

Findings:

Feedback from Nigeria's exchange partners did not raise any specific concerns with respect to their ability to process the information received from Nigeria and therefore with respect to Nigeria's implementation of these requirements. More generally, one of Nigeria's exchange partners reported rejecting more than 25% of the files received, reporting that it rejected 50% of files received, due to the technical requirements not being met. This is broadly in line with the general experience of other jurisdictions. It was noted that Nigeria has already successfully addressed the issues raised.

Based on these findings it was concluded that Nigeria is fully meeting expectations in relation to sorting, preparing and validating the information. Nigeria is encouraged to continue its implementation process accordingly, to ensure its ongoing effectiveness.

Recommendations:

No recommendations made.

SR 2.5 Jurisdictions should agree and use, with each exchange partner, transmission methods that meet appropriate minimum standards to ensure the confidentiality and integrity of the data throughout the transmission, including its encryption to a minimum secure standard.

Findings:

In order to put in place an agreed transmission method that meets appropriate minimum standards in confidentiality, integrity of the data and encryption for use with each of its exchange partners, Nigeria linked to the CTS.

Based on these findings it was concluded that Nigeria is fully meeting expectations in relation to agreeing and using appropriate transmission methods with each of its partners. Nigeria is encouraged to continue to ensure the ongoing effectiveness of its implementation.

Recommendations:

No recommendations made.

SR 2.6 Jurisdictions should carry out all exchanges annually within nine months of the end of the calendar year to which the information relates.

Findings:

Feedback from Nigeria's exchange partners did not raise any concerns with respect to timeliness of the exchanges by Nigeria and therefore with respect to Nigeria's implementation of this requirement.

Based on these findings it was concluded that Nigeria is fully meeting expectations in relation to exchanging the information in a timely manner. Nigeria is encouraged to continue to ensure the ongoing effectiveness of its implementation.

Recommendations:

No recommendations made.

SR 2.7 Jurisdictions should send the information in accordance with the agreed transmission methods and encryption standards.

Findings:

Feedback from Nigeria's exchange partners did not raise any concerns with respect to Nigeria's use of the agreed transmission methods and therefore with Nigeria's implementation of this requirement.

Based on these findings it was concluded that Nigeria is fully meeting expectations in relation to sending the information in accordance with the agreed transmission methods and encryption standards. Nigeria is encouraged to continue to ensure the ongoing effectiveness of its implementation.

Recommendations:

No recommendations made.

SR 2.8 Jurisdictions should have the systems in place to receive information and, once it has been received, should send a status message to the sending jurisdictions in accordance with the CRS Status Message XML Schema and the related User Guide.

Findings:

11 exchange partners highlighted delays in the sending of status messages by Nigeria, representing 13% of its partners. This represents a very high proportion of partners. It was noted that this was due to a technical issue which has since been resolved and that Nigeria has since sent status messages as required, including the messages impacted by the technical issue.

Based on these findings it was concluded that, Nigeria is meeting expectations in relation to the receipt of the information. Nigeria should continue its implementation process to ensure its effectiveness.

Recommendations:

No recommendations made.

SR 2.9 Jurisdictions should respond to a notification from an exchange partner as referred to in Section 4 of the Model CAA (which may include Status Messages) in accordance with the timelines set out in the Commentary to Section 4 of the Model CAA. In all other cases, jurisdictions should send corrected, amended or additional information received from a Reporting Financial Institution as soon as possible after it has been received.

Findings:

Nigeria appears ready to respond to notifications and to provide corrected, amended or additional information in a timely manner and no such concerns were raised by Nigeria's exchange partners and therefore with respect to Nigeria's implementation of these requirements.

Based on these findings it was concluded that Nigeria appears to be meeting expectations in relation to responding to notifications from exchange partners and the sending of corrected, amended or additional information. Nigeria is encouraged to continue to ensure the ongoing effectiveness of its implementation.

Recommendations:

No recommendations made.

Comments by the assessed jurisdiction

Nigeria acknowledges and appreciates the good work of the team of Assessors and their painstaking efforts to determine the state of affairs of the AEOI in practice in Nigeria, and to provide guidance for improvement of AEOI practices. We hereby state our continual commitment to conduct the AEOI system in conformity with the internationally agreed standards and to ensure we remain a reliable AEOI partner jurisdiction.

Oman

This report analyses the implementation of the AEOI Standard in Oman with respect to the requirements of the AEOI Terms of Reference. It assesses both the legal frameworks put in place to implement the AEOI Standard and the effectiveness of the implementation of the AEOI Standard in practice.

The methodology used for the peer reviews and that therefore underpins this report is outlined in Chapter 2.

Overall findings

AEOI legal framework

Oman's legal framework implementing the AEOI Standard is in place and is fully consistent with the requirements of the AEOI Terms of Reference. This includes Oman's domestic legislative framework requiring Reporting Financial Institutions to conduct the due diligence and reporting procedures (CR1) and its international legal framework to exchange the information with all of Oman's Interested Appropriate Partners (CR2).

Overall determination on the legal framework: In Place

Effectiveness of AEOI in practice

Oman's implementation of the AEOI Standard is partially compliant with the requirements of the AEOI Terms of Reference to ensure the effectiveness of the AEOI Standard in practice. This is because there are significant issues with respect to ensuring that Reporting Financial Institutions correctly conduct the due diligence and reporting procedures (CR1) and with respect to exchanging the information in an effective and timely manner (CR2).

Overall rating in relation to the effectiveness in practice: Partially Compliant

General context

Oman commenced exchanges under the AEOI Standard on a non-reciprocal basis in 2020 (i.e. it sends but does not receive information).

In order to provide for Reporting Financial Institutions to collect and report the information to be exchanged, Oman:

- amended the Income Tax Law 28/2009; and
- issued the Chairman of the Tax Authority Decision No. 78/2020 On Standards for Automatic Exchange of Financial Account Information.

Under this framework Reporting Financial Institutions were required to commence the due diligence procedures in relation to New Accounts from 1 July 2019. With respect to Preexisting Accounts, Reporting Financial Institutions were required to complete the due diligence procedures on High-Value Individual Accounts by 31 December 2019 and on Preexisting Lower Value Individual Accounts and Entity Accounts by 31 December 2020.

Following the initial Global Forum review, Oman amended its legislative framework to address issues identified, effective from 29 April 2024.

With respect to the exchange of the information under the AEOI Standard, Oman is a Party to the Convention on Mutual Administrative Assistance in Tax Matters and activated the associated CRS Multilateral Competent Authority Agreement in time for exchanges in 2020.

Table 1 sets out the number of Financial Institutions in Oman that reported information on Financial Accounts in 2023 as defined in the AEOI Standard (essentially because they maintained Financial Accounts for Account Holders, or that related to Controlling Persons, resident in a Reportable Jurisdiction). It also sets out the number of Financial Accounts that they reported in 2023. In this regard, it should be noted that Oman requires the reporting of Financial Accounts based on a prescribed list of exchange partners and some accounts may be required to be reported more than once (e.g. jointly held accounts or accounts with multiple related Controlling Persons), which is reflected in the figures below. These figures provide key contextual information to the development and implementation of Oman's administrative compliance strategy, which is analysed in the subsequent sections of this report.

Table.4. Number of Financial Institutions reporting and Financial Accounts reported

	Number
Number of Financial Institutions reporting Financial Accounts in 2023	32
Number of Financial Accounts reported in 2023	28,254

Table 2 sets out the number of exchange partners to which information was successfully sent by Oman in the past few years (including where the necessary frameworks were in place, containing an obligation on Reporting Financial Institutions to report information, but no relevant Reportable Accounts were identified). These figures provide key contextual information in relation to Oman's exchanges in practice, which is also analysed in subsequent sections of this report.

Table.5. Number of exchange partners to which information was successfully sent

	2020	2021	2022	2023
Number of exchange partners to which information was successfully sent	28	28	39	35

In order to provide for the effective implementation of the AEOI Standard, in Oman:

- the Oman Tax Authority (OTA), as the Competent Authority for AEOI purposes, has responsibility for ensuring the effective implementation of the due diligence and reporting obligations by Reporting Financial Institutions that are not supervised by certain other regulatory authorities, for taking enforcement action in respect of non-compliance with the AEOI, and for exchanging the information with Oman's exchange partners. The other regulatory authorities responsible for the effective implementation of the AEOI by Reporting Financial Institutions under their supervision are the Central Bank of Oman (CBO, the authority responsible for the supervision of banks, finance and leasing companies and money exchange companies, and also performs AML supervisory functions in these sectors) and the Financial Services Authority (FSA, the authority responsible for the supervision of the capital market and the insurance sector, and also performs AML supervisory functions in the two sectors);
- technical solutions necessary to receive and validate the information reported by Reporting Financial Institutions were put in place by establishing a secure platform for reporting that includes a validation system; and
- the Common Transmission System (CTS) is used for the exchange of the information, along with the associated file preparation and encryption requirements.

It should be noted that the review of Oman's legal frameworks implementing the AEOI Standard concluded with the determination that Oman's domestic legal framework is In Place and its international legal framework is In Place. This has been taken into account when reviewing the effectiveness of Oman's implementation of the AEOI Standard in practice.

Findings and conclusions on the legal frameworks

The detailed findings and conclusions on the AEOI legal frameworks for Oman are below, organised per Core Requirement (CR) and then per sub-requirement (SR) as extracted from the AEOI Terms of Reference (see Annex B).

CR1 Domestic legal framework: Jurisdictions should have a domestic legislative framework in place that requires all Reporting Financial Institutions to conduct the due diligence and reporting procedures in the CRS, and that provides for the effective implementation of the CRS as set out therein.

Determination: In Place

Oman's domestic legislative framework is in place and contains all of the key aspects of the CRS and its Commentary requiring Reporting Financial Institutions to conduct the due diligence and reporting procedures (SRs 1.1 – 1.3). It also provides for a framework to enforce the requirements (SR 1.4).

SR 1.1 Jurisdictions should define the scope of Reporting Financial Institutions consistently with the CRS.

Oman has defined the scope of Reporting Financial Institutions in its domestic legislative framework in accordance with the CRS and its Commentary.

Recommendations:

No recommendations made.

SR 1.2 Jurisdictions should define the scope of Financial Accounts and Reportable Accounts consistently with the CRS and incorporate the due diligence procedures to identify them.

Oman has defined the scope of the Financial Accounts that are required to be reported in its domestic legislative framework and incorporated the due diligence procedures that must be applied to identify them in accordance with the CRS and its Commentary.

Recommendations:

No recommendations made.

SR 1.3 Jurisdictions should incorporate the reporting requirements contained in Section I of the CRS into their domestic legislative framework.

Oman has incorporated the reporting requirements in its domestic legislative framework in accordance with the CRS and its Commentary.

Recommendations:

No recommendations made.

SR 1.4 Jurisdictions should have a legislative framework in place that allows for the enforcement of the requirements of the CRS in practice.

Oman has a legislative framework in place to enforce the requirements in accordance with the CRS and its Commentary.

Recommendations:

No recommendations made.

CR2 International legal framework: Jurisdictions should have exchange relationships in effect with all Interested Appropriate Partners as committed to and that provide for the exchange of information in accordance with the Model CAA.

Determination: In Place

Oman's international legal framework to exchange the information is in place, is consistent with the Model CAA and its Commentary and provides for exchange with all of Oman's Interested Appropriate Partners (i.e. all jurisdictions that are interested in receiving information from Oman and that meet the required standard in relation to confidentiality and data safeguards) (SRs 2.1 – 2.3).

SR 2.1 Jurisdictions should have exchange agreements in effect with all Interested Appropriate Partners that permit the automatic exchange of CRS information.

Oman has exchange agreements that permit the automatic exchange of CRS information in effect with all its Interested Appropriate Partners.

Recommendations:

No recommendations made.

SR 2.2 Such an exchange agreement should be put in place without undue delay, following the receipt of an expression of interest from an Interested Appropriate Partner.

Oman put in place its exchange agreements without undue delay.

Recommendations:

No recommendations made.

SR 2.3 Jurisdictions should ensure that the exchange agreements in effect provide for the exchange of information in accordance with the requirements of the Model CAA.

Oman's exchange agreements provide for the exchange of information in accordance with the requirements of the Model CAA.

Recommendations:

No recommendations made.

Assessed jurisdiction's comments on the assessment of its legal frameworks

No comments made.

Findings and conclusions in relation to effectiveness in practice

The detailed findings and conclusions in relation to effectiveness in practice of AEOI for Oman are below, organised per Core Requirement (CR) and then per sub-requirement (SR) as extracted from the AEOI Terms of Reference (see Annex B).

CR1 Effectiveness in practice: Jurisdictions should ensure that in practice Reporting Financial Institutions correctly implement the due diligence and reporting procedures, which includes a requirement for jurisdictions to have in place an administrative framework to ensure the effective implementation of the CRS.

Rating: Partially Compliant

Oman's implementation of the AEOI Standard is partially compliant with respect to ensuring that Reporting Financial Institutions are correctly conducting the due diligence and reporting procedures. More specifically, there are significant issues in relation to Oman ensuring effectiveness in a domestic context, such as through having an effective administrative compliance framework and related procedures (SR 1.5), and collaborating with exchange partners to ensure effectiveness (SR 1.6). Oman should continue its implementation process to ensure its effectiveness, including by addressing the recommendations made.

SR 1.5 Jurisdictions should ensure that in practice Reporting Financial Institutions identify the Financial Accounts they maintain, identify the Reportable Accounts among those Financial Accounts, as well as their Account Holders, and where relevant Controlling Persons, by correctly conducting the due diligence procedures and collect and report the required information with respect to each Reportable Account. This includes having in place:

- an effective administrative compliance framework to ensure the effective implementation of, and compliance with, the CRS. This framework should:
  - i. be based on a strategy that facilitates compliance by Reporting Financial Institutions and which is informed by a risk assessment in respect of the effective implementation of the CRS that takes into account relevant information sources (including third party sources);
  - ii. include procedures to ensure that Financial Institutions correctly apply the definitions of Reporting Financial Institutions and Non-Reporting Financial Institutions;
  - iii. include procedures to periodically verify Reporting Financial Institutions' compliance, conducted by authorities that have adequate powers with respect to the reviewed Reporting Financial Institutions, with procedures to access the records they maintain; and
- effective procedures to ensure that Financial Institutions, persons or intermediaries do not circumvent the due diligence and reporting procedures;
- effective enforcement mechanisms to address non-compliance by Reporting Financial Institutions;
- strong measures to ensure that valid self-certifications are always obtained for New Accounts;
- effective procedures to ensure that each, or each type of, jurisdiction-specific Non-Reporting Financial Institution and Excluded Account continue to present a low risk of being used to evade tax; and
- effective procedures to follow up with a Reporting Financial Institution when undocumented accounts are reported in order to establish the reasons why such information is being reported.

Findings:

In order to ensure that Reporting Financial Institutions correctly conduct the due diligence and reporting procedures, Oman implemented many of the requirements in accordance with expectations. However, significant issues were identified. The key findings were as follows:

- Oman has recently put in place a comprehensive strategy in relation to its administrative framework to monitor the implementation of the AEOI Standard, based on a risk assessment that takes into account a range of relevant information sources. In addition, communication and outreach activities have been carried out to help raise awareness and promote compliance amongst the Financial Institution population. This includes continuous dialogue with Financial Institutions via email, phone and the publication of relevant materials and information on the Tax Authority's website, as well as the organisation of webinars, seminars and meetings aimed at improving Financial Institutions' understanding and implementation of compliance requirements. Oman's strategy has been documented in its "CRS Administrative Compliance Strategy". A formalised annual review plan has also been developed to implement the strategy, including defined procedures to review and verify compliance. Activities also appear to be underway to ensure that the interaction between Oman's AEOI and AML frameworks always results in reporting in accordance with the AEOI Standard.

- Oman has adopted a multi-faceted approach, utilising various methods and sources of information to ensure that it has effectively identified Reporting Financial Institutions on an ongoing basis. Its starting point in determining the Reporting Financial Institution population is its mandatory CRS registration and nil reporting requirements by RFIs in relation to the AEOI Standard. Oman maintains a list of Reporting Financial Institutions, which is informed by the lists of regulated Financial Institutions maintained by the financial regulators and which will be supplemented using the list of Foreign Financial Institutions for FATCA purposes, the Oman Business Register and feedback from partner jurisdictions. Oman plans to cross-check the lists of Entities that could be Reporting Financial Institutions against the list of Entities that register as RFIs to identify Entities that may be incorrectly not registered and reporting to ensure that they have classified themselves correctly and are reporting information as required. The regulatory authorities have procedures in place to monitor and follow up on failures to report and the reasons for nil reporting by Reporting Financial Institutions. Oman intends to keep its understanding of the Financial Institution population up to date on a routine basis.
- The institutions responsible for implementing Oman's compliance strategy appear to have the necessary powers to discharge their functions, although this has not yet been fully tested in practice. With respect to resourcing, the Oman Tax Authority and each of the regulatory authorities have assigned the equivalent of 1-2 full time staff with specified skills and experience to monitor and ensure compliance by Reporting Financial Institutions, which have access to IT systems and tools to conduct risk assessments. Furthermore, the CBO includes some AEOI queries in its AML supervision activities with respect to the Entities it oversees, and there is a formalised arrangement to plan, manage or assess the impact of the activities in the context of the AEOI Standard. Furthermore, based on the risk assessment process and overarching compliance plan developed, the resources allocated appear to be sufficient to ensure the effectiveness of the AEOI Standard.
- It appears that the regulatory authorities have procedures in place to effectively enforce the requirements for regulated Financial Institutions, such as conducting desk-based reviews and onsite reviews, including through the inspection of records of Reporting Financial Institutions and the application of dissuasive penalties or sanctions. In addition to some verification activities carried out on an ad hoc basis, the Omani regulatory authorities plan to verify the full range of due diligence requirements by Reporting Financial Institutions under their respective supervision from 2024. As part of Oman's CRS Administrative Compliance Strategy, clearly defined procedures are in place to ensure that self-certifications are obtained as required.
- It appears that Oman is ready to take effective action to address circumvention of the requirements if such circumvention is detected, although it is only at an initial stage of implementation.
- Oman appears to have clearly defined procedures to follow up with Reporting Financial Institutions when undocumented accounts are reported, although it is at an early stage of implementation.
- It is noted that Oman does not have a jurisdiction-specific list of Non-Reporting Financial Institutions or Excluded Accounts for ongoing monitoring.

Table 3 provides a summary of the specific activities undertaken, or that are planned to be undertaken, in relation to each of the key parts of the framework described above.

Table.6. Activities undertaken

Activity type	Activities undertaken
Communication and outreach	Oman has carried out communication and outreach activities, including continuous dialogue with Financial Institutions via email, phone and the publication of relevant materials and information on the Tax Administration's website, as well as the organisation of webinars, seminars and meetings aimed at improving Financial Institutions' understanding and implementation of the requirements.
Verifying that Financial Institutions are reporting as required	Oman introduced mandatory registration and nil reporting requirements for Reporting Financial Institutions. Oman has also carried out some ad hoc verification activities to ensure that Financial Institutions are reporting as required, including following up with Entities that may be incorrectly not reporting and automated reminders generated through the reporting system. Oman intends to cross-check its list of registered RFIs against the lists of regulated Entities held by other relevant regulatory bodies and the FATCA FFI list. Oman has procedures and plans in place to conduct comprehensive verification activities to ensure that Financial Institutions are reporting as required.
Verifying whether the information reported is complete and accurate	Oman has conducted a desk-based analysis to verify whether the information being reported is complete and accurate, although it is unclear what this analysis consisted of. The CBO has added AEOI queries to its AML checks in relation to the Entities it oversees, and this has recently been formalised. Oman has not yet conducted in-depth audits, but has plans to do so in the near future. It has accordingly not yet identified any issues.
Enforcement	Following the activities mentioned above, Oman has not yet imposed penalties and sanctions but there are clearly defined procedures and plans to do so in the near future.

Oman was not able to confirm that it collects and monitors information on the proportion of Financial Accounts that are reported that include information on the Tax Identification Numbers and dates of birth with respect to the individuals associated with them. These data points are key to exchange partners to effectively utilise the information and are important to developing an effective compliance strategy to ensure the AEOI Standard is being effectively implemented. Oman was not able to confirm that it correctly collects and monitors information on the number of undocumented accounts reported by its Reporting Financial Institutions. This information is crucial to implementing the requirement to follow up on undocumented accounts.

Feedback was also received from Oman's exchange partners indicating that, compared to what they generally experience in relation to the information received from all of their exchange partners, they achieved a relatively low level of success when seeking to match information received from Oman with their taxpayer database. Furthermore, seven exchange partners highlighted issues with respect to the information received such as missing TINs, names and addresses and invalid information. Follow-up discussions confirmed that Oman is aware of these issues and is seeking to improve the situation.

Based on these findings it was concluded that Oman is partially meeting expectations in ensuring that Reporting Financial Institutions correctly conduct the due diligence and reporting procedures, including by having in place the required administrative compliance framework and related procedures. More specifically, significant issues have been identified, including with respect to the implementation of its plans to carry out verification activities to identify non-compliance by Reporting Financial Institutions and the implementation of an effective enforcement framework to address such non-compliance. Oman should therefore continue its implementation process accordingly, including by addressing the recommendations made.

Recommendations:

Oman should implement its plan to monitor and verify compliance and commence its verification activities to ensure that the information reported is complete and accurate, including appropriate verification activities to identify non-compliance in key areas, such as whether Reporting Financial Institutions are obtaining valid self-certifications as required.

Oman should implement its plan to enforce the requirements, including the application of penalties where appropriate.

Oman should implement its plan to follow up with all Reporting Financial Institutions reporting undocumented accounts, including to understand the reasons for it and to ensure that they are correctly applying the definition.

Oman should implement systems to monitor the reporting of Tax Identification Numbers and dates of birth by Reporting Financial Institutions to inform its compliance strategy.

Oman should address the issues raised by its exchange partners.

SR 1.6 Jurisdictions should collaborate on compliance and enforcement. This requires jurisdictions to:

c) use all appropriate measures available under the jurisdiction's domestic law to address errors or non-compliance notified to the jurisdiction by an exchange partner; and

d) have in place effective procedures to notify an exchange partner of errors that may have led to incomplete or incorrect information reporting or non-compliance with the due diligence or reporting procedures by a Reporting Financial Institution in the jurisdiction of the exchange partner.

It should be noted that, as Oman exchanged information on a non-reciprocal basis and did not therefore receive information, it was not required to have in place procedures to notify its exchange partners. SR 1.6 b) has therefore not been assessed in this case.

Findings:

In terms of cooperation on compliance and enforcement, it appears that Oman has not implemented all of the requirements in relation to issues notified to them (i.e. under Section 4 of the MCAA or equivalent) as expected. In particular, Oman received two notifications from its partners in 2023, indicating issues of missing/invalid TINs and DoBs, which it is still in the process of investigating and subsequently providing responses to the partners, due to the ongoing process of rebuilding and upgrading to a new AEOI system in Oman and the inability to access and process the necessary data. There is still no assurance that effective implementation will be ensured.

Based on these findings it was concluded that Oman is fully meeting expectations in relation to collaborating with its exchange partners to ensure that Reporting Financial Institutions correctly conduct the due diligence and reporting procedures. Oman is encouraged to continue its implementation process accordingly, to ensure its ongoing effectiveness.

Recommendations:

Oman should implement its documented procedures and take all appropriate measures to address errors or non-compliance notified by an exchange partner.

CR2 Effectiveness in practice: Jurisdictions should exchange the information effectively in practice, in a timely manner, including by sorting, preparing, validating and transmitting it in accordance with the AEOI Standard.

Rating: Partially Compliant

Oman's implementation of the AEOI Standard is partially compliant with respect to exchanging the information effectively in practice and in a timely manner. More specifically, while Oman appears to be meeting expectations with respect to providing corrections, amendments or additions (SR 2.9), there are significant issues with respect to Oman sorting, preparing and validating the information (SR 2.4) and correctly transmitting the information and in a timely manner (SR.s 2.5 – 2.8). Oman should continue its implementation process to ensure its effectiveness, including by addressing the recommendations made.

SR 2.4 Jurisdictions should sort, prepare and validate the information in accordance with the CRS XML Schema and the associated requirements in the CRS XML Schema User Guide and the File Error and Correction-related validations in the Status Message User Guide (i.e. the 50000 and 80000 range).

Findings:

Feedback from Oman's exchange partners did not raise any specific concerns with respect to their ability to process the information received from Oman and therefore with respect to Oman's implementation of these requirements. More generally, three (or 4.8%) of Oman's exchange partners reported rejecting 50% or more of the files received, due to the technical requirements not being met. This is partially in line with the general experience of other jurisdictions, and the number of files from Oman that were rejected has reduced over time. It was noted that Oman is working to resolve the issues raised, has contacted some of the partners and will contact the remaining ones. Many of the issues are still to be addressed.

Figure.1. Technical issues raised by Oman's exchange partners

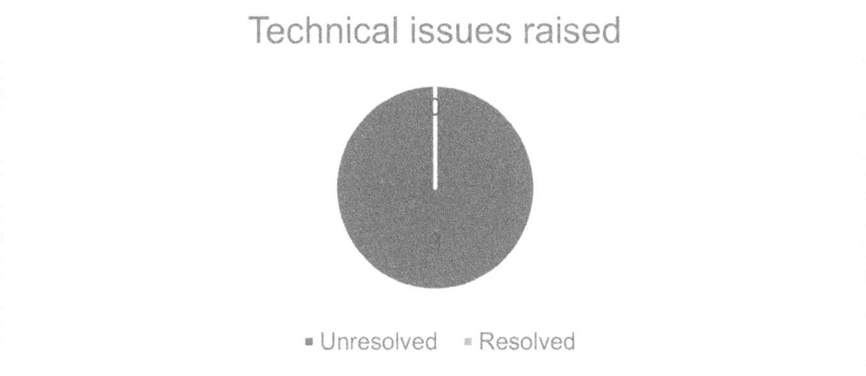

Based on these findings it was concluded that Oman is partially meeting expectations in relation to sorting, preparing and validating the information. However, some issues have been identified, including with respect to working with exchange partners to address the issues raised. Oman should therefore continue its implementation process accordingly, including by addressing the recommendations made.

Recommendations:

Oman should review its systems and procedures to sort, prepare and validate the information to ensure they meet the requirements of the AEOI Standard.

Oman should continue to work with its exchange partners to address the issues raised.

SR 2.5 Jurisdictions should agree and use, with each exchange partner, transmission methods that meet appropriate minimum standards to ensure the confidentiality and integrity of the data throughout the transmission, including its encryption to a minimum secure standard.

Findings:

In order to put in place an agreed transmission method that meets appropriate minimum standards in confidentiality, integrity of the data and encryption for use with each of its exchange partners, Oman linked to the Common Transmission System.

Based on these findings it was concluded that Oman is fully meeting expectations in relation to agreeing and using appropriate transmission methods with each of its partners. Oman is encouraged to continue to ensure the ongoing effectiveness of its implementation.

Recommendations:

No recommendations made.

SR 2.6 Jurisdictions should carry out all exchanges annually within nine months of the end of the calendar year to which the information relates.

Findings:

Two exchange partners highlighted delays in the sending of information by Oman (representing 3.2% of its partners). This represents a relatively high proportion of exchange partners, although the overall timeliness of the exchanges by Oman has improved over time. Furthermore, all these partners stated that the information has still not been received.

Based on these findings it was concluded that Oman is partially meeting expectations in relation to exchanging the information in a timely manner. More specifically, significant issues have been identified, including with respect to sending information on time. Oman should continue its implementation process to ensure its effectiveness, including by addressing the recommendation made.

Recommendations:

Oman should ensure it sends information to all of its exchange partners in a timely manner.

SR 2.7 Jurisdictions should send the information in accordance with the agreed transmission methods and encryption standards.

Findings:

Feedback from Oman's exchange partners did not raise any concerns with respect to Oman's use of the agreed transmission methods and therefore with Oman's implementation of this requirement.

Based on these findings it was concluded that Oman is fully meeting expectations in relation to sending the information in accordance with the agreed transmission methods and encryption standards. Oman is encouraged to continue to ensure the ongoing effectiveness of its implementation.

Recommendations:

No recommendations made.

SR 2.8 Jurisdictions should have the systems in place to receive information and, once it has been received, should send a status message to the sending jurisdictions in accordance with the CRS Status Message XML Schema and the related User Guide.

Findings:

It should be noted that, as Oman exchanged information on a non-reciprocal basis and did not receive information, it was not required to have in place systems to receive the information and provide status messages. SR 2.8 has therefore not been assessed in this case.

Recommendations:

No recommendations made.

SR 2.9 Jurisdictions should respond to a notification from an exchange partner as referred to in Section 4 of the Model CAA (which may include Status Messages) in accordance with the timelines set out in the Commentary to Section 4 of the Model CAA. In all other cases, jurisdictions should send corrected, amended or additional information received from a Reporting Financial Institution as soon as possible after it has been received.

Findings:

While Oman has procedures in place to address notifications received from partners, to date it has not yet resolved two notifications received from its exchange partners in 2023 due to the ongoing process of rebuilding and upgrading to a new AEOI system in Oman and the inability to access and process the necessary data, although Oman stated that it provides updates to exchange partners every 90 days. It therefore appears that Oman's approach does not ensure that corrected, amended or additional information is provided in a timely manner.

Based on these findings it was concluded that Oman is not meeting expectations in relation to responding to notifications from exchange partners and the sending of corrected, amended or additional information. Oman is encouraged to continue to ensure the ongoing effectiveness of its implementation, including by addressing the recommendation made.

Recommendations:

Oman should implement procedures to effectively respond to partners when they notify Oman of errors or suspected non-compliance by its Reporting Financial Institutions.

Assessed jurisdiction's comments on the assessment of effectiveness in practice

No comments made.

Peru

This report analyses the implementation of the AEOI Standard in Peru with respect to the requirements of the AEOI Terms of Reference. It assesses both the legal frameworks put in place to implement the AEOI Standard and the effectiveness of the implementation of the AEOI Standard in practice.

The methodology used for the peer reviews and that therefore underpins this report is outlined in Chapter 2.

Overall findings

AEOI legal framework

Peru's legal framework implementing the AEOI Standard is in place but needs improvement in order to be fully consistent with the requirements of the AEOI Terms of Reference. While Peru's international legal framework to exchange the information with all of Peru's Interested Appropriate Partners (CR2) is consistent with the requirements, its domestic legislative framework requiring Reporting Financial Institutions to conduct the due diligence and reporting procedures (CR1) has deficiencies significant to the proper functioning of elements of the AEOI Standard. More specifically, deficiencies have been identified in relation to the scope of Reporting Financial Institutions and Financial Accounts and there are deficiencies in the enforcement framework.

Overall determination on the legal framework: In Place But **Needs Improvement**

Effectiveness of AEOI in practice

Peru's implementation of the AEOI Standard is on track with respect to the requirements of the AEOI Terms of Reference to ensure the effectiveness of the AEOI Standard in practice. This includes ensuring Reporting Financial Institutions correctly conduct the due diligence and reporting procedures (CR1) and exchanging the information in an effective and timely manner (CR2). Peru is encouraged to continue its implementation process accordingly, to ensure its ongoing effectiveness.

Overall rating in relation to the effectiveness in practice: On Track

General context

Peru commenced exchanges under the AEOI Standard in 2020.

In order to provide for Reporting Financial Institutions to collect and report the information to be exchanged, Peru:

- relies on Article 87(7), Article 175(7 and 8) and Article 177(2, 3, 15, 27 and 28) of the Tax Code;
- relies on Articles 427 and 438 of the Criminal Code; and
- enacted Supreme Decree 256-2018-EF (Regulation establishing the financial information that shall be provided to SUNAT to conduct the automatic Exchange of information as set forth in international agreements and the Decisions of the Andean Community Commission).

Under this framework Reporting Financial Institutions were required to commence the due diligence procedures in relation to New Accounts from 1 January 2019. With respect to Preexisting Accounts, Reporting Financial Institutions were required to complete the due diligence procedures on High-Value

Individual Accounts by 31 December 2019 and on Preexisting Lower Value Individual Accounts and Entity Accounts by 31 December 2020.

With respect to the exchange of the information under the AEOI Standard, Peru is a Party to the Convention on Mutual Administrative Assistance in Tax Matters and activated the associated CRS Multilateral Competent Authority Agreement in time for exchanges in 2020.

Table 1 sets out the number of Financial Institutions in Peru that reported information on Financial Accounts in 2023 as defined in the AEOI Standard (essentially because they maintained Financial Accounts for Account Holders, or relating to Controlling Persons, resident in a Reportable Jurisdiction). It also sets out the number of Financial Accounts that they reported in 2023. In this regard, it should be noted that Peru requires the reporting of Financial Accounts based on a prescribed list of exchange partners and some accounts may be required to be reported more than once (e.g. jointly held accounts or accounts with multiple related Controlling Persons), which is reflected in the figures below. These figures provide key contextual information to the development and implementation of Peru's administrative compliance strategy, which is analysed in the subsequent sections of this report.

Table.7. Number of Financial Institutions reporting and Financial Accounts reported

	Number
Number of Financial Institutions reporting Financial Accounts in 2023	140
Number of Financial Accounts reported in 2023	22 750

Table 2 sets out the number of exchange partners to which information was successfully sent by Peru in the past few years (including where the necessary frameworks were in place, containing an obligation on Reporting Financial Institutions to report information, but no relevant Reportable Accounts were identified). These figures provide key contextual information in relation to Peru's exchanges in practice, which is also analysed in subsequent sections of this report.

Table.8. Number of exchange partners to which information was successfully sent

	2021	2022	2023
Number of exchange partners to which information was successfully sent	45	61	73

In order to provide for the effective implementation of the AEOI Standard, in Peru:

- the *Superintendencia Nacional de Aduanas y de Administración Tributaria* (SUNAT, the tax authority) has the responsibility to ensure the effective implementation of the due diligence and reporting obligations by Reporting Financial Institutions and for exchanging the information with Peru's exchange partners;
- technical solutions necessary to receive and validate the information reported by Reporting Financial Institutions were put in place through the Integral System of Reception and Automatic Exchange of Information, which is based on the Multiple Data Exchange Solution (MDES) and allows for validation of the data received from Reporting Financial Institutions; and
- the Common Transmission System (CTS) is used for the exchange of the information, along with the associated file preparation and encryption requirements.

It should be noted that the review of Peru's legal frameworks implementing the AEOI Standard concluded with the determination that Peru's domestic legal framework is In Place But Needs Improvement and its international legal framework is In Place. This has been taken into account when reviewing the effectiveness of Peru's implementation of the AEOI Standard in practice and where particular identified gaps in Peru's legal frameworks directly impact its implementation in practice, these are mentioned below.

Findings and conclusions on the legal frameworks

The detailed findings and conclusions on the AEOI legal frameworks for Peru are below, organised per Core Requirement (CR) and sub-requirement (SR), as extracted from the AEOI Terms of Reference (see Annex C).

CR1 Domestic legal framework: Jurisdictions should have a domestic legislative framework in place that requires all Reporting Financial Institutions to conduct the due diligence and reporting procedures in the CRS, and that provides for the effective implementation of the CRS as set out therein.

Determination: In Place But **Needs Improvement**

Peru's domestic legislative framework is in place and contains most of the key aspects of the CRS and its Commentary requiring Reporting Financial Institutions to conduct the due diligence and reporting procedures, but it needs improvement in relation to the scope of Reporting Financial Institutions required to report information (SR 1.1), the scope of Financial Accounts required to be reported (SR 1.2) and the framework to enforce the requirements (SR 1.4). Most significantly, Peru's legislative framework does not define Financial Institutions in accordance with the AEOI Standard nor does it contain rules to prevent practices intended to circumvent the reporting and due diligence procedures as required.

SR 1.1 Jurisdictions should define the scope of Reporting Financial Institutions consistently with the CRS.

Peru has defined the scope of Reporting Financial Institutions in its domestic legislative framework in a manner that is largely consistent with the CRS and its Commentary. However, a deficiency has been identified. More specifically, Peru has defined Financial Institutions with reference to entities described in other financial law, which will include entities that are not Financial Institutions under the AEOI Standard. The scope of Reporting Financial Institutions is material to the proper functioning of the AEOI Standard.

Recommendations:

Peru should amend its domestic legislative framework to ensure that the meaning of "Custodial Institution", "Investment Entity" and "Specified Insurance Company" are defined in line with the AEOI Standard.

SR 1.2 Jurisdictions should define the scope of Financial Accounts and Reportable Accounts consistently with the CRS and incorporate the due diligence procedures to identify them.

Peru has defined the Financial Accounts that are required to be reported in its domestic legislative framework and incorporated the due diligence procedures that must be applied to identify them in a manner that is largely consistent with the CRS and its Commentary. However, deficiencies have been identified. More significantly, Peru's legislative framework:

- does not limit the use of a mailing address when applying the residence address test only to the special circumstances as contemplated in the Commentary; and
- does not define annuity contracts in line with the AEOI Standard.

The scope of Financial Accounts and the due diligence procedures are material to the proper functioning of the AEOI Standard.

Recommendations:

Peru should amend its domestic legislative framework to ensure that a mailing address is only permitted to be used in the special circumstances permitted under the AEOI Standard.

Peru should amend its domestic legislative framework to ensure that the exclusion of retirement income contracts from the definition of annuity contract is in line with the AEOI Standard.

SR 1.3 Jurisdictions should incorporate the reporting requirements contained in Section I of the CRS into their domestic legislative framework.

Peru has incorporated the reporting requirements in its domestic legislative framework in accordance with the CRS and its Commentary.

Recommendations:

No recommendations made.

SR 1.4 Jurisdictions should have a legislative framework in place that allows for the enforcement of the requirements of the CRS in practice.

Peru has a legislative framework in place to enforce the requirements in a manner that is largely consistent with the CRS and its Commentary. However, deficiencies have been identified. More specifically, Peru's legislative framework:

- does not include rules to prevent all relevant persons (including Reporting Financial Institutions, other persons and intermediaries) from adopting any practices intended to circumvent the reporting and due diligence procedures as required; and
- does not impose sanctions on Account Holders and Controlling Persons for the provision of a false self-certification.

These are the key elements of the required enforcement framework relates to and are therefore material to the proper functioning of the AEOI Standard.

Recommendations:

Peru should amend its domestic legislative framework to introduce rules to prevent Financial Institutions, persons and intermediaries from adopting practices intended to circumvent the due diligence and reporting procedures.

Peru should amend its domestic legislative framework to include sanctions on Account Holders and Controlling Persons for the provision of a false self-certification.

CR2 International legal framework: Jurisdictions should have exchange relationships in effect with all Interested Appropriate Partners as committed to and that provide for the exchange of information in accordance with the Model CAA.

Determination: In Place

Peru's international legal framework to exchange the information is **in place**, is consistent with the Model CAA and its Commentary and provides for exchange with all of Peru's Interested Appropriate Partners (i.e. all jurisdictions that are interested in receiving information from Peru and that meet the required standard in relation to confidentiality and data safeguards) (SRs 2.1 – 2.3).

SR 2.1 Jurisdictions should have exchange agreements in effect with all Interested Appropriate Partners that permit the automatic exchange of CRS information.

Peru has exchange agreements that permit the automatic exchange of CRS information in effect with all its Interested Appropriate Partners.

Recommendations:

No recommendations made.

SR 2.2 Such an exchange agreement should be put in place without undue delay, following the receipt of an expression of interest from an Interested Appropriate Partner.

Peru put in place its exchange agreements without undue delay.

Recommendations:

No recommendations made.

SR 2.3 Jurisdictions should ensure that the exchange agreements in effect provide for the exchange of information in accordance with the requirements of the Model CAA.

Peru's exchange agreements provide for the exchange of information in accordance with the requirements of the Model CAA.

Recommendations:

No recommendations made.

Assessed jurisdiction's comments on the assessment of its legal frameworks

Please note that Peru has introduced amended Supreme Decree N° 256-2018-EF by means of Supreme Decree N° 139-2024-EF in order to remedy the deficiencies identified in the AEOI peer review related with sub requirements 1.1 and 1.2.

Findings and conclusions in relation to effectiveness in practice

The following table contains the detailed findings for Peru, organised per Core Requirement (CR) and then per sub-requirement (SR) as extracted from the AEOI Terms of Reference.

CR1 Effectiveness in practice: Jurisdictions should ensure that in practice Reporting Financial Institutions correctly implement the due diligence and reporting procedures, which includes a requirement for jurisdictions to have in place an administrative framework to ensure the effective implementation of the CRS.

Rating: On Track

Peru's implementation of the AEOI Standard is on track with respect to ensuring that Reporting Financial Institutions are correctly conducting the due diligence and reporting procedures and are therefore reporting complete and accurate information. This includes ensuring effectiveness in a domestic context, such as through having an effective administrative compliance framework and related procedures (SR 1.5), and collaborating with exchange partners to ensure effectiveness (SR 1.6). Peru is encouraged to continue its implementation process to ensure its ongoing effectiveness.

SR 1.5 Jurisdictions should ensure that in practice Reporting Financial Institutions identify the Financial Accounts they maintain, identify the Reportable Accounts among those Financial Accounts, as well as their Account Holders, and where relevant Controlling Persons, by correctly conducting the due diligence procedures and collect and report the required information with respect to each Reportable Account. This includes having in place:

a) an effective administrative compliance framework to ensure the effective implementation of, and compliance with, the CRS. This framework should:

    i. be based on a strategy that facilitates compliance by Reporting Financial Institutions and which is informed by a risk assessment in respect of the effective implementation of the CRS that takes into account relevant information sources (including third party sources);

    ii. include procedures to ensure that Financial Institutions correctly apply the definitions of Reporting Financial Institutions and Non-Reporting Financial Institutions;

    iii. include procedures to periodically verify Reporting Financial Institutions' compliance, conducted by authorities that have adequate powers with respect to the reviewed Reporting Financial Institutions, with procedures to access the records they maintain; and

b) effective procedures to ensure that Financial Institutions, persons or intermediaries do not circumvent the due diligence and reporting procedures;

c) effective enforcement mechanisms to address non-compliance by Reporting Financial Institutions;

d) strong measures to ensure that valid self-certifications are always obtained for New Accounts;

e) effective procedures to ensure that each, or each type of, jurisdiction-specific Non-Reporting Financial Institution and Excluded Account continue to present a low risk of being used to evade tax; and

f) effective procedures to follow up with a Reporting Financial Institution when undocumented accounts are reported in order to establish the reasons why such information is being reported.

Findings:

In order to ensure that Reporting Financial Institutions correctly conduct the due diligence and reporting procedures, Peru implemented most of the requirements in accordance with expectations. The key findings were as follows:

- Peru implemented an overarching strategy to ensure compliance with the AEOI Standard and has conducted a risk assessment that took into account a range of relevant information sources, such as the type and size of the RFIs, information from the AML regulator, compliance behaviour for domestic tax purposes regimes, as well as an analysis of the information reported under the AEOI Standard. Peru's compliance strategy facilitates compliance and incorporates a credible approach to enforcement. Peru intends to keep its compliance strategy and risk assessment under review to ensure its effectiveness on an ongoing basis.
- Peru has taken action to understand its population of Reporting Financial Institutions utilising relevant information sources such as the list of companies with reporting obligations to the SUNAT (e.g. the Financial Information Report, by which all financial accounts opened in Peru are required to be declared and reporting in relation to withholding tax obligations on mutual funds, investment funds and *fideicomisos*), information from the Financial Intelligence Unit (FIU), from the tax databases and from industry associations, information on the companies regulated by the Superintendency of Banks, Insurance and Private Pension Funds, and the list of Foreign Financial Institutions for FATCA purposes. Peru is taking action to ensure that Reporting Financial Institutions identified are classifying themselves correctly under its domestic rules and ensuring that they report information as required. Peru intends to keep its understanding of its Financial Institution population up to date on a routine basis.
- The SUNAT, the institution responsible for implementing Peru's compliance strategy, appears to have the necessary powers and resources to discharge its functions. With respect to resourcing, Peru has assigned twelve staff to monitor and ensure compliance by Reporting Financial Institutions, to conduct risk assessment as well as to receive information from RFIs and subsequently exchanging it with exchange partners, which have

access to IT systems and tools to carry out their functions. The staff are only allocated full time to AEOI-related tasks on reporting/exchange period. Overall, they appear to have effectively started to implement an operational plan to verify compliance with the requirements, incorporating appropriate compliance activities.

- Peru has started conducting some compliance activities based on a risk-based approach, in particular desk-based reviews, which can include the inspection of records held by Reporting Financial Institutions. So far, the reviews have led to the identification of several Reportable Accounts for which information was not reported or for which information was incorrectly reported. Peru is also planning to expand its in-depth verification activities through carrying out onsite audits in the near future.
- Peru has defined procedures to ensure self-certifications are obtained as required, although has not yet begun to implement them. Peru follows up on undocumented accounts when they are reported.
- Peru has developed and documented procedures to enforce the requirements, including the application of penalties and sanctions for non-compliance when it is identified. It has imposed sanctions on Reporting Financial Institutions that have failed to report on time.
- Peru does not yet have a complete plan to take action to address circumvention of the requirements when such circumvention is detected, although it is taking steps to develop such plan. This reflects its lack of a legal basis to do so, although it is noted that such cases have not yet been identified. Peru is working to implement an anti-avoidance rule applicable to the AEOI Standard.
- It is noted that Peru does not have a jurisdiction-specific list of Non-Reporting Financial Institutions or Excluded Accounts for ongoing monitoring.

Table 3 provides a summary of the specific activities undertaken, or that are planned to be undertaken, in relation to each of the key parts of the framework described above.

Table.9. Activities undertaken

Activity type	Activities undertaken
Communication and outreach	Peru has carried out substantial communication and outreach activities, such as meetings held by the SUNAT with the financial sector, the creation of dedicated email addresses to receive queries from Financial Institutions, the publication of guidance and other types of communications on the SUNAT's webpage and social media accounts to assist Financial Institutions with their obligations under the AEOI Standard.
Verifying that Financial Institutions are reporting as required	Peru has carried out substantial verification activities to ensure that Financial Institutions are reporting as required, such as requiring nil returns, cross-checking relevant information sources, carrying out communicational campaigns and engaging with the Reporting Financial Institutions that had not reported. Peru identified many Financial Institutions incorrectly not reporting and it is following up on these issues with a view to ensuring future compliance.
Verifying whether the information reported is complete and accurate	Peru has started conducting desk-based checks to verify whether the information being reported is complete and accurate, which can include the review of the underlying documentation. It accordingly identified many issues, commonly concerning Reportable Accounts not being reported and accounts reported with issues on TINs and/or DoBs. It is following up on these issues with a view to ensuring future compliance. Although Peru has not yet conducted in-depth audits/onsite visits, it plans to do so in the near future.
Enforcement	Peru has imposed some penalties and sanctions, mainly for Reporting Financial Institutions not reporting information or reporting information with a delay. It is monitoring the impact of these penalties and sanctions with a view to ensuring future compliance. Peru is also reviewing the cases where Reportable Accounts were not reported and where incorrect information was reported to identify suitable enforcement measures.

With respect to the Financial Account information collected and exchanged by Peru, the presence of the key data points of Tax Identification Numbers and the level of undocumented accounts appeared to be in line with most other jurisdictions.

While the collection and reporting of dates of birth is generally higher across jurisdictions, Peru nevertheless reported a much lower rate of collection of dates of birth when compared to other jurisdictions. This is a key data point for exchange partners to effectively utilise the information. Follow-up discussions confirmed that Peru is aware of these issues and is taking steps to address them.

Feedback from Peru's exchange partners indicated that, compared to what they generally experience when seeking to match information received from their exchange partners with their taxpayer database, they achieved a relatively lower level of success when seeking to match information received from Peru. Furthermore, one exchange partner highlighted an issue with respect to the information received related to an abnormal variance in the balance of an account, which was communicated informally to Peru. Follow-up discussions confirmed that Peru is aware of these issues and is seeking to improve the situation.

Based on these findings it was concluded that, overall, Peru is meeting expectations in ensuring that Reporting Financial Institutions correctly conduct the due diligence and reporting procedures, including by having in place the required administrative compliance framework and related procedures. It was also noted that there is room for improvement with respect to the full implementation of the compliance strategy, including in-depth reviews and the review of self-certifications. Peru is therefore encouraged to continue its implementation process accordingly, including by addressing the recommendations made.

Recommendations:

Peru should continue to implement and expand its activities to verify that Reporting Financial Institutions are correctly conducting their due diligence and reporting obligations, specifically including in-depth reviews.

Peru should put in place a clearly defined policy to ensure that, where circumvention of the AEOI Standard is identified, action is taken to address it. Reference is made to the recommendation made when assessing Peru's legal frameworks implementing the AEOI Standard.

Peru should implement its plans to monitor and verify whether Reporting Financial Institutions are obtaining valid self-certifications as required.

SR 1.6 Jurisdictions should collaborate on compliance and enforcement. This requires jurisdictions to:

a) use all appropriate measures available under the jurisdiction's domestic law to address errors or non-compliance notified to the jurisdiction by an exchange partner; and

b) have in place effective procedures to notify an exchange partner of errors that may have led to incomplete or incorrect information reporting or non-compliance with the due diligence or reporting procedures by a Reporting Financial Institution in the jurisdiction of the exchange partner.

Findings:

In order to collaborate on compliance and enforcement, it appears that Peru implemented all of the requirements in relation to issues notified to them (i.e. under Section 4 of the MCAA or equivalent) in accordance with expectations. While no such notifications have yet been received, Peru has the necessary systems and procedures to process them as required. It also appears that Peru will notify its partners effectively of errors or suspected non-compliance it identified when utilising the information received.

Based on these findings it was concluded that Peru is fully meeting expectations in relation to collaborating with its exchange partners to ensure that Reporting Financial Institutions correctly conduct the due diligence and reporting procedures. Peru is encouraged to continue its implementation process accordingly, to ensure its ongoing effectiveness.

Recommendations:

No recommendations made.

CR2 Effectiveness in practice: Jurisdictions should exchange the information effectively in practice, in a timely manner, including by sorting, preparing, validating and transmitting it in accordance with the AEOI Standard

Rating: On Track

Peru's implementation of the AEOI Standard is on track with respect to exchanging the information effectively in practice, including in relation to correctly transmitting the information in a timely manner (SRs 2.5 – 2.8) and providing corrections, amendments or additions to the information (SR 2.9). However, some issues were found with respect to sorting, preparing and validating the information (SR 2.4). Peru is encouraged to continue its implementation process accordingly, to ensure its ongoing effectiveness.

SR 2.4 Jurisdictions should sort, prepare and validate the information in accordance with the CRS XML Schema and the associated requirements in the CRS XML Schema User Guide and the File Error and Correction-related validations in the Status Message User Guide (i.e. the 50000 and 80000 range).

Findings:

13 exchange partners highlighted particular issues with respect to preparation and format of the information sent by Peru (representing 17% of its partners). These generally related to particular file errors, e.g. errors when identifying resent files. More generally, 11 (or 14.5%) of Peru's exchange partners reported rejecting 25% or more of the files received, of which 3 (or 4%) reported rejecting more than 50% of files received, due to the technical requirements not being met. This is a relatively very high amount when compared to other jurisdictions and it has not improved over time. It was noted that Peru has already successfully addressed all of the issues.

Figure.2. Technical issues raised by Peru's exchange partners

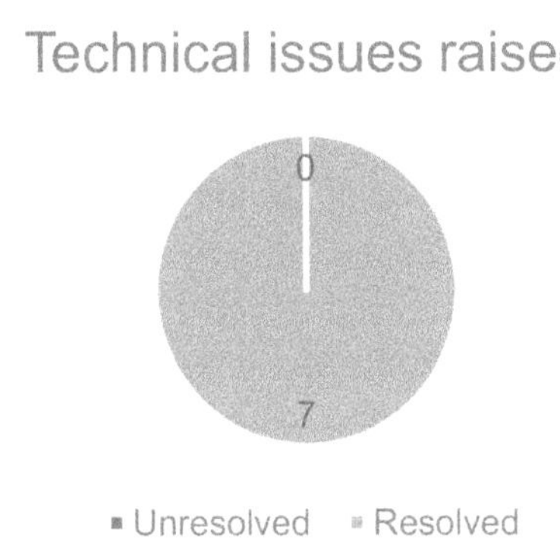

Based on these findings it was concluded that, overall, Peru is meeting expectations in relation to sorting, preparing and validating the information. It was also noted that there is room for improvement with respect to validation and preparation of files before they are sent. Peru is therefore encouraged to continue its implementation process accordingly, including in relation to the areas highlighted.

Recommendations:

Peru should review its systems and procedures for sorting, preparing and validating the information to send to its exchange partners, to ensure they meet the requirements of the AEOI Standard.

SR 2.5 Jurisdictions should agree and use, with each exchange partner, transmission methods that meet appropriate minimum standards to ensure the confidentiality and integrity of the data throughout the transmission, including its encryption to a minimum secure standard.

Findings:

In order to put in place an agreed transmission method that meets appropriate minimum standards in confidentiality, integrity of the data and encryption for use with each of its exchange partners, Peru linked to the CTS.

Based on these findings it was concluded that Peru is fully meeting expectations in relation to agreeing and using appropriate transmission methods with each of its partners. Peru is encouraged to continue to ensure the ongoing effectiveness of its implementation.

Recommendations:

No recommendations made.

SR 2.6 Jurisdictions should carry out all exchanges annually within nine months of the end of the calendar year to which the information relates.

Findings:

Feedback from Peru's exchange partners did not raise any concerns with respect to timeliness of the exchanges by Peru and therefore with respect to Peru's implementation of this requirement.

Based on these findings it was concluded that Peru is fully meeting expectations in relation to exchanging the information in a timely manner. Peru is encouraged to continue to ensure the ongoing effectiveness of its implementation.

Recommendations:

No recommendations made.

SR 2.7 Jurisdictions should send the information in accordance with the agreed transmission methods and encryption standards.

Findings:

Feedback from Peru's exchange partners did not raise any concerns with respect to Peru's use of the agreed transmission methods and therefore with Peru's implementation of this requirement.

Based on these findings it was concluded that Peru is fully meeting expectations in relation to sending the information in accordance with the agreed transmission methods and encryption standards. Peru is encouraged to continue to ensure the ongoing effectiveness of its implementation.

Recommendations:

No recommendations made.

SR 2.8 Jurisdictions should have the systems in place to receive information and, once it has been received, should send a status message to the sending jurisdictions in accordance with the CRS Status Message XML Schema and the related User Guide.

Findings:

12 exchange partners highlighted delays in the sending of status messages by Peru, representing 12.5% of its partners. This represents a very high proportion of partners and has not improved over time. It was noted that Peru successfully addressed all of the issues and sent the status messages to its exchange partners.

Based on these findings it was concluded that, overall, Peru is meeting expectations in relation to the receipt of the information. It was also noted that there is room for improvement with respect to sending status messages to partner jurisdictions in a timely manner. Peru is encouraged to continue to ensure the ongoing effectiveness of its implementation, including in relation to the area highlighted.

Recommendations:

Peru should ensure it sends status messages to all of its exchange partners in a timely manner.

SR 2.9 Jurisdictions should respond to a notification from an exchange partner as referred to in Section 4 of the Model CAA (which may include Status Messages) in accordance with the timelines set out in the Commentary to Section 4 of the Model CAA. In all other cases, jurisdictions should send corrected, amended or additional information received from a Reporting Financial Institution as soon as possible after it has been received.

Findings:

Peru appears ready to respond to notifications and to provided corrected, amended or additional information in a timely manner and no such concerns were raised by Peru's exchange partners and therefore with respect to Peru's implementation of these requirements.

Based on these findings it was concluded that Peru appears to be meeting expectations in relation to responding to notifications from exchange partners and the sending of corrected, amended or additional information. Peru is encouraged to continue to ensure the ongoing effectiveness of its implementation.

Recommendations:

No recommendations made.

Comments by the assessed jurisdiction

No comments made.

Poland

Overall findings

Poland's legal framework implementing the AEOI Standard is in place but needs improvement in order to be fully consistent with the requirements of the AEOI Terms of Reference. While Poland's international legal framework to exchange the information with all of Poland's Interested Appropriate Partners (CR2) is consistent with the requirements, its domestic legislative framework requiring Reporting Financial Institutions to conduct the due diligence and reporting procedures (CR1) has deficiencies affecting the proper functioning of elements of the AEOI Standard. Most significantly, Poland's legislative framework does not define the scope of Reporting Financial Institutions in line with the requirements.

The methodology used for the peer reviews and that therefore underpins this report is outlined in Chapter 2.

Overall determination on the legal framework: In Place But **Needs Improvement**

Conclusions on the legal framework

General context

Poland commenced exchanges under the AEOI Standard in 2017.

In order to provide for Reporting Financial Institutions to collect and report the information to be exchanged, Poland:

- enacted the Act of March 9, 2017 on exchange of tax information with other countries; and
- made reference to the Act of November 16, 2000 on countering money laundering and terrorism financing for the purposes of the identification of Controlling Persons under the AEOI Standard.

Under this framework Reporting Financial Institutions were required to commence the due diligence procedures in relation to New Accounts from 1 January 2016. With respect to Preexisting Accounts, Reporting Financial Institutions were required to complete the due diligence procedures on High Value Individual Accounts by 31 December 2017 and on Lower Value Individual Accounts and Entity Accounts by 31 December 2018.

With respect to the exchange of information under the AEOI Standard, Poland:

- is a Party to the Convention on Mutual Administrative Assistance in Tax Matters and activated the associated CRS Multilateral Competent Authority Agreement in time for exchanges in 2017;
- has in place European Directive 2011/16/EU on Administrative Cooperation in the Field of Taxation as amended by Directive 2014/107/EU; and
- has in place European Union agreements with five European third countries.[1]

Detailed findings

The detailed findings for Poland are below, organised per Core Requirement (CR) and sub-requirement (SR), as extracted from the AEOI Terms of Reference (see Annex B).

CR1 Domestic legal framework: Jurisdictions should have a domestic legislative framework in place that requires all Reporting Financial Institutions to conduct the due diligence and reporting procedures in the CRS, and that provides for the effective implementation of the CRS as set out therein.

Determination: In Place But **Needs Improvement**

Poland's domestic legislative framework is in place and contains most of the key aspects of the CRS and its Commentary requiring Reporting Financial Institutions to conduct the due diligence and reporting procedures, but it needs improvement in relation to the scope of Reporting Financial Institutions required to report information (SR 1.1) the due diligence procedures to be applied (SR 1.2), and the framework to enforce the requirements (SR1.4). Most significantly, Poland's legislative framework does not fully define Investment Entities in accordance with the requirements.

SR 1.1 Jurisdictions should define the scope of Reporting Financial Institutions consistently with the CRS.

Poland has defined the scope of Reporting Financial Institutions in its domestic legislative framework in a manner that is largely consistent with the CRS and its Commentary. However, a deficiency has been identified. More specifically, while Poland's legislative framework has the required definition of Investment Entity, it does not include in binding law a requirement that the definition be interpreted consistently with the similar language defining "financial institution" in the Financial Action Task Force Recommendations. This is a key element to the definition of Reporting Financial Institution and is therefore material to the proper functioning of the AEOI Standard.

Recommendations:

Poland should amend its domestic legislative framework to require the term Investment Entity to be interpreted consistently with the language defining "financial institution" in the Financial Action Task Force Recommendation, although it is noted that the non-binding Explanatory Memorandum instructs that the interpretation of the Act be commensurate with the Commentary.

SR 1.2 Jurisdictions should define the scope of Financial Accounts and Reportable Accounts consistently with the CRS and incorporate the due diligence procedures to identify them.

Poland has defined the scope of the Financial Accounts that are required to be reported in its domestic legislative framework and incorporated the due diligence procedures that must be applied to identify them in accordance with the CRS and its Commentary. While a deficiency has been identified concerning New Accounts opened during a transitory period, as alternative procedures were required and as the transitional period ended in on 30 April 2017, this is considered to be relatively minor and its impact not to be material.

Recommendations:

Poland should ensure that New Accounts opened during the transitory period of 1 January 2016 to 30 April 2017 are subjected to due diligence procedures that are in accordance with the AEOI Standard.

SR 1.3 Jurisdictions should incorporate the reporting requirements contained in Section I of the CRS into their domestic legislative framework.

Poland has incorporated the reporting requirements in its domestic legislative framework in accordance with the CRS and its Commentary.

Recommendations:

No recommendations made.

SR 1.4 Jurisdictions should have a legislative framework in place that allows for the enforcement of the requirements of the CRS in practice.

Poland has a legislative framework in place to enforce the requirements in a manner that is largely consistent with the CRS and its Commentary. While a deficiency has been identified with respect to a lack of an explicit legal basis to enforce a sanction where a Reporting Financial Institution is a legal arrangement, it is considered relatively minor and does not materially undermine the implementation of SR 1.4. This is because such Reporting Financial Institutions have so far not been known to exist in Poland and are considered unlikely to exist under Poland's financial and legal frameworks.

Recommendations:

Poland should amend its domestic legislative framework to ensure that it is able to sanction noncompliance by a Reporting Financial Institution that is a legal arrangement.

CR2 International legal framework: Jurisdictions should have exchange relationships in effect with all Interested Appropriate Partners as committed to and that provide for the exchange of information in accordance with the Model CAA.

Determination: In Place

Poland's international legal framework to exchange the information is in place, is consistent with the Model CAA and its Commentary and provides for exchange with all of Poland's Interested Appropriate Partners (i.e. all jurisdictions that are interested in receiving information from Poland and that meet the required standard in relation to confidentiality and data safeguards) (SRs 2.1 – 2.3).

SR 2.1 Jurisdictions should have exchange agreements in effect with all Interested Appropriate Partners that permit the automatic exchange of CRS information.

Poland has exchange agreements that permit the automatic exchange of CRS information in effect with all its Interested Appropriate Partners.

Recommendations:

No recommendations made.

SR 2.2 Such an exchange agreement should be put in place without undue delay, following the receipt of an expression of interest from an Interested Appropriate Partner.

Poland put in place its exchange agreements without undue delay.

Recommendations:

No recommendations made.

SR 2.3 Jurisdictions should ensure that the exchange agreements in effect provide for the exchange of information in accordance with the requirements of the Model CAA.

Poland's exchange agreements provide for the exchange of information in accordance with the requirements of the Model CAA.

Recommendations:

No recommendations made.

Comments by the assessed jurisdiction

No comments made.

Note

[1] Andorra, Liechtenstein, Monaco, San Marino and Switzerland.

Portugal

Overall findings

Portugal's legal framework implementing the AEOI Standard is in place but needs improvement in order to be fully consistent with the requirements of the AEOI Terms of Reference. While Portugal's international legal framework to exchange the information with all of Portugal's Interested Appropriate Partners (CR2) is consistent with the requirements, its domestic legislative framework requiring Reporting Financial Institutions to conduct the due diligence and reporting procedures (CR1) has a deficiency significant to the proper functioning of elements of the AEOI Standard. More specifically, the deficiency relates to the approach to non-Participating Jurisdictions.

The methodology used for the peer reviews and that therefore underpins this report is outlined in Chapter 2.

Overall determination on the legal framework: In Place But **Needs Improvement**

Conclusions on the legal framework

General context

Portugal commenced exchanges under the AEOI Standard in 2017.

In order to provide for Reporting Financial Institutions to collect and report the information to be exchanged, Portugal:

- enacted Decree-Law No. 64/2016, of 11 October (as amended by Decree-Law No. 83/2017); and
- introduced several Ministerial Orders.

Under this framework Reporting Financial Institutions were required to commence the due diligence procedures in relation to New Accounts from 1 January 2016. With respect to Preexisting Accounts, Reporting Financial Institutions were required to complete the due diligence procedures on High Value Individual Accounts by 31 December 2016 and on Lower Value Individual Accounts and Entity Accounts by 31 December 2017.

With respect to the exchange of information under the AEOI Standard, Portugal:

- is a Party to the Convention on Mutual Administrative Assistance in Tax Matters and activated the associated CRS Multilateral Competent Authority Agreement in time for exchanges in 2017;
- has in place European Directive 2011/16/EU on Administrative Cooperation in the Field of Taxation as amended by Directive 2014/107/EU;
- has in place European Union agreements with five European third countries;[1] and
- put in place a bilateral agreement.[2]

Detailed findings

The detailed findings for Portugal are below, organised per Core Requirement (CR) and sub-requirement (SR), as extracted from the AEOI Terms of Reference (see Annex B).

CR1 Domestic legal framework: Jurisdictions should have a domestic legislative framework in place that requires all Reporting Financial Institutions to conduct the due diligence and reporting procedures in the CRS, and that provides for the effective implementation of the CRS as set out therein.

Determination: In Place But **Needs Improvement**

Portugal's domestic legislative framework is in place and contains most of the key aspects of the CRS and its Commentary requiring Reporting Financial Institutions to conduct the due diligence and reporting procedures, but it needs improvement in relation to defining the term Particpating Jurisdiction (SR 1.2)..

SR 1.1 Jurisdictions should define the scope of Reporting Financial Institutions consistently with the CRS.

Portugal has defined the scope of Reporting Financial Institutions in its domestic legislative framework in accordance with the CRS and its Commentary.

Recommendations:

No recommendations made.

SR 1.2 Jurisdictions should define the scope of Financial Accounts and Reportable Accounts consistently with the CRS and incorporate the due diligence procedures to identify them.

Portugal has defined the scope of the Financial Accounts that are required to be reported in its domestic legislative framework and incorporated the due diligence procedures that must be applied to identify them in a manner that is largely consistent with the CRS and its Commentary. However, a deficiency has been identified. More specifically, Portugal's legislative framework does not incorporate the requirements in relation to certain Entities not located in Participating Jurisdictions in line with the AEOI Standard. This deficiency is material to the proper functioning of the AEOI Standard as it does not ensure that all Investment Entities that are not in Participating Jurisdictions are subject to the "look-through" approach to identify their Controlling Persons.

Recommendations:

Portugal should amend its domestic legislative framework to ensure that the approach taken with respect to the eight jurisdictions defined as Participating Jurisdictions and with which Portugal does not have an agreement to exchange CRS information with (and which have not implemented the AEOI Standard), is in accordance with the AEOI Standard.

SR 1.3 Jurisdictions should incorporate the reporting requirements contained in Section I of the CRS into their domestic legislative framework.

Portugal has incorporated the reporting requirements in its domestic legislative framework in accordance with the CRS and its Commentary.

Recommendations:

No recommendations made.

SR 1.4 Jurisdictions should have a legislative framework in place that allows for the enforcement of the requirements of the CRS in practice.

Portugal has a legislative framework in place to enforce the requirements in accordance with the CRS and its Commentary.

Recommendations:

No recommendations made.

CR2 International legal framework: Jurisdictions should have exchange relationships in effect with all Interested Appropriate Partners as committed to and that provide for the exchange of information in accordance with the Model CAA.

Determination: In Place

Portugal's international legal framework to exchange the information is in place, is consistent with the Model CAA and its Commentary and provides for exchange with all of Portugal's Interested Appropriate Partners (i.e. all jurisdictions that are interested in receiving information from Portugal and that meet the required standard in relation to confidentiality and data safeguards) (SRs 2.1 – 2.3).

SR 2.1 Jurisdictions should have exchange agreements in effect with all Interested Appropriate Partners that permit the automatic exchange of CRS information.

Portugal has exchange agreements that permit the automatic exchange of CRS information in effect with all its Interested Appropriate Partners.

Recommendations:

No recommendations made.

SR 2.2 Such an exchange agreement should be put in place without undue delay, following the receipt of an expression of interest from an Interested Appropriate Partner.

Portugal put in place its exchange agreements without undue delay.

Recommendations:

No recommendations made.

SR 2.3 Jurisdictions should ensure that the exchange agreements in effect provide for the exchange of information in accordance with the requirements of the Model CAA.

Portugal's exchange agreements provide for the exchange of information in accordance with the requirements of the Model CAA.

Recommendations:

No recommendations made.

Comments by the assessed jurisdiction

Portugal agrees with the contents and conclusions of this assessment. To address the recommendation made, Portugal has recently amended its regulations concerning the implementation of the term "Participating Jurisdictions" for the purposes of the AEOI Standard, by the Order (Despacho) no. 150/2024-XXIV, of 23 October 2024, of the Secretary of State for Tax Affairs.

Notes

[1] Andorra, Liechtenstein, Monaco, San Marino and Switzerland.

[2] With Hong Kong (China).

Saint Kitts and Nevis

Overall findings

Saint Kitts and Nevis's legal framework implementing the AEOI Standard is in place but needs improvement in order to be fully consistent with the requirements of the AEOI Terms of Reference. While Saint Kitts and Nevis' international legal framework to exchange the information with all of Saint Kitts and Nevis' Interested Appropriate Partners (CR2) is consistent with the requirements, its domestic legislative framework requiring Reporting Financial Institutions to conduct the due diligence and reporting procedures (CR1) has deficiencies significant to the proper functioning of elements of the AEOI Standard. More specifically, there are deficiencies in the enforcement framework.

The methodology used for the peer reviews and that therefore underpins this report is outlined in Chapter 2.

Overall determination on the legal framework: In Place **But Needs Improvement**

Conclusions on the legal framework

General context

Saint Kitts and Nevis commenced exchanges under the AEOI Standard in 2018.

In order to provide for Reporting Financial Institutions to collect and report the information to be exchanged, Saint Kitts and Nevis:

- enacted the Common Reporting Standard (Automatic Exchange of Financial Account Information) Act 2016, as amended in 2018; and
- introduced the Common Reporting Standard (Automatic Exchange of Financial Account Information) Regulations 2016, as amended in 2018.

Under this framework Reporting Financial Institutions were required to commence the due diligence procedures in relation to New Accounts from 1 January 2017. With respect to Preexisting Accounts, Reporting Financial Institutions were required to complete the due diligence procedures on High Value Individual Accounts by 31 December 2017 and on Lower Value Individual Accounts and Entity Accounts by 31 December 2018.

Following the initial Global Forum peer review, Saint Kitts and Nevis made various amendments to its legislative framework to address issues identified, the last of which was effective from 16 August 2018.

With respect to the exchange of information under the AEOI Standard, Saint Kitts and Nevis is a Party to the Convention on Mutual Administrative Assistance in Tax Matters and activated the associated CRS Multilateral Competent Authority Agreement in time for exchanges in 2018.

Detailed findings

The detailed findings for Saint Kitts and Nevis are below, organised per Core Requirement (CR) and sub-requirement (SR), as extracted from the AEOI Terms of Reference (see Annex B).

CR1 Domestic legal framework: Jurisdictions should have a domestic legislative framework in place that requires all Reporting Financial Institutions to conduct the due diligence and reporting procedures in the CRS, and that provides for the effective implementation of the CRS as set out therein.

Determination: In Place **But Needs Improvement**

Saint Kitts and Nevis' domestic legislative framework is in place and contains most of the key aspects of the CRS and its Commentary requiring Reporting Financial Institutions to conduct the due diligence and reporting procedures, but it needs improvement in relation to the scope of due diligence procedures (SR 1.2) and the framework to enforce the requirements (SR 1.4). Most significantly, Saint Kitts and Nevis's legislative framework has an anti-circumvention rule that does not cover all relevant persons that may engage in practices to avoid due diligence and reporting and it does not include an explicit legal basis to impose or enforce a sanction where a Reporting Financial Institution is a legal arrangement.

SR 1.1 Jurisdictions should define the scope of Reporting Financial Institutions consistently with the CRS.

Saint Kitts and Nevis has defined the scope of Reporting Financial Institutions in its domestic legislative framework in accordance with the CRS and its Commentary.

Recommendations:

No recommendations made.

SR 1.2 Jurisdictions should define the scope of Financial Accounts and Reportable Accounts consistently with the CRS and incorporate the due diligence procedures to identify them.

Saint Kitts and Nevis has defined the scope of the Financial Accounts that are required to be reported in its domestic legislative framework and incorporated the due diligence procedures that must be applied to identify them in a manner that is largely consistent with the CRS and its Commentary. While a deficiency has been identified with respect to defining the term Participating Jurisdiction, it is considered relatively minor and does not materially undermine the implementation of SR 1.2. Saint Kitts and Nevis has taken all necessary steps to ensure relevant agreements are in place.

Recommendations:

Saint Kitts and Nevis should amend its domestic legislative framework to ensure that the approach taken with respect to the nine jurisdictions defined as Participating Jurisdictions and with which Saint Kitts and Nevis does not have an agreement to exchange CRS information with, is in accordance with the AEOI Standard.

SR 1.3 Jurisdictions should incorporate the reporting requirements contained in Section I of the CRS into their domestic legislative framework.

Saint Kitts and Nevis has incorporated the reporting requirements in its domestic legislative framework in accordance with the CRS and its Commentary.

Recommendations:

No recommendations made.

SR 1.4 Jurisdictions should have a legislative framework in place that allows for the enforcement of the requirements of the CRS in practice.

Saint Kitts and Nevis has a legislative framework in place to enforce the requirements in a manner that is largely consistent with the CRS and its Commentary. However, deficiencies have been identified. More specifically, Saint Kitts and Nevis's legislative framework legislative framework has an anti-circumvention rule that does not cover all relevant persons that may engage in practices to avoid due diligence and reporting and Saint Kitts and Nevis does not include an explicit legal basis to enforce a sanction where a Reporting Financial Institution is a legal arrangement. These deficiencies relates to key elements of the AEOI Standard and are therefore material to its proper functioning.

Recommendations:

Saint Kitts and Nevis should ensure that its anti-avoidance rule covers avoidance of CRS reporting and due diligence when entered into by Account Holders or intermediaries, not just by Financial Institutions.

Saint Kitts and Nevis should amend its legislative framework to ensure that there is an explicit legal basis to enforce a sanction when there is non-compliance by a Reporting Financial Institution that is a legal arrangement.

CR2 International legal framework: Jurisdictions should have exchange relationships in effect with all Interested Appropriate Partners as committed to and that provide for the exchange of information in accordance with the Model CAA.

Determination: In Place

Saint Kitts and Nevis' international legal framework to exchange the information in place, is consistent with the Model CAA and its Commentary and provides for exchange with all of Saint Kitts and Nevis's Interested Appropriate Partners (i.e. all jurisdictions that are interested in receiving information from Saint Kitts and Nevis and that meet the required standard in relation to confidentiality and data safeguards) (SRs 2.1 – 2.3).

SR 2.1 Jurisdictions should have exchange agreements in effect with all Interested Appropriate Partners that permit the automatic exchange of CRS information.

Saint Kitts and Nevis has exchange agreements that permit the automatic exchange of CRS information in effect with all its Interested Appropriate Partners.

Recommendations:

No recommendations made.

SR 2.2 Such an exchange agreement should be put in place without undue delay, following the receipt of an expression of interest from an Interested Appropriate Partner.

Saint Kitts and Nevis put in place its exchange agreements without undue delay.

Recommendations:

No recommendations made.

SR 2.3 Jurisdictions should ensure that the exchange agreements in effect provide for the exchange of information in accordance with the requirements of the Model CAA.

Saint Kitts and Nevis's exchange agreements provide for the exchange of information in accordance with the requirements of the Model CAA.

Recommendations:

No recommendations made.

Comments by the assessed jurisdiction

No comments made.

Saint Lucia

Overall findings

Saint Lucia's legal framework implementing the AEOI Standard is in place but needs improvement in order to be fully consistent with the requirements of the AEOI Terms of Reference. While Saint Lucia's international legal framework to exchange the information with all of Saint Lucia's Interested Appropriate Partners (CR2) is consistent with the requirements, its domestic legislative framework requiring Reporting Financial Institutions to conduct the due diligence and reporting procedures (CR1) has deficiencies significant to the proper functioning of elements of the AEOI Standard. Most significantly, Saint Lucia's legislative framework provides for a category of jurisdiction-specific Excluded Account that is not in accordance with the requirements and deficiencies have been identified in the enforcement framework.

The methodology used for the peer reviews and that therefore underpins this report is outlined in Chapter 2.

Overall determination on the legal framework: In Place But **Needs Improvement**

Conclusions on the legal framework

General context

Saint Lucia commenced exchanges under the AEOI Standard in 2018.

In order to provide for Reporting Financial Institutions to collect and report the information to be exchanged, Saint Lucia:

- enacted the Automatic Exchange of Financial Account Information Act No. 22 of 2016, which was subsequently amended by the Automatic Exchange of Financial Account Information (Amendment) Act No. 10 of 2017, the Automatic Exchange of Financial Account Information (Amendment Schedule 2) Order S.I. 105 of 2017 and the Automatic Exchange of Financial Account Information (Amendment) Act No. 7 of 2018;
- introduced the Automatic Exchange of Financial Account Information (Designation of Excluded Accounts) Order No. 106 of 2017 and the Automatic Exchange of Financial Account Information (Designation of Non-Reporting Financial Institution) Order No. 107 of 2017, which were subsequently amended by the Automatic Exchange of Financial Account Information (Designation of Excluded Accounts) Order No. 119 of 2017, the Automatic Exchange of Financial Account Information (Designation of Non-Reporting Financial Institution) Order No. 7 of 2019 and the Automatic Exchange of Financial Account Information (Designation of Excluded Accounts) Order No. 8 of 2019; and
- issued further guidance, which is not legally binding.

Under this framework Reporting Financial Institutions were required to commence the due diligence procedures in relation to New Accounts from 1 January 2017. With respect to Preexisting Accounts, Reporting Financial Institutions were required to complete the due diligence procedures on High Value Individual Accounts by 31 December 2017 and on Lower Value Individual Accounts and Entity Accounts by 31 December 2018.

Following the initial Global Forum peer review, Saint Lucia made various amendments to its legislative framework to address issues identified, the last of which was effective from 11 February 2019.

With respect to the exchange of information under the AEOI Standard, Saint Lucia is a Party to the Convention on Mutual Administrative Assistance in Tax Matters and activated the associated CRS Multilateral Competent Authority Agreement in time for exchanges in 2018.

Detailed findings

The detailed findings for Saint Lucia are below, organised per Core Requirement (CR) and sub-requirement (SR), as extracted from the AEOI Terms of Reference (see Annex B).

CR1 Domestic legal framework: Jurisdictions should have a domestic legislative framework in place that requires all Reporting Financial Institutions to conduct the due diligence and reporting procedures in the CRS, and that provides for the effective implementation of the CRS as set out therein.

Determination: In Place But **Needs Improvement**

Saint Lucia's domestic legislative framework is in place and contains most of the key aspects of the CRS and its Commentary requiring Reporting Financial Institutions to conduct the due diligence and reporting procedures, but it needs improvement in relation to the scope of Financial Accounts required to be reported (SR 1.2) and the enforcement framework (SR 1.4). Most significantly, Saint Lucia provides for a category of jurisdiction-specific Excluded Account that is not in accordance with the requirements, the power to access to records to verify compliance is limited only to records held by a Reporting Financial Institution, and there is no explicit legal basis to enforce a sanction where a Reporting Financial Institution is a legal arrangement.

SR 1.1 Jurisdictions should define the scope of Reporting Financial Institutions consistently with the CRS.

Saint Lucia has defined the scope of Reporting Financial Institutions in its domestic legislative framework in accordance with the CRS and its Commentary.

Recommendations:

No recommendations made.

SR 1.2 Jurisdictions should define the scope of Financial Accounts and Reportable Accounts consistently with the CRS and incorporate the due diligence procedures to identify them.

Saint Lucia has defined the scope of the Financial Accounts that are required to be reported in its domestic legislative framework and incorporated the due diligence procedures that must be applied to identify them largely in accordance with the CRS and its Commentary. However, a deficiency has been identified. More specifically, Saint Lucia has provided for a jurisdiction-specific Excluded Account that is not in accordance with the requirements. The scope of Financial Accounts, including the provision of Excluded Accounts, is material to the proper functioning of the AEOI Standard.

Recommendations:

Saint Lucia should amend its domestic legislative framework to remove the Pension Fund Accounts from its jurisdiction-specific list of Excluded Accounts as they do not meet the requirements in the AEOI Standard, such as full reporting to the authorities with respect to the Account Holders and penalties on early withdrawals.

SR 1.3 Jurisdictions should incorporate the reporting requirements contained in Section I of the CRS into their domestic legislative framework.

Saint Lucia has incorporated the reporting requirements in its domestic legislative framework in accordance with the CRS and its Commentary.

Recommendations:

No recommendations made.

SR 1.4 Jurisdictions should have a legislative framework in place that allows for the enforcement of the requirements of the CRS in practice.

Saint Lucia has a legislative framework in place to enforce the requirements in a manner that is largely consistent with the CRS and its Commentary. However, deficiencies have been identified. Most significantly, Saint Lucia's legislative framework does not impose sanctions on Account Holders and Controlling Persons for the provision of a false self-certification, access to records is limited only to records held by a Reporting Financial Institution, and there is no explicit legal basis to enforce a sanction where a Reporting Financial Institution is a legal arrangement. These are key elements of the required enforcement framework and are therefore material to the proper functioning of the AEOI Standard.

Recommendations:

Saint Lucia should ensure that its anti-avoidance rule covers avoidance of CRS reporting and due diligence when entered into by Account Holders or intermediaries, not just by Financial Institutions.

Saint Lucia should amend its domestic legislative framework to include sanctions on Account Holders and Controlling Persons for the provision of a false self-certification.

Saint Lucia should amend its domestic legislative framework to require Reporting Financial Institutions to maintain records of self-certifications for at least five years from the deadline to report the information, rather than six years from the date when an account is closed.

Saint Lucia should amend its domestic legislative framework to provide the appropriate authorities with the power to directly access the records and evidence held by persons that are not Reporting Financial Institutions that are relevant for verifying and enforcing the AEOI Standard.

Saint Lucia should amend its legislative framework to ensure that there is an explicit legal basis to enforce a sanction when there is non-compliance by a Reporting Financial Institution that is a legal arrangement.

CR2 International legal framework: Jurisdictions should have exchange relationships in effect with all Interested Appropriate Partners as committed to and that provide for the exchange of information in accordance with the Model CAA.

Determination: In Place

Saint Lucia's international legal framework to exchange the information is in place, is consistent with the Model CAA and its Commentary and provides for exchange with all of Saint Lucia's Interested Appropriate Partners (i.e. all jurisdictions that are interested in receiving information from Saint Lucia and that meet the required standard in relation to confidentiality and data safeguards) (SRs 2.1 – 2.3).

SR 2.1 Jurisdictions should have exchange agreements in effect with all Interested Appropriate Partners that permit the automatic exchange of CRS information.

Saint Lucia has exchange agreements that permit the automatic exchange of CRS information in effect with all its Interested Appropriate Partners.

Recommendations:

No recommendations made.

SR 2.2 Such an exchange agreement should be put in place without undue delay, following the receipt of an expression of interest from an Interested Appropriate Partner.

Saint Lucia put in place its exchange agreements without undue delay.

Recommendations:

No recommendations made.

SR 2.3 Jurisdictions should ensure that the exchange agreements in effect provide for the exchange of information in accordance with the requirements of the Model CAA.

Saint Lucia's exchange agreements provide for the exchange of information in accordance with the requirements of the Model CAA.

Recommendations:

No recommendations made.

Comments by the assessed jurisdiction

No comments made.

Saint Vincent and the Grenadines

Overall findings

Saint Vincent and the Grenadines' legal framework implementing the AEOI Standard is in place but needs improvement in order to be fully consistent with the requirements of the AEOI Terms of Reference. While Saint Vincent and the Grenadines' international legal framework to exchange the information with all of Saint Vincent and the Grenadines Interested Appropriate Partners (CR2) is consistent with the requirements, its domestic legislative framework requiring Reporting Financial Institutions to conduct the due diligence and reporting procedures (CR1) has deficiencies significant to the proper functioning of elements of the AEOI Standard. More specifically, Saint Vincent and the Grenadines' legislative framework provides for jurisdiction-specific Non-Reporting Financial Institutions that are not in accordance with the requirements and there are deficiencies in the enforcement framework.

The methodology used for the peer reviews and that therefore underpins this report is outlined in Chapter 2.

Overall determination on the legal framework: In Place But **Needs Improvement**

Conclusions on the legal framework

General context

Saint Vincent and the Grenadines commenced exchanges under the AEOI Standard in 2018.

In order to provide for Reporting Financial Institutions to collect and report the information to be exchanged, Saint Vincent and the Grenadines:

- enacted the Automatic Exchange of Information (Common reporting Standards) Act 2016; and
- introduced the Automatic Exchange of Information (Common reporting Standards) Regulations 2016.

Under this framework Reporting Financial Institutions were required to commence the due diligence procedures in relation to New Accounts from 1 January 2017. With respect to Preexisting Accounts, Reporting Financial Institutions were required to complete the due diligence procedures on High Value Individual Accounts by 31 December 2017 and on Lower Value Individual Accounts and Entity Accounts by 31 December 2018.

With respect to the exchange of information under the AEOI Standard, Saint Vincent and the Grenadines is a Party to the Convention on Mutual Administrative Assistance in Tax Matters and activated the associated CRS Multilateral Competent Authority Agreement in time for exchanges in 2018.

Detailed findings

The detailed findings for Saint Vincent and the Grenadines are below, organised per Core Requirement (CR) and sub-requirement (SR), as extracted from the AEOI Terms of Reference (see Annex B).

CR1 Domestic legal framework: Jurisdictions should have a domestic legislative framework in place that requires all Reporting Financial Institutions to conduct the due diligence and reporting procedures in the CRS, and that provides for the effective implementation of the CRS as set out therein.

Determination: In Place But **Needs Improvement**

Saint Vincent and the Grenadines' domestic legislative framework is in place and contains most of the key aspects of the CRS and its Commentary requiring Reporting Financial Institutions to conduct the due diligence and reporting procedures, but it needs improvement in relation to the scope of Reporting Financial Institutions required to report information (SR 1.1) and the framework to enforce the requirements (SR 1.4). More specifically, Saint Vincent and the Grenadines provides for jurisdiction-specific Non-Reporting Financial Institutions that are not in accordance with the requirements and there are deficiencies in the enforcement framework in place.

SR 1.1 Jurisdictions should define the scope of Reporting Financial Institutions consistently with the CRS.

Saint Vincent and the Grenadines has defined the scope of Reporting Financial Institutions in its domestic legislative framework in a manner that is largely consistent with the CRS and its Commentary. However, certain specific deficiencies have been identified, namely Saint Vincent and the Grenadines provides for two jurisdiction-specific Non-Reporting Financial Institutions that are not in accordance with the requirements. The scope of Reporting Financial Institutions, including the provision of Non-Reporting Financial Institutions, is material to the proper functioning of the AEOI Standard.

Recommendations:

Saint Vincent and the Grenadines should amend its domestic legislative framework to remove Friendly Societies from its jurisdiction-specific list of Non-Reporting Financial Institutions as they do not meet the requirements of the AEOI Standard such as in relation to the purpose of the deposits and the restrictions on the contributions and withdrawals.

Saint Vincent and the Grenadines should amend its domestic legislative framework to remove Non-Profit Organisations from its jurisdiction-specific list of Non-Reporting Financial Institutions as they do not meet the requirements in the AEOI Standard.

SR 1.2 Jurisdictions should define the scope of Financial Accounts and Reportable Accounts consistently with the CRS and incorporate the due diligence procedures to identify them.

Saint Vincent and the Grenadines has defined the scope of the Financial Accounts that are required to be reported in its domestic legislative framework and incorporated the due diligence procedures that must be applied to identify them in a manner that is largely consistent with the CRS and its Commentary. However, a deficiency has been identified. More specifically, Saint Vincent and the Grenadines' legislative framework does not incorporate the requirements in relation to certain Entities not located in Participating Jurisdictions in line with the AEOI Standard. This deficiency is material to the proper functioning of the AEOI Standard as it does not ensure that all Investment Entities that are not in Participating Jurisdictions are subject to the "look-through" approach to identify their Controlling Persons.

Recommendations:

Saint Vincent and the Grenadines should amend its domestic legislative framework to ensure that the approach taken with respect to the 17 jurisdictions defined as Participating Jurisdictions and with which Saint Vincent and the Grenadines does not have an agreement to exchange CRS information with (11 of which have not implemented the CRS), is in accordance with the AEOI Standard.

SR 1.3 Jurisdictions should incorporate the reporting requirements contained in Section I of the CRS into their domestic legislative framework.

Saint Vincent and the Grenadines has incorporated the reporting requirements in its domestic legislative framework in accordance with the CRS and its Commentary.

Recommendations:

No recommendations made.

SR 1.4 Jurisdictions should have a legislative framework in place that allows for the enforcement of the requirements of the CRS in practice.

Saint Vincent and the Grenadines has a legislative framework in place to enforce the requirements in a manner that is largely consistent with the CRS and its Commentary. However, deficiencies have been identified. More specifically, Saint Vincent and the Grenadines' legislative framework does not include sanctions on Reporting Financial Institutions for failing to apply due diligence procedures in accordance with the AEOI Standard and its anti-circumvention rule does not cover all relevant persons that may engage in practices to avoid due diligence and reporting. These are key elements of the required enforcement framework and are therefore material to the proper functioning of the AEOI Standard.

Recommendations:

Saint Vincent and the Grenadines should ensure that its anti-avoidance rule covers avoidance of CRS reporting and due diligence when entered into by Account Holders or intermediaries, not just by Financial Institutions.

Saint Vincent and the Grenadines should amend its domestic legislative framework to include sanctions for failure to apply the due diligence and reporting procedures, rather than being limited to failures leading to incorrect reporting.

CR2 International legal framework: Jurisdictions should have exchange relationships in effect with all Interested Appropriate Partners as committed to and that provide for the exchange of information in accordance with the Model CAA.

Determination: In Place

Saint Vincent and the Grenadines' international legal framework to exchange the information is in place, is consistent with the Model CAA and its Commentary and provides for exchange with all of Saint Vincent and the Grenadines' Interested Appropriate Partners (i.e. all jurisdictions that are interested in receiving information from Saint Vincent and the Grenadines and that meet the required standard in relation to confidentiality and data safeguards) (SRs 2.1 – 2.3).

SR 2.1 Jurisdictions should have exchange agreements in effect with all Interested Appropriate Partners that permit the automatic exchange of CRS information.

Saint Vincent and the Grenadines has exchange agreements that permit the automatic exchange of CRS information in effect with all its Interested Appropriate Partners.

Recommendations:

No recommendations made.

SR 2.2 Such an exchange agreement should be put in place without undue delay, following the receipt of an expression of interest from an Interested Appropriate Partner.

Saint Vincent and the Grenadines put in place its exchange agreements without undue delay.

Recommendations:

No recommendations made.

SR 2.3 Jurisdictions should ensure that the exchange agreements in effect provide for the exchange of information in accordance with the requirements of the Model CAA.

Saint Vincent and the Grenadines' exchange agreements provide for the exchange of information in accordance with the requirements of the Model CAA.

Recommendations:

No recommendations made.

Comments by the assessed jurisdiction

No comments made.

Samoa

Overall findings

Samoa's legal framework implementing the AEOI Standard is in place but needs improvement in order to be fully consistent with the requirements of the AEOI Terms of Reference. While Samoa's international legal framework to exchange the information with all of Samoa's Interested Appropriate Partners (CR2) is consistent with the requirements, its domestic legislative framework requiring Reporting Financial Institutions to conduct the due diligence and reporting procedures (CR1) has deficiencies significant to the proper functioning of an element of the AEOI Standard. More specifically, there are deficiencies in the enforcement framework.

The methodology used for the peer reviews and that therefore underpins this report is outlined in Chapter 2.

Overall determination on the legal framework: In Place But **Needs Improvement**

Conclusions on the legal framework

General context

Samoa commenced exchanges under the AEOI Standard in 2018.

In order to provide for Reporting Financial Institutions to collect and report the information to be exchanged, Samoa enacted the Tax Information Exchange Amendment Act 2017, which is an amendment to the Tax Information Exchange Act 2012.

Under this framework Reporting Financial Institutions were required to commence the due diligence procedures in relation to New Accounts from 1 January 2017. With respect to Preexisting Accounts, Reporting Financial Institutions were required to complete the due diligence procedures on High Value Individual Accounts by 31 December 2017 and on Lower Value Individual Accounts and Entity Accounts by 31 December 2018.

With respect to the exchange of information under the AEOI Standard, Samoa is a Party to the Convention on Mutual Administrative Assistance in Tax Matters and activated the associated CRS Multilateral Competent Authority Agreement in time for exchanges in 2018.

Detailed findings

The detailed findings for Samoa are below, organised per Core Requirement (CR) and sub-requirement (SR), as extracted from the AEOI Terms of Reference (see Annex B).

CR1 Domestic legal framework: Jurisdictions should have a domestic legislative framework in place that requires all Reporting Financial Institutions to conduct the due diligence and reporting procedures in the CRS, and that provides for the effective implementation of the CRS as set out therein.

Determination: In Place But **Needs Improvement**

Samoa's domestic legislative framework is in place and contains most of the key aspects of the CRS and its Commentary requiring Reporting Financial Institutions to conduct the due diligence and reporting procedures, but it needs improvement in relation to the framework to enforce the requirements (SR 1.4). Most significantly, Samoa's legislative framework does not fully provide for sanctions on Reporting Financial Institutions for filing incorrect information and it does not have an explicit legal basis to enforce a sanction for non-compliance if the Reporting Financial Institution is a legal arrangement.

SR 1.1 Jurisdictions should define the scope of Reporting Financial Institutions consistently with the CRS.

Samoa has defined the scope of Reporting Financial Institutions in its domestic legislative framework in accordance with the CRS and its Commentary.

Recommendations:

No recommendations made.

SR 1.2 Jurisdictions should define the scope of Financial Accounts and Reportable Accounts consistently with the CRS and incorporate the due diligence procedures to identify them.

Samoa has defined the scope of the Financial Accounts that are required to be reported in its domestic legislative framework and incorporated the due diligence procedures that must be applied to identify them in accordance with the CRS and its Commentary.

Recommendations:

No recommendations made.

SR 1.3 Jurisdictions should incorporate the reporting requirements contained in Section I of the CRS into their domestic legislative framework.

Samoa has incorporated the reporting requirements in its domestic legislative framework in accordance with the CRS and its Commentary.

Recommendations:

No recommendations made.

SR 1.4 Jurisdictions should have a legislative framework in place that allows for the enforcement of the requirements of the CRS in practice.

Samoa has a legislative framework in place to enforce the requirements in a manner that is largely consistent with the CRS and its Commentary. However, deficiencies have been identified. More specifically, Samoa's legislative framework:

- does not include rules to prevent all relevant persons (including Reporting Financial Institutions, other persons and intermediaries) from adopting any practices intended to circumvent the reporting and due diligence procedures as required;
- does not include an explicit legal basis to enforce a sanction where a Reporting Financial Institution is a legal arrangement; and
- has sanctions for noncompliance only when it is intentional or due to recklessness, which does not cover a sufficiently broad range of behaviours causing noncompliance.

These are the key elements of the required enforcement framework relates to and are therefore material to the proper functioning of the AEOI Standard

Recommendations:

Samoa should ensure that its anti-avoidance rule covers avoidance of CRS reporting and due diligence when entered into by Account Holders or intermediaries, not just by Financial Institutions.

Samoa should amend its legislative framework to ensure that there is an explicit legal basis to enforce a sanction when there is non-compliance by a Reporting Financial Institution that is a legal arrangement.

Samoa should amend its domestic legislative framework to ensure that sanctions are not limited to noncompliance that is intentional or due to recklessness.

CR2 International legal framework: Jurisdictions should have exchange relationships in effect with all Interested Appropriate Partners as committed to and that provide for the exchange of information in accordance with the Model CAA.

Determination: In Place

Samoa's international legal framework to exchange the information is in place, is consistent with the Model CAA and its Commentary and provides for exchange with all of Samoa's Interested Appropriate Partners (i.e. all jurisdictions that are interested in receiving information from Samoa and that meet the required standard in relation to confidentiality and data safeguards) (SRs 2.1 – 2.3).

SR 2.1 Jurisdictions should have exchange agreements in effect with all Interested Appropriate Partners that permit the automatic exchange of CRS information.

Samoa has exchange agreements that permit the automatic exchange of CRS information in effect with all its Interested Appropriate Partners.

Recommendations:

No recommendations made.

SR 2.2 Such an exchange agreement should be put in place without undue delay, following the receipt of an expression of interest from an Interested Appropriate Partner.

Samoa put in place its exchange agreements without undue delay.

Recommendations:

No recommendations made.

SR 2.3 Jurisdictions should ensure that the exchange agreements in effect provide for the exchange of information in accordance with the requirements of the Model CAA.

Samoa's exchange agreements provide for the exchange of information in accordance with the requirements of the Model CAA.

Recommendations:

No recommendations made.

Comments by the assessed jurisdiction

No comments made.

Sint Maarten

Overall findings

Sint Maarten's legal framework implementing the AEOI Standard is in place but needs improvement in order to be fully consistent with the requirements in the AEOI Terms of Reference. While Sint Maarten's international legal framework to exchange the information with all of Sint Maarten's Interested Appropriate Partners (CR2) is consistent with the requirements, its domestic legislative framework requiring Reporting Financial Institutions to conduct the due diligence and reporting procedures (CR1) has deficiencies significant to the proper functioning of elements of the AEOI Standard. More specifically, deficiencies have been identified in relation to the scope of Financial Accounts and there are deficiencies in the enforcement framework.

The methodology used for the peer reviews and that therefore underpins this report is outlined in Chapter 2.

Overall determination on the legal framework: In Place But **Needs Improvement**

Conclusions on the legal framework

General context

Sint Maarten committed to commence the exchanges under the AEOI Standard on a non-reciprocal basis in 2018 (i.e. it will send but not receive information), although was delayed in delivering its commitment and is expecting to commence exchanges in September 2022.

In order to provide for Reporting Financial Institutions to collect and report the information to be exchanged, Sint Maarten:

- enacted amendments to the General National Ordinance on National Taxes (amended by National Ordinance No. 48 of 2020); and
- introduced National Decree No. 77 of 2021, in force from 31 January 2022 and with retroactive effect from 1 January 2018.

Under this framework Reporting Financial Institutions were required to apply the due diligence procedures in relation to New Accounts from 1 January 2018. With respect to Preexisting Accounts, Reporting Financial Institutions were required to apply the due diligence procedures on Preexisting Individual Accounts and Entity Accounts by 31 December 2018.

With respect to the exchange of the information under the AEOI Standard, Sint Maarten has the Convention on Mutual Administrative Assistance in Tax Matters[1] in place, which entered into force from 10 October 2010, and activated the associated CRS Multilateral Competent Authority Agreement in time for exchanges in 2022.

In order to provide for the effective implementation of the AEOI Standard, in Sint Maarten:

- the Sint Maarten's Competent Authority for purposes of the AEOI Standard has the responsibility to ensure the effective implementation of the due diligence and reporting obligations by Reporting Financial Institutions and for exchanging the information with Sint Maarten's exchange partners;
- technical solutions necessary to receive and validate the information reported by Reporting Financial Institutions were put in place through the Multi Data Exchange System; and

- the Common Transmission System (CTS) will be used to carry out the exchanges of information, along with the associated file preparation and encryption requirements.

Detailed findings

The detailed findings for Sint Maarten are below, organised per Core Requirement (CR) and sub-requirement (SR), as extracted from the AEOI Terms of Reference (see Annex B).

CR1 Domestic legal framework: Jurisdictions should have a domestic legislative framework in place that requires all Reporting Financial Institutions to conduct the due diligence and reporting procedures in the CRS, and that provides for the effective implementation of the CRS as set out therein.

Determination: In Place But **Needs Improvement**

Sint Maarten's domestic legislative framework is in place and contains most of the key aspects of the CRS and its Commentary requiring Reporting Financial Institutions to conduct the due diligence and reporting procedures, but it needs improvement in relation to the due diligence procedures that must be applied to Financial Accounts (SR 1.2) and the framework to enforce the requirements (SR 1.4). Most significantly, Sint Maarten's legislative framework does not fully incorporate the definition and processes related to the identification of Controlling Persons of trusts and similar arrangements.

SR 1.1 Jurisdictions should define the scope of Reporting Financial Institutions consistently with the CRS.

Sint Maarten has defined the scope of Reporting Financial Institutions in its domestic legislative framework in accordance with the CRS and its Commentary.

Recommendations:

No recommendations made.

SR 1.2 Jurisdictions should define the scope of Financial Accounts and Reportable Accounts consistently with the CRS and incorporate the due diligence procedures to identify them.

Sint Maarten has defined the Financial Accounts that are required to be reported in its domestic legislative framework and incorporated the due diligence procedures that must be applied to identify them in a manner that is largely consistent with the CRS and its Commentary. However, deficiencies have been identified. Most significantly, Sint Maarten's legislative framework:

- does not incorporate the definition of Documentary Evidence in accordance with the CRS and its relevant Commentary; and
- does not fully incorporate the definition of Controlling Persons as required and does not fully incorporate the due diligence procedures to identify Controlling Persons.

The due diligence procedures are material to the proper functioning of the AEOI Standard.

Recommendations:

Sint Maarten should amend its domestic legislative framework to require Reporting Financial Institutions to always identify and determine the reportable status of the Controlling Persons of trusts and similar legal arrangements in accordance with the AEOI Standard.

Sint Maarten should amend its domestic legislative framework to ensure that its Financial Institutions apply the definition of Controlling Persons in the AEOI Standard.

Sint Maarten should amend its domestic legislative framework to require Reporting Financial Institutions to only use Documentary Evidence in relation to the due diligence procedures for Preexisting Entity

Accounts in accordance with the conditions in the AEOI Standard.

SR 1.3 Jurisdictions should incorporate the reporting requirements contained in Section I of the CRS into their domestic legislative framework.

Sint Maarten has incorporated the reporting requirements in its domestic legislative framework in accordance with the CRS and its Commentary.

Recommendations:

No recommendations made.

SR 1.4 Jurisdictions should have a legislative framework in place that allows for the enforcement of the requirements of the CRS in practice.

Sint Maarten has a legislative framework in place to enforce the requirements in a manner that is largely consistent with the CRS and its Commentary. However, deficiencies have been identified. More specifically, Sint Maarten's legislative framework:

- does not include rules to prevent all relevant persons (including Reporting Financial Institutions, other persons and intermediaries) from adopting any practices intended to circumvent the reporting and due diligence procedures as required;
- does not impose sanctions on Account Holders and Controlling Persons for the provision of a false self-certification; and
- only has sanctions for noncompliance where it is intentional or due to gross negligence, which does not cover a sufficiently broad range of behaviours causing noncompliance.

These are the key elements of the required enforcement framework relates to and are therefore material to the proper functioning of the AEOI Standard.

Recommendations:

Sint Maarten should amend its legislative framework to prevent Financial Institutions, intermediaries and other persons from adopting practices intended to circumvent the reporting and due diligence procedures.

Sint Maarten should amend its domestic legislative framework to include sanctions on Account Holders and Controlling Persons for the provision of a false self-certification.

Sint Maarten should amend its domestic legislative framework to ensure that sanctions are not limited to noncompliance that is intentional or due to gross negligence.

CR2 International legal framework: Jurisdictions should have exchange relationships in effect with all Interested Appropriate Partners as committed to and that provide for the exchange of information in accordance with the Model CAA.

Determination: In Place

Sint Maarten's international legal framework to exchange the information is in place, is consistent with the Model CAA and its Commentary and provides for exchange with all of Sint Maarten's Interested Appropriate Partners (i.e. all jurisdictions that are interested in receiving information from Sint Maarten and that meet the required standard in relation to confidentiality and data safeguards) (SRs 2.1 – 2.3).

SR 2.1 Jurisdictions should have exchange agreements in effect with all Interested Appropriate Partners that permit the automatic exchange of CRS information.

Sint Maarten has exchange agreements that permit the automatic exchange of CRS information in effect with all its Interested Appropriate Partners.

Recommendations:

No recommendations made.

SR 2.2 Such an exchange agreement should be put in place without undue delay, following the receipt of an expression of interest from an Interested Appropriate Partner.

Sint Maarten put in place its exchange agreements without undue delay.

Recommendations:

No recommendations made.

SR 2.3 Jurisdictions should ensure that the exchange agreements in effect provide for the exchange of information in accordance with the requirements of the Model CAA.

Sint Maarten's exchange agreements provide for the exchange of information in accordance with the requirements of the Model CAA.

Recommendations:

No recommendations made.

Comments by the assessed jurisdiction

No comments made.

Note

[1] Through a territorial extension by the Netherlands.

Slovak Republic

Overall findings

The Slovak Republic's legal framework implementing the AEOI Standard is in place and is consistent with the requirements of the AEOI Terms of Reference. This includes the Slovak Republic's domestic legislative framework requiring Reporting Financial Institutions to conduct the due diligence and reporting procedures (CR1) and its international legal framework to exchange the information with all of the Slovak Republic's Interested Appropriate Partners (CR2).

The methodology used for the peer reviews and that therefore underpins this report is outlined in Chapter 2.

Overall determination on the legal framework: In Place

Conclusions on the legal framework

General context

The Slovak Republic commenced exchanges under the AEOI Standard in 2017.

In order to provide for Reporting Financial Institutions to collect and report the information to be exchanged, the Slovak Republic:

- enacted Act 359/2015 Coll., as amended by Act 300/2016 and Act 305/2019; and
- introduced Decree 446/2015 Coll., as amended by Decree 348/2018.

Under this framework Reporting Financial Institutions were required to commence the due diligence procedures in relation to New Accounts from 1 January 2016. With respect to Preexisting Accounts, Reporting Financial Institutions were required to complete the due diligence procedures on High Value Individual Accounts by 31 December 2016 and on Lower Value Individual Accounts and Entity Accounts by 31 December 2017.

Following the initial Global Forum peer review, the Slovak Republic made various amendments to its legislative framework to address issues identified, the last of which was effective from 1 January 2021.

With respect to the exchange of information under the AEOI Standard, the Slovak Republic:

- is a Party to the Convention on Mutual Administrative Assistance in Tax Matters and activated the associated CRS Multilateral Competent Authority Agreement in time for exchanges in 2017;
- has in place European Directive 2011/16/EU on Administrative Cooperation in the Field of Taxation as amended by Directive 2014/107/EU; and
- has in place European Union agreements with five European third countries.[1]

Detailed findings

The detailed findings for the Slovak Republic are below, organised per Core Requirement (CR) and sub-requirement (SR), as extracted from the AEOI Terms of Reference (see Annex B).

CR1 Domestic legal framework: Jurisdictions should have a domestic legislative framework in place that requires all Reporting Financial Institutions to conduct the due diligence and reporting procedures in the CRS, and that provides for the effective implementation of the CRS as set out therein.

Determination: In Place

The Slovak Republic's domestic legislative framework is in place and contains all of the key aspects of the CRS and its Commentary requiring Reporting Financial Institutions to conduct the due diligence and reporting procedures (SRs 1.1 – 1.3). It also provides a framework to enforce the requirements (SR 1.4).

SR 1.1 Jurisdictions should define the scope of Reporting Financial Institutions consistently with the CRS.

The Slovak Republic has defined the scope of Reporting Financial Institutions in its domestic legislative framework in accordance with the CRS and its Commentary.

Recommendations:

No recommendations made.

SR 1.2 Jurisdictions should define the scope of Financial Accounts and Reportable Accounts consistently with the CRS and incorporate the due diligence procedures to identify them.

The Slovak Republic has defined the scope of the Financial Accounts that are required to be reported in its domestic legislative framework and incorporated the due diligence procedures that must be applied to identify them in accordance with the CRS and its Commentary.

Recommendations:

No recommendations made.

SR 1.3 Jurisdictions should incorporate the reporting requirements contained in Section I of the CRS into their domestic legislative framework.

The Slovak Republic has incorporated the reporting requirements in its domestic legislative framework in accordance with the CRS and its Commentary.

Recommendations:

No recommendations made.

SR 1.4 Jurisdictions should have a legislative framework in place that allows for the enforcement of the requirements of the CRS in practice.

The Slovak Republic has a legislative framework in place to enforce the requirements in accordance with the CRS and its Commentary. While a deficiency has been identified with respect to a lack of an explicit legal basis to enforce a sanction where a Reporting Financial Institution is a legal arrangement, it is considered relatively minor and does not materially undermine the implementation of SR 1.4. This is because such Reporting Financial Institutions have so far not been known to exist in the Slovak Republic and are considered unlikely to exist under the Slovak Republic's financial and legal frameworks.

Recommendations:

The Slovak Republic should amend its legislative framework to ensure that there is an explicit legal basis to enforce a sanction when there is non-compliance by a Reporting Financial Institution that is a legal arrangement.

CR2 International legal framework: Jurisdictions should have exchange relationships in effect with all Interested Appropriate Partners as committed to and that provide for the exchange of information in accordance with the Model CAA.

Determination: In Place

The Slovak Republic's international legal framework to exchange the information is in place, is consistent with the Model CAA and its Commentary and provides for exchange with all of the Slovak Republic's Interested Appropriate Partners (i.e. all jurisdictions that are interested in receiving information from the Slovak Republic and that meet the required standard in relation to confidentiality and data safeguards) (SRs 2.1 – 2.3).

SR 2.1 Jurisdictions should have exchange agreements in effect with all Interested Appropriate Partners that permit the automatic exchange of CRS information.

The Slovak Republic has exchange agreements that permit the automatic exchange of CRS information in effect with all its Interested Appropriate Partners.

Recommendations:

No recommendations made.

SR 2.2 Such an exchange agreement should be put in place without undue delay, following the receipt of an expression of interest from an Interested Appropriate Partner.

The Slovak Republic put in place its exchange agreements without undue delay.

Recommendations:

No recommendations made.

SR 2.3 Jurisdictions should ensure that the exchange agreements in effect provide for the exchange of information in accordance with the requirements of the Model CAA.

The Slovak Republic's exchange agreements provide for the exchange of information in accordance with the requirements of the Model CAA.

Recommendations:

No recommendations made.

Comments by the assessed jurisdiction

The competent authority of the Slovak Republic is conducting the legislative process in order to address the remaining recommendation under SR 1.4 with a view to complete the process in the 1Q 2025.

Note

[1] Andorra, Liechtenstein, Monaco, San Marino and Switzerland.

Slovenia

Overall findings

Slovenia's legal framework implementing the AEOI Standard is in place but needs improvement in order to be fully consistent with the requirements of the AEOI Terms of Reference. While Slovenia's international legal framework to exchange the information with all of Slovenia's Interested Appropriate Partners (CR2) is consistent with the requirements, its domestic legislative framework requiring Reporting Financial Institutions to conduct the due diligence and reporting procedures (CR1) has deficiencies significant to the proper functioning of elements of the AEOI Standard. Most significantly, deficiencies have been identified in relation to Slovenia's enforcement framework.

The methodology used for the peer reviews and that therefore underpins this report is outlined in Chapter 2.

Overall determination on the legal framework: In Place But **Needs Improvement**

Conclusions on the legal framework

General context

Slovenia commenced exchanges under the AEOI Standard in 2017.

In order to provide for Reporting Financial Institutions to collect and report the information to be exchanged, Slovenia:

- amended the Tax Procedure Act (ZDavP-2I, as further amended in the OJ No. 69/2017 of 8 December 2017);
- amended the Rules on the implementation of the Tax Procedure Act; and
- issued further guidance, which is not legally binding.

Under this framework Reporting Financial Institutions were required to commence the due diligence procedures in relation to New Accounts from 1 January 2016. With respect to Preexisting Accounts, Reporting Financial Institutions were required to complete the due diligence procedures on High Value Individual Accounts by 31 December 2016 and on Lower Value Individual Accounts and Entity Accounts by 31 December 2017.

Following the initial peer review by the Global Forum, Slovenia amended its legislative framework to address issues identified, effective from 9 December 2017.

With respect to the exchange of information under the AEOI Standard, Slovenia:

- is a Party to the convention on Mutual Administrative Assistance in Tax Matters and activated the associated CRS Multilateral Competent Authority Agreement in time for exchanges in 2017;
- has implemented European Directive 2011/16/EU on Administrative Cooperation in the Field of Taxation, as amended by Directive 2014/107/EU; and
- has in place European Union agreements with five European third countries.[1]

Detailed findings

The detailed findings for Slovenia are below, organised per Core Requirement (CR) and sub-requirement (SR), as extracted from the AEOI Terms of Reference (see Annex B).

CR1 Domestic legal framework: Jurisdictions should have a domestic legislative framework in place that requires all Reporting Financial Institutions to conduct the due diligence and reporting procedures in the CRS, and that provides for the effective implementation of the CRS as set out therein.

Determination: In Place But **Needs Improvement**

Slovenia's domestic legislative framework is in place and contains most of the key aspects of the CRS and its Commentary requiring Reporting Financial Institutions to conduct the due diligence and reporting procedures, but it needs improvement in relation to the due diligence procedures to be applied (SR 1.2) and the framework to enforce the requirements (SR 1.4). Most significantly, Slovenia does not provide for sanctions on Reporting Financial Institutions for filing incorrect or incomplete information.

SR 1.1 Jurisdictions should define the scope of Reporting Financial Institutions consistently with the CRS.

Slovenia has defined the scope of Reporting Financial Institutions in its domestic legislative framework in accordance with the CRS and its Commentary.

Recommendations:

No recommendations made.

SR 1.2 Jurisdictions should define the scope of Financial Accounts and Reportable Accounts consistently with the CRS and incorporate the due diligence procedures to identify them.

Slovenia has defined the scope of the Financial Accounts that are required to be reported in its domestic legislative framework and incorporated the due diligence procedures that must be applied to identify them in a manner that is largely consistent with the CRS and its Commentary. While a deficiency has been identified with respect to defining the term Participating Jurisdiction it does not materially undermine the implementation of SR 1.2.

Recommendations:

Slovenia should amend its domestic legislative framework to include a definition of Participating Jurisdiction that is in accordance with the AEOI Standard.

SR 1.3 Jurisdictions should incorporate the reporting requirements contained in Section I of the CRS into their domestic legislative framework.

Slovenia has incorporated the reporting requirements in its domestic legislative framework in accordance with the CRS and its Commentary.

Recommendations:

No recommendations made.

SR 1.4 Jurisdictions should have a legislative framework in place that allows for the enforcement of the requirements of the CRS in practice.

Slovenia has a legislative framework in place to enforce the requirements in a manner that is largely consistent with the CRS and its Commentary. However, deficiencies have been identified. More specifically, Slovenia's domestic legislative framework does not include rules to prevent Financial Institutions, persons or intermediaries from adopting practices to circumvent the reporting and due diligence procedures, and does not provide for sanctions on Reporting Financial Institutions for filing incorrect or incomplete information. These are key elements of the required enforcement framework and are therefore material to its proper functioning.

Recommendations:

Slovenia should amend its legislative framework introduce an anti-avoidance provision in accordance with the Standard.

While Slovenia is able to impose penalties for failing to report, failing to carry out due diligence and failing to keep the required records, it is recommended to amend its legislative framework to ensure it is able to also impose penalties for filing incorrect or incomplete information.

CR2 International legal framework: Jurisdictions should have exchange relationships in effect with all Interested Appropriate Partners as committed to and that provide for the exchange of information in accordance with the Model CAA.

Determination: In Place

Slovenia's international legal framework to exchange the information is in place, is consistent with the Model CAA and its Commentary and provides for exchange with all of Slovenia's Interested Appropriate Partners (i.e. all jurisdictions that are interested in receiving information from Slovenia and that meet the required standard in relation to confidentiality and data safeguards) (SRs 2.1 – 2.3).

SR 2.1 Jurisdictions should have exchange agreements in effect with all Interested Appropriate Partners that permit the automatic exchange of CRS information.

Slovenia has exchange agreements that permit the automatic exchange of CRS information in effect with all its Interested Appropriate Partners.

Recommendations:

No recommendations made.

SR 2.2 Such an exchange agreement should be put in place without undue delay, following the receipt of an expression of interest from an Interested Appropriate Partner.

Slovenia put in place its exchange agreements without undue delay.

Recommendations:

No recommendations made.

SR 2.3 Jurisdictions should ensure that the exchange agreements in effect provide for the exchange of information in accordance with the requirements of the Model CAA.

Slovenia's exchange agreements provide for the exchange of information in accordance with the requirements of the Model CAA.

Recommendations:

No recommendations made.

Comments by the assessed jurisdiction

Slovenia wishes to express its gratitude and deep appreciation for the excellent work carried out by the Secretariat of the Global Forum and the AEOI Assessment Panel. Slovenia is confident that the AEOI legal determination report is a fair and accurate picture of the legal framework in force. We are satisfied with the conclusion that Slovenia's legal framework implementing the AEOI Standard is in place and is consistent with the requirements of the AEOI Terms of Reference and that there are no recommendations.

Note

[1] Andorra, Liechtenstein, Monaco, San Marino and Switzerland.

Sweden

Overall findings

Sweden's legal framework implementing the AEOI Standard is in place but needs improvement in order to be fully consistent with the requirements of the AEOI Terms of Reference. While Sweden's international legal framework to exchange the information with all of Sweden's Interested Appropriate Partners (CR2) is consistent with the requirements, its domestic legislative framework requiring Reporting Financial Institutions to conduct the due diligence and reporting procedures (CR1) has deficiencies significant to the proper functioning of an element of the AEOI Standard. More specifically, there are deficiencies in the enforcement framework.

The methodology used for the peer reviews and that therefore underpins this report is outlined in Chapter 2.

Overall determination on the legal framework: In Place But **Needs Improvement**

Conclusions on the legal framework

General context

Sweden commenced exchanges under the AEOI Standard in 2017.

In order to provide for Reporting Financial Institutions to collect and report the information to be exchanged, Sweden:

- amended its Tax Procedure Code (2011:1244) and the Tax Procedure Ordinance (2011:1261);
- enacted Act (2015:911) on the identification of reportable accounts with regard to automatic exchange of information on financial accounts;
- enacted Act (2015:912) on the automatic exchange of information on financial accounts; and
- introduced Ordinance (2015:921) on the identification of reportable accounts with regard to automatic exchange of information on financial accounts and Ordinance (2015:922) on the automatic exchange of information on financial accounts.

Under this framework Reporting Financial Institutions were required to commence the due diligence procedures in relation to New Accounts from 1 January 2016. With respect to Preexisting Accounts, Reporting Financial Institutions were required to complete the due diligence procedures on High Value Individual Accounts by 31 December 2016 and on Lower Value Individual Accounts and Entity Accounts by 31 December 2017.

Following the initial Global Forum peer review, Sweden amended its legislative framework to address issues identified, effective from 1 January 2019.

With respect to the exchange of information under the AEOI Standard, Sweden:

- is a Party to the Convention on Mutual Administrative Assistance in Tax Matters and activated the associated CRS Multilateral Competent Authority Agreement in time for exchanges in 2017;
- has in place European Directive 2011/16/EU on Administrative Cooperation in the Field of Taxation, as amended by Directive 2014/107/EU; and
- has in place European Union agreements with five European third countries.[1]

Detailed findings

The detailed findings for Sweden are below, organised per Core Requirement (CR) and sub-requirement (SR), as extracted from the AEOI Terms of Reference (see Annex B).

CR1 Domestic legal framework: Jurisdictions should have a domestic legislative framework in place that requires all Reporting Financial Institutions to conduct the due diligence and reporting procedures in the CRS, and that provides for the effective implementation of the CRS as set out therein.

Determination: In Place But **Needs Improvement**

Sweden's domestic legislative framework is in place and contains most of the key aspects of the CRS and its Commentary requiring Reporting Financial Institutions to conduct the due diligence and reporting procedures, but it needs improvement in relation to the framework to enforce the requirements (SR 1.4). More specifically, the enforcement framework does not have an anti-circumvention rule that can cover all persons that may engage in avoidance, has a sanction framework that does not explicitly cover an RFI that is a legal arrangement, and does not fully provide for sanctions on Reporting Financial Institutions in all cases for failing to carry out the due diligence procedures.

SR 1.1 Jurisdictions should define the scope of Reporting Financial Institutions consistently with the CRS.

Sweden has defined the scope of Reporting Financial Institutions in its domestic legislative framework in accordance with the CRS and its Commentary.

Recommendations:

No recommendations made.

SR 1.2 Jurisdictions should define the scope of Financial Accounts and Reportable Accounts consistently with the CRS and incorporate the due diligence procedures to identify them.

Sweden has defined the scope of the Financial Accounts that are required to be reported in its domestic legislative framework and incorporated the due diligence procedures that must be applied to identify them in accordance with the CRS and its Commentary.

Recommendations:

No recommendations made.

SR 1.3 Jurisdictions should incorporate the reporting requirements contained in Section I of the CRS into their domestic legislative framework.

Sweden has incorporated the reporting requirements in its domestic legislative framework in accordance with the CRS and its Commentary.

Recommendations:

No recommendations made.

SR 1.4 Jurisdictions should have a legislative framework in place that allows for the enforcement of the requirements of the CRS in practice.

Sweden has a legislative framework in place to enforce the requirements in a manner that is largely consistent with the CRS and its Commentary. However, deficiencies have been identified. More specifically, Sweden's legislative framework:

- has an anti-circumvention rule that does not cover all relevant persons that may engage in practices to avoid due diligence and reporting;
- does not include an explicit legal basis to enforce a sanction where a Reporting Financial Institution is a legal arrangement; and
- does not impose sanctions for failing to carry out the due diligence procedures required under the AEOI Standard, where it does not impact reporting.

These are key elements of the required enforcement framework that, taken together, are material to the proper functioning of the AEOI Standard.

Recommendations:

Sweden should ensure that its anti-avoidance rule covers avoidance of CRS reporting and due diligence by any person, not just by persons resident in Sweden.

Sweden should amend its legislative framework to ensure that there is an explicit legal basis to enforce a sanction when there is non-compliance by a Reporting Financial Institution that is a legal arrangement.

While Sweden is able to impose penalties for failing to report, for reporting incorrect information and for failing to keep the required records, it is recommended to amend its legislative framework to ensure it is able to also impose penalties in all cases for failing to carry out due diligence.

CR2 International legal framework: Jurisdictions should have exchange relationships in effect with all Interested Appropriate Partners as committed to and that provide for the exchange of information in accordance with the Model CAA.

Determination: In Place

Sweden's international legal framework to exchange the information is in place, is consistent with the Model CAA and its Commentary and provides for exchange with all of Sweden's Interested Appropriate Partners (i.e. all jurisdictions that are interested in receiving information from Sweden and that meet the required standard in relation to confidentiality and data safeguards) (SRs 2.1 – 2.3).

SR 2.1 Jurisdictions should have exchange agreements in effect with all Interested Appropriate Partners that permit the automatic exchange of CRS information.

Sweden has exchange agreements that permit the automatic exchange of CRS information in effect with all its Interested Appropriate Partners.

Recommendations:

No recommendations made.

SR 2.2 Such an exchange agreement should be put in place without undue delay, following the receipt of an expression of interest from an Interested Appropriate Partner.

Sweden put in place its exchange agreements without undue delay.

Recommendations:

No recommendations made.

SR 2.3 Jurisdictions should ensure that the exchange agreements in effect provide for the exchange of information in accordance with the requirements of the Model CAA.

Sweden's exchange agreements provide for the exchange of information in accordance with the requirements of the Model CAA.

Recommendations:

No recommendations made.

Comments by the assessed jurisdiction

On 5 September 2024 the Swedish government decided to submit a bill to the Parliament, containing all the amendments to the legislation that have been deemed necessary to address the recommendations made. The parliamentary process is on-going, and it is likely that the bill will be adopted by the end of October. We do not foresee any political or other impediments.

Note

[1] Andorra, Liechtenstein, Monaco, San Marino and Switzerland.

Switzerland

Overall findings

Switzerland's legal framework implementing the AEOI Standard is in place but needs improvement in order to be fully consistent with the requirements of the AEOI Terms of Reference. While Switzerland's international legal framework to exchange the information with all of Switzerland's Interested Appropriate Partners (CR2) is consistent with the requirements of the AEOI Terms of Reference, its domestic legislative framework requiring Reporting Financial Institutions to conduct the due diligence and reporting procedures (CR1) has deficiencies significant to the proper functioning of elements of the AEOI Standard. More specifically, Switzerland provides for jurisdiction-specific Non-Reporting Financial Institutions and Excluded Accounts that do not meet the requirements of the AEOI Standard, and there are deficiencies in the enforcement framework.

The methodology used for the peer reviews and that therefore underpins this report is outlined in Chapter 2.

Overall determination on the legal framework: In Place But **Needs Improvement**

Conclusions on the legal framework

General context

Switzerland commenced exchanges under the AEOI Standard in 2018.

In order to provide for Reporting Financial Institutions to collect and report the information to be exchanged, Switzerland:

- enacted the Federal Act of 18 December 2015 on the International Automatic Exchange of Information in Tax Matters; as amended on 9 October 2020;
- introduced the Ordinance of 23 November 2016 on the International Automatic Exchange of Information in Tax Matters; as amended on 9 October 2020;
- issued further guidance, which is legally binding; and
- made reference to the Federal Act of 12 December 2014 on the Implementation of the Revised FATF Recommendations of 2012 for the purposes of the identification of Controlling Persons under the AEOI Standard.

Under this framework Reporting Financial Institutions were required to commence the due diligence procedures in relation to New Accounts from 1 January 2017. With respect to Preexisting Accounts, Reporting Financial Institutions were required to complete the due diligence procedures on High Value Individual Accounts by 31 December 2017 and on Lower Value Individual Accounts and Entity Accounts by 31 December 2018.

Following the initial Global Forum peer review, Switzerland made various amendments to its legislative framework to address issues identified, the last of which will be effective from 1 January 2021.

With respect to the exchange of information under the AEOI Standard, Switzerland:

- is a Party to the Convention on Mutual Administrative Assistance in Tax Matters and activated the associated CRS Multilateral Competent Authority Agreement in time for exchanges in 2018;
- has in place an agreement with the European Union; and

- put in place two bilateral agreements.[1]

Detailed findings

The detailed findings for Switzerland are below, organised per Core Requirement (CR) and sub-requirement (SR), as extracted from the AEOI Terms of Reference (see Annex B).

CR1 Domestic legal framework: Jurisdictions should have a domestic legislative framework in place that requires all Reporting Financial Institutions to conduct the due diligence and reporting procedures in the CRS, and that provides for the effective implementation of the CRS as set out therein.

Determination: In Place But **Needs Improvement**

Switzerland's domestic legislative framework is in place and contains most of the key aspects of the CRS and its Commentary requiring Reporting Financial Institutions to conduct the due diligence and reporting procedures, but it needs improvement in relation to the scope of Reporting Financial Institutions required to report information (SR 1.1), and the scope of Financial Accounts required to be reported (SR 1.2).

More specifically, Switzerland provides for categories of jurisdiction-specific Non-Reporting Financial Institutions and Excluded Accounts that do not meet the requirements of the AEOI Standard, and it does not fully provide for sanctions on Reporting Financial Institutions for failing to comply with due diligence and reporting requirements.

SR 1.1 Jurisdictions should define the scope of Reporting Financial Institutions consistently with the CRS.

Switzerland has defined the scope of Reporting Financial Institutions in its domestic legislative framework in a manner that is largely consistent with the CRS and its Commentary. However, deficiencies have been identified. More specifically, Switzerland provides for two categories of jurisdiction-specific Non-Reporting Financial Institutions that do not correspond to any of the categories of Non-Reporting Financial Institutions foreseen in the AEOI Standard. The scope of Reporting Financial Institutions, including the provision on Non-Reporting Financial Institutions is material to the proper functioning of the AEOI Standard.

Recommendations:

Switzerland should amend its domestic legislative framework to remove two categories from its jurisdiction-specific list of Non-Reporting Financial Institutions as they do not correspond to any of the categories of Non-Reporting Financial Institutions foreseen in the AEOI Standard. The entries are: i) associations that pursue a non-commercial purpose, and ii) foundations that pursue a public, charitable or non-material purpose.

SR 1.2 Jurisdictions should define the scope of Financial Accounts and Reportable Accounts consistently with the CRS and incorporate the due diligence procedures to identify them.

Switzerland has defined the scope of the Financial Accounts that are required to be reported in its domestic legislative framework and incorporated the due diligence procedures that must be applied to them in a manner that is largely consistent with the CRS and its Commentary. However, deficiencies have been identified. More specifically, Switzerland provides for three jurisdiction-specific Excluded Accounts which are not in line with the requirements of the AEOI Standard. Two of the Excluded Accounts do not correspond to any of the categories of Excluded Accounts in the AEOI Standard. The capital contribution accounts have some similarity to escrow accounts, but do not relate to the sale, exchange or lease of real or personal property and do not have sufficiently similar characteristics to the requirements nor to ensure that these accounts pose a low risk of being used to evade tax. The scope of Financial Accounts, including the provision of Excluded Accounts, is material to the proper functioning of the AEOI Standard.

Recommendations:

Switzerland should amend its domestic legislative framework to remove three entries from its jurisdiction-specific list of Excluded Accounts as they do not meet the requirements. The entries are: i) accounts of associations that pursue a non-commercial purpose; ii) accounts of foundations that pursue a public, charitable or non-material purpose; and iii) capital contribution accounts.

SR 1.3 Jurisdictions should incorporate the reporting requirements contained in Section I of the CRS into their domestic legislative framework.

Switzerland has incorporated the reporting requirements in its domestic legislative framework in accordance with the CRS and its Commentary.

Recommendations:

No recommendations made.

SR 1.4 Jurisdictions should have a legislative framework in place that allows for the enforcement of the requirements of the CRS in practice.

Switzerland has a legislative framework in place to enforce the requirements in a manner that is largely consistent with the CRS and its Commentary. However, deficiencies have been identified. More specifically, Switzerland's legislative framework has sanctions for filing late, filing incorrect information or failing to carry out due diligence but the noncompliance must be shown to have been intentional. Furthermore, it does not provide for sanctions for failing keep records in accordance with the AEOI Standard. These deficiencies relate to key elements of the required enforcement framework and are therefore material to the proper functioning of the AEOI Standard

Recommendations:

Switzerland should ensure that it has sanction provisions applicable to Reporting Financial Institutions that fail to keep records in accordance with the AEOI Standard.

Switzerland should amend its domestic legislative framework to ensure that sanctions are not limited to intentional noncompliance.

CR2 International legal framework: Jurisdictions should have exchange relationships in effect with all Interested Appropriate Partners as committed to and that provide for the exchange of information in accordance with the Model CAA.

Determination: In Place

Switzerland's international legal framework to exchange the information is in place, is consistent with the Model CAA and its Commentary and provides for exchange with all of Switzerland's Interested Appropriate Partners (i.e. all jurisdictions that are interested in receiving information from Switzerland and that meet the required standard in relation to confidentiality and data safeguards) (SRs 2.1 – 2.3).

SR 2.1 Jurisdictions should have exchange agreements in effect with all Interested Appropriate Partners that permit the automatic exchange of CRS information.

Switzerland has exchange agreements that permit the automatic exchange of CRS information in effect with all its Interested Appropriate Partners.

Recommendations:

No recommendations made.

SR 2.2 Such an exchange agreement should be put in place without undue delay, following the receipt of an expression of interest from an Interested Appropriate Partner.

Switzerland put in place its exchange agreements without undue delay.

Recommendations:

No recommendations made.

SR 2.3 Jurisdictions should ensure that the exchange agreements in effect provide for the exchange of information in accordance with the requirements of the Model CAA.

Switzerland's exchange agreements provide for the exchange of information in accordance with the requirements of the Model CAA.

Recommendations:

No recommendations made.

Comments by the assessed jurisdiction

No comments made.

Note

[1] With Hong Kong (China) and Singapore.

Thailand

Overall findings

Thailand's legal framework implementing the AEOI Standard is in place but needs improvement in order to be fully consistent with the requirements of the AEOI Terms of Reference. While Thailand's international legal framework to exchange the information with all of Thailand's Interested Appropriate Partners (CR2) is consistent with the requirements, its domestic legislative framework requiring Reporting Financial Institutions to conduct the due diligence and reporting procedures (CR1) has deficiencies significant to the proper functioning of elements of the AEOI Standard. More specifically, the deficiencies relate to defining Controlling Persons, Participating Jurisdictions and the enforcement framework.

The methodology used for the peer reviews and that therefore underpins this report is outlined in Chapter 2.

Overall determination on the legal framework: In Place **But Needs Improvement**

Conclusions on the legal framework

General context

Thailand commenced exchanges under the AEOI Standard in 2023.

In order to provide for Reporting Financial Institutions to collect and report the information to be exchanged, Thailand relies on:

- Emergency Decree on Exchange of Information for Implementation of the International Agreement on Taxation B.E. 2566 (2023), in force from 31 March 2023;
- Ministerial Regulation on the Exchange of Information for Implementation of the International Agreement on Taxation, B.E. 2566 (2023), in force from 16 August 2023;
- Notification of the Ministry of Finance, Re: Determination of Reportable Jurisdictions and Participating Jurisdictions under Competent Authority Agreement on the Automatic Exchange of Information, in force from 16 August 2023;
- Notification of the Ministry of Finance Re: Determination of Non-Reportable Person under Emergency Decree on Exchange of Information for Implementation of the International Agreement on Taxation B.E. 2566 (2023), in force from 16 August 2023;
- Notification of the Director-General of the Revenue Department on Rules, Procedures, Conditions and Formats for Submitting Financial Account Information under Competent Authority Agreement on the Automatic Exchange of Information, in force from 16 August 2023; and
- Notification of the Ministry of Finance, Re: Determination of Reporting Financial Institution for Reportable Financial Account Information under Emergency Decree on Exchange of Information for Implementation of the International Agreement on Taxation B.E. 2566 (2023), in force from 27 April 2024.

Under this framework Reporting Financial Institutions were required to commence the due diligence procedures in relation to New Accounts from 16 August 2023. With respect to Preexisting Accounts, Reporting Financial Institutions were required to complete due diligence procedures on High Value Individual Accounts by 15 September 2023 or 30 June 2024 and on Lower Value Individual Accounts and Entity Accounts by 30 June 2024.

With respect to the exchange of information under the AEOI Standard, Thailand is a Party to the Convention on Mutual Administrative Assistance in Tax Matters and activated the associated CRS Multilateral Competent Authority Agreement in time for exchanges in 2023.

Detailed findings

The detailed findings for Thailand are below, organised per Core Requirement (CR) and sub-requirement (SR), as extracted from the AEOI Terms of Reference (see Annex B).

CR1 Domestic legal framework: Jurisdictions should have a domestic legislative framework in place that requires all Reporting Financial Institutions to conduct the due diligence and reporting procedures in the CRS, and that provides for the effective implementation of the CRS as set out therein.

Overall determination on the legal framework: In Place **But Needs Improvement**

Thailand's domestic legislative framework is in place and contains many of the key aspects of CRS and its Commentary requiring Reporting Financial Institutions to conduct the due diligence and reporting procedures, but it needs improvement in relation to the due diligence procedures that must be applied to Financial Accounts (SR 1.2) and the framework to enforce the requirements (SR 1.4). More specifically, Thailand's domestic legislative framework does not define the term Controlling Persons in accordance with the requirements, its approach with respect to Participating Jurisdictions is not in line with the AEOI Standard and there are deficiencies in Thailand's enforcement framework.

SR 1.1 Jurisdictions should define the scope of Reporting Financial Institutions consistently with the CRS.

Thailand has defined the scope of Reporting Financial Institutions in its domestic legislative framework in accordance with the CRS and its Commentary.

Recommendations:

No recommendations made.

SR 1.2 Jurisdictions should define the scope of Financial Accounts and Reportable Accounts consistently with the CRS and incorporate the due diligence procedures to identify them.

Thailand has defined the scope of the Financial Accounts that are required to be reported in its domestic legislative framework and has incorporated the due diligence procedures that must be applied to identify them in a manner that is largely consistent with the CRS and its Commentary. However, deficiencies have been identified. More specifically, Thailand's legislative framework does not define Controlling Persons in accordance with the requirements and its approach with respect to Participating Jurisdictions is not in line with the AEOI Standard.

Recommendation:

Thailand should amend its domestic legislative framework to ensure that "Controlling Person" is defined in accordance with the AEOI Standard.

Thailand should amend its domestic legislative framework to ensure that the approach taken with respect to the 44 jurisdictions defined as Participating Jurisdictions and with which Thailand does not have an agreement to exchange CRS information with (two of which have not implemented the AEOI Standard), is in accordance with the AEOI Standard

SR 1.3 Jurisdictions should incorporate the reporting requirements contained in Section I of the CRS into their domestic legislative framework.

Thailand has incorporated the reporting requirements in its domestic legislative framework in accordance with the CRS and its Commentary.

Recommendations:

No recommendations made.

SR 1.4 Jurisdictions should have a legislative framework in place that allows for the enforcement of the requirements of the CRS in practice.

Thailand has a legislative framework in place to enforce the requirements in a manner that is largely consistent with the CRS and its Commentary. However, deficiencies have been identified. More specifically, Thailand's legislative framework:

- does not provide the relevant authorities with the power to directly access the records held by Reporting Financial Institutions in relation to the due diligence procedures applied;
- has sanctions on Reporting Financial Institutions for failing to report information that have a limited deterrent effect, as they depend on an order to report information being issued and are not applicable if the order is complied with;
- has limited sanctions for filing incorrect information as the incorrect filing must be shown to have been intentional;
- does not impose sanctions for failing to carry out the due diligence procedures required under the AEOI Standard, where it does not impact reporting;
- does not include an explicit legal basis to impose or enforce a sanction where a Reporting Financial Institution is a legal arrangement; and
- does not include measures to ensure that valid self-certifications are always obtained and validated for New Accounts.

These are the key elements of the required enforcement framework and are therefore material to the proper functioning of the AEOI Standard.

Recommendations:

Thailand should amend its domestic legislative framework to provide the appropriate authorities with the power to directly access the records and evidence relevant for verifying and enforcing the AEOI Standard

Thailand should amend its domestic legislative framework to ensure that sanctions for failure to report information are capable of being applied even where the noncompliance is corrected.

Thailand should amend its domestic legislative framework to ensure that sanctions for filing incorrect information are not limited to intentional reporting of incorrect information.

Thailand should ensure that it has sanction provisions applicable to Reporting Financial Institutions that fail to conduct the due diligence requirements in accordance with the AEOI Standard, regardless of the impact on reporting.

Thailand should amend its legislative framework to ensure that it is able to sanction non-compliance by any legal arrangement that is a Reporting Financial Institution.

Thailand should introduce measures to ensure that valid self-certifications are always obtained and validated for New Accounts.

CR2 International legal framework: Jurisdictions should have exchange relationships in effect with all Interested Appropriate Partners as committed to and that provide for the exchange of information in accordance with the Model CAA.

Determination: In Place

Thailand's international legal framework to exchange the information is in place, is consistent with the Model CAA and its Commentary and provides for exchange with all of Thailand's Interested Appropriate Partners (i.e. all jurisdictions that are interested in receiving information from Thailand and that meet the required standard in relation to confidentiality and data safeguards) (SRs 2.1 – 2.3).

SR 2.1 Jurisdictions should have exchange agreements in effect with all Interested Appropriate Partners that permit the automatic exchange of CRS information.

Thailand has exchange agreements that permit the automatic exchange of CRS information in effect with all its Interested Appropriate Partners.

Recommendations:

No recommendations made.

SR 2.2 Such an exchange agreement should be put in place without undue delay, following the receipt of an expression of interest from an Interested Appropriate Partner.

Thailand put in place its exchange agreements without undue delay.

Recommendations:

No recommendations made.

SR 2.3 Jurisdictions should ensure that the exchange agreements in effect provide for the exchange of information in accordance with the requirements of the Model CAA.

Thailand's exchange agreements provide for the exchange of information in accordance with the requirements of the Model CAA.

Recommendations:

No recommendations made.

Comments by the assessed jurisdiction

No comments made.

United Kingdom

Overall findings

The United Kingdom's legal framework implementing the AEOI Standard is in place but needs improvement in order to be fully consistent with the requirements of the AEOI Terms of Reference. While the United Kingdom's international legal framework to exchange the information with all of the United Kingdom's Interested Appropriate Partners (CR2) is consistent with the requirements, its domestic legislative framework requiring Reporting Financial Institutions to conduct the due diligence and reporting procedures (CR1) has a deficiency significant to the proper functioning of elements of the AEOI Standard. More specifically, the rules in the United Kingdom's legislative framework to prevent the adoption of practices intended to circumvent the reporting and due diligence procedures are insufficient in scope.

The methodology used for the peer reviews and that therefore underpins this report is outlined in Chapter 2.

Overall determination on the legal framework: In Place But **Needs Improvement**

Conclusions on the legal framework

General context

The United Kingdom commenced exchanges under the AEOI Standard in 2017.

In order to provide for Reporting Financial Institutions to collect and report the information to be exchanged, the United Kingdom:

- enacted Section 222 of the Finance Act 2013;
- introduced the International Tax Compliance Regulations 2015 as amended by Statutory Instruments 1839 of 2015, 899 of 2016, 598 of 2017, 490 of 2018, 881 of 2019 and 438 of 2020; and
- issued further guidance, which is not legally binding.

Under this framework Reporting Financial Institutions were required to commence the due diligence procedures in relation to New Accounts from 1 January 2016. With respect to Preexisting Accounts, Reporting Financial Institutions were required to complete the due diligence procedures on High Value Individual Accounts by 31 December 2016 and on Lower Value Individual Accounts and Entity Accounts by 31 December 2017.

Following the initial Global Forum peer review, the United Kingdom made various amendments to its legislative framework to address issues identified, the last of which was effective from 13 May 2020.

With respect to the exchange of information under the AEOI Standard, the United Kingdom:

- is a Party to the Convention on Mutual Administrative Assistance in Tax Matters and activated the associated CRS Multilateral Competent Authority Agreement in time for exchanges in 2017; and
- put in place 12 bilateral agreements.[1]

Detailed findings

The detailed findings for the United Kingdom are below, organised per Core Requirement (CR) and sub-requirement (SR), as extracted from the AEOI Terms of Reference (see Annex B).

CR1 Domestic legal framework: Jurisdictions should have a domestic legislative framework in place that requires all Reporting Financial Institutions to conduct the due diligence and reporting procedures in the CRS, and that provides for the effective implementation of the CRS as set out therein.

Determination: In Place But **Needs Improvement**

The United Kingdom's domestic legislative framework is in place and contains most of the key aspects of the CRS and its Commentary requiring Reporting Financial Institutions to conduct the due diligence and reporting procedures, but it needs improvement in one area relating to the framework to enforce the requirements (SR 1.4). More specifically, the rules in the United Kingdom's legislative framework to prevent persons from adopting practices intended to circumvent the reporting and due diligence procedures are insufficient in scope as they do not cover all relevant persons and circumstances.

SR 1.1 Jurisdictions should define the scope of Reporting Financial Institutions consistently with the CRS.

The United Kingdom has defined the scope of Reporting Financial Institutions in its domestic legislative framework in accordance with the CRS and its Commentary.

Recommendations:

No recommendations made.

SR 1.2 Jurisdictions should define the scope of Financial Accounts and Reportable Accounts consistently with the CRS and incorporate the due diligence procedures to identify them.

The United Kingdom has defined the scope of the Financial Accounts that are required to be reported in its domestic legislative framework and incorporated the due diligence procedures that must be applied to identify them in accordance with the CRS and its Commentary.

Recommendations:

No recommendations made.

SR 1.3 Jurisdictions should incorporate the reporting requirements contained in Section I of the CRS into their domestic legislative framework.

The United Kingdom has incorporated the reporting requirements in its domestic legislative framework in accordance with the CRS and its Commentary.

Recommendations:

No recommendations made.

SR 1.4 Jurisdictions should have a legislative framework in place that allows for the enforcement of the requirements of the CRS in practice.

The United Kingdom has a legislative framework in place to enforce the requirements in a manner that is largely consistent with the CRS and its Commentary. However, a deficiency has been identified. More specifically, the United Kingdom's legislative framework has an anti-circumvention rule that does not cover all relevant persons that may engage in practices to avoid due diligence and reporting. This is a key element of the required enforcement framework and is therefore material to the proper functioning of the AEOI Standard.

Recommendations:

The United Kingdom should ensure that its anti-avoidance rule covers avoidance of CRS reporting and due diligence when entered into by Account Holders or intermediaries, not just by Financial Institutions.

CR2 International legal framework: Jurisdictions should have exchange relationships in effect with all Interested Appropriate Partners as committed to and that provide for the exchange of information in accordance with the Model CAA.

Determination: In Place

The United Kingdom's international legal framework to exchange the information is in place, is consistent with the Model CAA and its Commentary and provides for exchange with all of the United Kingdom's Interested Appropriate Partners (i.e. all jurisdictions that are interested in receiving information from the United Kingdom and that meet the required standard in relation to confidentiality and data safeguards) (SRs 2.1 – 2.3).

SR 2.1 Jurisdictions should have exchange agreements in effect with all Interested Appropriate Partners that permit the automatic exchange of CRS information.

The United Kingdom has exchange agreements that permit the automatic exchange of CRS information in effect with all its Interested Appropriate Partners.

Recommendations:

No recommendations made.

SR 2.2 Such an exchange agreement should be put in place without undue delay, following the receipt of an expression of interest from an Interested Appropriate Partner.

The United Kingdom put in place its exchange agreements without undue delay.

Recommendations:

No recommendations made.

SR 2.3 Jurisdictions should ensure that the exchange agreements in effect provide for the exchange of information in accordance with the requirements of the Model CAA.

The United Kingdom's exchange agreements provide for the exchange of information in accordance with the requirements of the Model CAA.

Recommendations:

No recommendations made.

Comments by the assessed jurisdiction

No comments made.

Note

[1] With Anguilla, Bermuda, the British Virgin Islands, the Cayman Islands, Guernsey, Hong Kong (China), the Isle of Man, Jersey, Montserrat, Qatar, Singapore and the Turks and Caicos Islands. The United Kingdom has also activated a relationship under the CRS MCAA with Qatar.

Vanuatu

Overall findings

Vanuatu's legal framework implementing the AEOI Standard is in place but needs improvement in order to be fully consistent with the requirements of the AEOI Terms of Reference. While Vanuatu's international legal framework to exchange the information with all of Vanuatu's Interested Appropriate Partners (CR2) is consistent with the requirements, its domestic legislative framework requiring Reporting Financial Institutions to conduct the due diligence and reporting procedures (CR1) has a deficiency significant to the proper functioning of elements of the AEOI Standard. More specifically, a deficiency has been identified in relation to Vanuatu's enforcement framework.

The methodology used for the peer reviews and that therefore underpins this report is outlined in Chapter 2.

Overall determination on the legal framework: In Place But **Needs Improvement**

Conclusions on the legal framework

General context

Vanuatu commenced exchanges under the AEOI Standard in 2018.

In order to provide for Reporting Financial Institutions to collect and report the information to be exchanged, Vanuatu:

- enacted International Tax Cooperation Act No. 7 of 2016 that was subsequently replaced by Tax Administration Act No. 37 of 2018 (with full effect from 1 January 2020);
- introduced Automatic Exchange of Information Regulations Order No. 76 of 2017 that was subsequently replaced by the Tax Administration Regulation Order No. 154 of 2019 (with full effect from 1 January 2020), as amended with effect from 14 September 2020; and
- issued further guidance, which is not legally binding.

Under this framework Reporting Financial Institutions were required to commence the due diligence procedures in relation to New Accounts from 30 June 2017. With respect to Preexisting Accounts, Reporting Financial Institutions were required to complete the due diligence procedures on High Value Individual Accounts by 31 December 2017 and on Lower Value Individual Accounts and Entity Accounts by 31 December 2018.

Following the initial Global Forum peer review, Vanuatu made various amendments to its legislative framework to address issues identified, the last of which was effective from 14 September 2020.

With respect to the exchange of information under the AEOI Standard, Vanuatu is a Party to the Convention on Mutual Administrative Assistance in Tax Matters and activated the associated CRS Multilateral Competent Authority Agreement in time for exchanges in 2018.

Detailed findings

The detailed findings for Vanuatu are below, organised per Core Requirement (CR) and sub-requirement (SR), as extracted from the AEOI Terms of Reference (see Annex B).

CR1 Domestic legal framework: Jurisdictions should have a domestic legislative framework in place that requires all Reporting Financial Institutions to conduct the due diligence and reporting procedures in the CRS, and that provides for the effective implementation of the CRS as set out therein.

Determination: In Place But **Needs Improvement**

Vanuatu's domestic legislative framework is in place and contains all of the key aspects of the CRS and its Commentary requiring Reporting Financial Institutions to conduct the due diligence and reporting procedures (SRs 1.1 – 1.3), but it needs improvement in relation to the framework to enforce the requirements (SR 1.4). More specifically, Vanuatu's legislative framework does not have an explicit legal basis to impose or enforce a sanction for non-compliance if the Reporting Financial Institution is a legal arrangement.

SR 1.1 Jurisdictions should define the scope of Reporting Financial Institutions consistently with the CRS.

Vanuatu has defined the scope of Reporting Financial Institutions in its domestic legislative framework in accordance with the CRS and its Commentary.

Recommendations:

No recommendations made.

SR 1.2 Jurisdictions should define the scope of Financial Accounts and Reportable Accounts consistently with the CRS and incorporate the due diligence procedures to identify them.

Vanuatu has defined the scope of the Financial Accounts that are required to be reported in its domestic legislative framework and incorporated the due diligence procedures that must be applied to identify them in accordance with the CRS and its Commentary.

Recommendations:

No recommendations made.

SR 1.3 Jurisdictions should incorporate the reporting requirements contained in Section I of the CRS into their domestic legislative framework.

Vanuatu has incorporated the reporting requirements in its domestic legislative framework in accordance with the CRS and its Commentary.

Recommendations:

No recommendations made.

SR 1.4 Jurisdictions should have a legislative framework in place that allows for the enforcement of the requirements of the CRS in practice.

Vanuatu has a legislative framework in place to enforce the requirements in a manner that is largely consistent with the CRS and its Commentary. However, a deficiency has been identified. More specifically, Vanuatu's legislative framework does not include an explicit legal basis to enforce a sanction where a Reporting Financial Institution is a legal arrangement. This deficiency relates to a key element of the AEOI Standard and is therefore material to the proper functioning of the AEOI Standard.

Recommendations:

Vanuatu should amend its legislative framework to ensure that there is an explicit legal basis to enforce a sanction when there is non-compliance by a Reporting Financial Institution that is a legal arrangement.

CR2 International legal framework: Jurisdictions should have exchange relationships in effect with all Interested Appropriate Partners as committed to and that provide for the exchange of information in accordance with the Model CAA.

Determination: In Place

Vanuatu's international legal framework to exchange the information is in place, is consistent with the Model CAA and its Commentary and provides for exchange with all of Vanuatu's Interested Appropriate Partners (i.e. all jurisdictions that are interested in receiving information from Vanuatu and that meet the required standard in relation to confidentiality and data safeguards) (SRs 2.1 – 2.3).

SR 2.1 Jurisdictions should have exchange agreements in effect with all Interested Appropriate Partners that permit the automatic exchange of CRS information.

Vanuatu has exchange agreements that permit the automatic exchange of CRS information in effect with all its Interested Appropriate Partners.

Recommendations:

No recommendations made.

SR 2.2 Such an exchange agreement should be put in place without undue delay, following the receipt of an expression of interest from an Interested Appropriate Partner.

Vanuatu put in place its exchange agreements without undue delay.

Recommendations:

No recommendations made.

SR 2.3 Jurisdictions should ensure that the exchange agreements in effect provide for the exchange of information in accordance with the requirements of the Model CAA.

Vanuatu's exchange agreements provide for the exchange of information in accordance with the requirements of the Model CAA.

Recommendations:

No recommendations made.

Comments by the assessed jurisdiction

No comments made.

Annex A. Details of the exchange agreements in place

The table below presents information on the exchange agreements in place by the jurisdictions that have been newly assessed in relation to their legal frameworks they have in place with respect to the AEOI Standard. This includes agreements activated through multilateral frameworks (such as the CRS Multilateral Competent Authority Agreement or in a European Union context) as well as bilateral agreements.

For the latest information, please refer to the section on Activated Exchange Relationships for CRS Information on the AEOI Portal (www.oecd.org/tax/automatic-exchange).

Jurisdiction	Exchange agreements in place:
Jamaica (77)	Anguilla, Argentina, Aruba, Australia, Austria, Azerbaijan, Barbados, Belgium, Bermuda, Brazil, Bulgaria, Canada, Cayman Islands, Chile, Colombia, Cook Islands, Costa Rica, Croatia, Curaçao, Cyprus, Czechia, Denmark, Dominica, Estonia, Finland, France, Germany, Ghana, Gibraltar, Greece, Guernsey, Hong Kong, China, Hungary, Iceland, India, Indonesia, Ireland, Isle of Man, Israel, Italy, Japan, Jersey, Korea, Kuwait, Liechtenstein, Lithuania, Luxembourg, Macau, China, Malaysia, Malta, Mauritius, Monaco, Netherlands, New Zealand, Norway, Panama, Poland, Portugal, Romania, Russia, Saint Kitts and Nevis, Saint Lucia, Saint Vincent and the Grenadines, San Marino, Saudi Arabia, Singapore, Slovak Republic, Slovenia, South Africa, Spain, Sweden, Switzerland, Türkiye, Turks and Caicos Islands, United Kingdom, Uruguay, Vanuatu
Jordan	None
Maldives (88)	Albania, Andorra, Argentina, Aruba, Australia, Austria, Azerbaijan, Bahrain, Belgium, Bermuda, Brazil, Brunei Darussalam, Bulgaria, Cayman Islands, Chile, China, Colombia, Cook Islands, Costa Rica, Croatia, Curaçao, Cyprus, Czechia, Denmark, Dominica, Ecuador, Estonia, Finland, France, Georgia, Germany, Ghana, Gibraltar, Greece, Guernsey, Hong Kong, China, Hungary, Iceland, India, Indonesia, Ireland, Isle of Man, Israel, Italy, Japan, Jersey, Kazakhstan, Kenya, Korea, Kuwait, Liechtenstein, Lithuania, Luxembourg, Macau, China, Malaysia, Malta, Mauritius, Mexico, Moldova, Monaco, Netherlands, New Caledonia, New Zealand, Nigeria , Norway, Peru, Poland, Portugal, Romania, Russia, Saint Kitts and Nevis, San Marino, Saudi Arabia, Singapore, Slovak Republic, Slovenia, South Africa, Spain, Sweden, Switzerland, Thailand, Türkiye, Turks and Caicos Islands, Ukraine, United Arab Emirates, United Kingdom, Uruguay, Vanuatu
Montenegro	None
Thailand (70)	Albania, Argentina, Aruba, Australia, Austria, Azerbaijan, Belgium, Bermuda, Bulgaria, Cayman Islands, Chile, Colombia, Cook Islands, Costa Rica, Croatia, Curaçao, Cyprus, Czechia, Denmark, Dominica, Ecuador, Estonia, Faroe Islands, Finland, Germany, Greece, Guernsey, Hong Kong, China, Hungary, India, Indonesia, Ireland, Isle of Man, Italy, Japan, Jersey, Kenya, Korea, Liechtenstein, Lithuania, Luxembourg, Macau, China, Malaysia, Maldives, Malta, Monaco, Netherlands, New Zealand, Nigeria , Norway, Peru, Poland, Portugal, Romania, Russia, Saint Kitts and Nevis, San Marino, Saudi Arabia, Singapore, Slovak Republic, Slovenia, South Africa, Spain, Sweden, Switzerland, Türkiye, Turks and Caicos Islands, United Kingdom, Uruguay, Vanuatu

Annex B. The AEOI Terms of Reference

Below are the Core Requirements and Sub-Requirements of the AEOI Terms of Reference with respect to the implementation of the AEOI Standard.

CR1 Legal framework: Jurisdictions should have a domestic legislative framework in place that requires all Reporting Financial Institutions to conduct the due diligence and reporting procedures in the CRS, and that provides for the effective implementation of the CRS as set out therein

Defining Reporting Financial Institutions

SR 1.1 Jurisdictions should define the scope of Reporting Financial Institutions consistently with the CRS, in particular by:

a) incorporating the definitions contained in paragraph A of Section VIII of the CRS into their domestic legislative framework; and

b) ensuring that any Financial Institution or category of Financial Institutions defined domestically as a Non-Reporting Financial Institution meets the requirements for its status as a Non-Reporting Financial Institution as set out in paragraph B of Section VIII of the CRS.

Defining the Financial Accounts to be reported and incorporating the due diligence procedures to identify them

SR 1.2 Jurisdictions should define the scope of Financial Accounts and Reportable Accounts consistently with the CRS and incorporate the due diligence procedures to identify them, in particular by:

a) incorporating the definitions contained in subparagraphs C. 1 to 16, and paragraphs D and E of Section VIII of the CRS into their domestic legislative framework.

b) defining New Accounts as those opened from the first day of the calendar year (or other appropriate reporting period) prior to the year of first exchange and Preexisting Accounts as those that are open on the last day of the preceding calendar year (or other appropriate reporting period).

c) incorporating the due diligence procedures contained in Sections II to VII of the CRS into their domestic legislative framework.[1]

d) ensuring that any Financial Account or category of Financial Accounts defined in their domestic legislative framework as an Excluded Account meets the requirements for its status as an Excluded Account as set out in subparagraph C. 17 of Section VIII of the CRS.

Reporting the information

SR 1.3 Jurisdictions should incorporate the reporting requirements contained in Section I of the CRS into their domestic legislative framework.[2]

Enforcement

SR 1.4 Jurisdictions should have a legislative framework in place that allows for the enforcement of the requirements of the CRS in practice, including through rules to:

a) prevent Financial Institutions, persons or intermediaries from adopting practices intended to circumvent the due diligence and reporting procedures;
b) require Reporting Financial Institutions to keep records of the steps undertaken and any evidence relied upon for the due diligence procedures for at least five years following the end of the period within which the Reporting Financial Institution must report the information required to be reported under Section I of the CRS;
c) ensure that valid self-certifications are always obtained for New Accounts; and
d) address non-compliance with the requirements of the CRS.

CR1 Effectiveness in practice: Jurisdictions should ensure that in practice Reporting Financial Institutions correctly implement the due diligence and reporting procedures, which includes a requirement for jurisdictions to have in place an administrative framework to ensure the effective implementation of the CRS

Ensuring effectiveness domestically

SR 1.5 Jurisdictions should ensure that in practice Reporting Financial Institutions identify the Financial Accounts they maintain, identify the Reportable Accounts among those Financial Accounts, as well as their Account Holders, and where relevant Controlling Persons, by correctly conducting the due diligence procedures and collect and report the required information with respect to each Reportable Account. This includes having in place:

a) an effective administrative compliance framework to ensure the effective implementation of, and compliance with, the CRS. This framework should:
   i. be based on a strategy that facilitates compliance by Reporting Financial Institutions and which is informed by a risk assessment in respect of the effective implementation of the CRS that takes into account relevant information sources (including third party sources);
   ii. include procedures to ensure that Financial Institutions correctly apply the definitions of Reporting Financial Institutions and Non-Reporting Financial Institutions;
   iii. include procedures to periodically verify Reporting Financial Institutions' compliance,[3] conducted by authorities that have adequate powers with respect to the reviewed Reporting Financial Institutions, with procedures to access the records they maintain;[4] and
b) effective procedures to ensure that Financial Institutions, persons or intermediaries do not circumvent the due diligence and reporting procedures;
c) effective enforcement mechanisms to address non-compliance by Reporting Financial Institutions;
d) strong measures to ensure that valid self-certifications are always obtained for New Accounts;[5]
e) effective procedures to ensure that each, or each type of, jurisdiction-specific Non-Reporting Financial Institution and Excluded Account continue to present a low risk of being used to evade tax;[6] and
f) effective procedures to follow up with a Reporting Financial Institution when undocumented accounts are reported in order to establish the reasons why such information is being reported.[7]

International collaboration to ensure effectiveness

SR 1.6 Jurisdictions should collaborate on compliance and enforcement. This requires jurisdictions to:

a) use all appropriate measures available under the jurisdiction's domestic law to address errors or non-compliance notified to the jurisdiction by an exchange partner;[8] and

b) have in place effective procedures to notify an exchange partner of errors that may have led to incomplete or incorrect information reporting or non-compliance with the due diligence or reporting procedures by a Reporting Financial Institution in the jurisdiction of the exchange partner.[9]

CR2 Legal framework: Jurisdictions should have exchange relationships in effect with all Interested Appropriate Partners as committed to and that provide for the exchange of information in accordance with the Model CAA

Putting in place the exchange agreements on time

SR 2.1 Jurisdictions should have exchange agreements in effect with all Interested Appropriate Partners that permit the automatic exchange of CRS information.

SR 2.2 Such an exchange agreement should be put in place without undue delay, following the receipt of an expression of interest from an Interested Appropriate Partner.[10]

The contents of the agreements

SR 2.3 Jurisdictions should ensure that the exchange agreements in effect provide for the exchange of information in accordance with the requirements of the Model CAA,[11] including with respect to:

a) the categories of information to be exchanged;[12]

b) the timing of the exchange of information;[13]

c) the notifying of an exchange partner when the jurisdiction has reason to believe that an error may have led to incomplete or incorrect information reporting or there is non-compliance with the due diligence or reporting procedures by a Reporting Financial Institution, located in the exchange partner;[14] and

d) taking all appropriate measures available under the jurisdiction's domestic law to address errors or non-compliance notified to it.[15]

CR2 Effectiveness in practice: Jurisdictions should exchange the information effectively in practice, in a timely manner, including by sorting, preparing, validating and transmitting it in accordance with the AEOI Standard

Preparing and validating the information

SR 2.4 Jurisdictions should sort, prepare and validate the information in accordance with the CRS XML Schema and the associated requirements in the CRS XML Schema User Guide[16] and the File Error and Correction-related validations in the Status Message User Guide (i.e. the 50000 and 80000 range).[17]

Transmitting the information

SR 2.5 Jurisdictions should agree and use, with each exchange partner, transmission methods that meet appropriate minimum standards to ensure the confidentiality and integrity of the data throughout the transmission, including its encryption to a minimum secure standard.[18]

SR 2.6 Jurisdictions should carry out all exchanges annually within nine months of the end of the calendar year to which the information relates.[19]

SR 2.7 Jurisdictions should send the information in accordance with the agreed transmission methods and encryption standards.[20]

SR 2.8 Jurisdictions should have the systems in place to receive information and, once it has been received, should send a status message to the sending jurisdictions in accordance with the CRS Status Message XML Schema and the related User Guide.

Providing corrections, amendments or additions

SR 2.9 Jurisdictions should respond to a notification from an exchange partner as referred to in Section 4 of the Model CAA (which may include Status Messages) in accordance with the timelines set out in the Commentary to Section 4 of the Model CAA. In all other cases, jurisdictions should send corrected, amended or additional information received from a Reporting Financial Institution as soon as possible after it has been received.[21]

CR3: Jurisdictions should keep the information exchanged confidential and properly safeguarded, and use it in accordance with the exchange agreement under which it was exchanged SR

SR 3.1 Jurisdictions should meet the confidentiality and data safeguard requirements, including on the use of the information, referred to in Section 5 of the Model CAA to be able to receive information under the AEOI Standard.

Notes

1 Sections II to VII of the CRS set out the General Due Diligence Requirements, the Due Diligence for Preexisting Individual Accounts, the Due Diligence for New Individual Accounts, the Due Diligence for Preexisting Entity Accounts, the Due Diligence for New Entity Accounts, the Special Due Diligence Rules and the Defined Terms respectively. Paragraphs D and E of 3 Section VIII of the CRS set out the definitions relevant to the due diligence procedures.

2 Section I of the CRS sets out the General Reporting Requirements, specifying the information that must be reported with respect to each Reportable Account.

3 Paragraph A. 3 of Section IX of the CRS

4 Paragraph A. 2 of Section IX of the CRS

5 Paragraph 18 of the Commentary on Section IX of the CRS

6 Paragraph A. 4 of Section IX of the CRS

7 Paragraph A. 3 of Section IX of the CRS

8 Section 4 of the Model CAA

9 Section 4 of the Model CAA

10 Exchange agreements are expected to be put in place in time for exchanges from the date committed to unless the expression of interest indicates a later date for the commencement of exchanges or the expression of interest is not received in time. Whether the expression of interest is received in time for exchanges to commence in a particular year will depend on the specific circumstances, including the approach to the implementation of the AEOI Standard taken by the potential exchange partners.

11 Note that the agreements can take various forms. What is key is that both exchange partners are satisfied that the arrangement in place delivers the outcomes specified in the requirements.

12 Section 2 of the Model CAA

13 Section 3 of the Model CAA

14 Section 4 of the Model CAA

15 Section 4 of the Model CAA

16 Paragraph 5 of Section 3 of the Model CAA

17 If using the Common Transmission System, the information should be prepared in accordance with the File Preparation and Encryption User Guide.

18 Paragraph 6 of Section 3 of the Model CAA and the File Preparation and Encryption User Guide

19 Paragraph 3 of Section 3 of the Model CAA also states that information is only required to be exchanged with respect to a calendar year if both jurisdictions have in effect legislation that requires reporting with respect to such calendar year that is consistent with the scope of exchange required (Section 2 of the Model CAA) and the reporting and due diligence procedures contained in the CRS.

20 Paragraph 6 of Section 3 of the Model CAA and the File Preparation and Encryption User Guide

21 Commentary on Section 2 of the Model CAA

www.ingramcontent.com/pod-product-compliance
Ingram Content Group UK Ltd.
Pitfield, Milton Keynes, MK11 3LW, UK
UKHW051500290926
15471UKWH00008B/1311

9 789264 555105